THE SILENT GOSPEL
The Science of Divinity
Creation of the Shroud of Turin

James Andrew Barrett

Tamaso maa jyotir gamaya

(Lead us from darkness into Light)

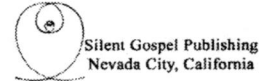
Silent Gospel Publishing
Nevada City, California

The Silent Gospel
The Science of Divinity
Creation of The Shroud of Turin

Copyrighted © 2006 by James Andrew Barrett

All Rights Reserved. No part of this book may be used or reproduced by any means, graphic, electronic, or mechanical, including photocopying, recording, taping or by any information storage retrieval system without the written permission of the publisher except in the case of brief quotations embodied in critical articles and reviews.

www.silentgospel.com

ISBN
978-0-9794355-0-8

Silent Gospel Publishing
Nevada City, California
95959
contact: info@silentgospel.com

Dedication:

*To my children Shawn and Rebecca-Anne
In appreciation for the continuing gifts that I receive from their light and presence.*

Acknowledgements:

*Special love and thanks to my love, friend and partner Patti,
For without her continuing love and support this work would never have been completed.*

A special thanks to Leeya Thompson, her patience and dedication to assist me in the completion of this work have been invaluable.

Also special acknowledgements to Dr. Konstantin Korokov, Andrew Junker, Ph.D., Beverly Rubik, Ph.D., Candace B. Pert, PH.D., Dean Shrock, Ph.D., Linda Russek, Ph.D., Bruce Rawles, Gary Schwartz, Ph.D., their insights and courage inspires, and to William Tiller for his continuing exploration of reality.

Finally deepest gratitude to Kathleen Egenes for her support in the completion of this effort.

Contents

Preface: 1
    Biological Dance - Touching between Realms

Introduction: A Question of Life: 7

PART ONE: The Shroud, East Meets West: 10

Chapter One: le Coeur de Mystère: 11
    The Shroud,
    S.T.U.R.P.,
    The Image,
    The Death of Public Interest
    Mapping of the Shroud,
    Sudarium of Oviedo,
    Facts on the Shroud,
    The Mystery:
    What a man can do,

Chapter Two: Placebo & Faith: 25
    Faith,
    Mr. Wright,
    Communication,
    Lebhon,

Chapter Three: The Rainbow, Wisdom or Golden Body 'Ja'-lus in Tibetan: 38
    Ramalinga Swamigal,
    Dzogpa Chenpo,
    Khenpo A Chung,
    The Rainbow Body,
    Paramahansa Yogananda,
    Master Zi Sheng Wang,
    Milarepa,
    Sri Aurobindo,
    Loung Pordaeng,
    H.E. Chagdud Tulku Rinpoche,

Chapter Four: The Guru Jesus: 52
    The Man Jesus,

Cross Pollination,
Religious Environment During Jesus' Time,
Trade,
Higher Education,
Epiphany,
The Word,
Background,
The Transfiguration,

Chapter Five: Resurrection: 76
Luke.24:,
Summary,

Chapter Six: Have Heart: 85
Heart of the Matter,
Aims of the Heart,
The Center of Self: First comes Sraddha: The Virtue of Love,
Info-Energy,
Fifth Way,
Heart Facts,
The Open Heart,
Sacred or Purified Heart,

Chapter Seven: Truth: 105
Signposts of Truth,
Psychological Factors,
Components of Integrity,

Chapter Eight: Heart Intelligence: 113
Science of the Heart,
Wave Theory,
Synergy,

Chapter Nine: Intent & Compassion: 121
Truth is Truth,
Surfing the Flux of the Infinite Womb,
Compassion,
Compassion is Divine Mind's Primal Intent, The *Divine Creative Feminine,*
Metta, Loving-kindness, Karuna and Tong Len,
Practice of Tong-Len,
Bodhicitta,

Chapter Ten: Breath: 135

Giving Breath A Quality,
Anatomy of Breath,

Chapter Eleven: Heart Rate Variability: 142
Heart Rate Variability (HRV),
Frequency,
Pranayama,
 Patanjali,
Eightfold Path,

Chapter Twelve: Siddhas & Siddhis: 154
Pilot Baba,
Keiko Aikawa,
Pam Reynolds,
In the Blink of an Eye,

PART TWO: The Science of Divinity; Illusion of Identity: 159

Chapter Thirteen: Awareness; No Subject, Object nor Action, An elaborate presentation on No-thing: 160
The Arising of "I",
Identities of Mind – Forming of "I",
Ego,
Soul,
Heart,
The Template of "I",
Qualitative Nature of Awareness,
Ground of Reality
Dharma,
St. Clare,

Chapter Fourteen: Quantum Zero Point & the Holographic Web: 184
The Split,
Physics of Life,
Quantum Physics
The Science of Movement,
Superposition,
Light Facts,
Consciousness,
Holographic Fractality,
Zero Point Energy or the Electromagnetic Quantum Vacuum,

Primary Perspective,
Gaia,
Shift of attitude and perspective,

Chapter Fifteen: Resonance: 213

Chapter Sixteen: Tuning to the Divine: 220
Coherency occurs at Equilibrium,
Sun Rise on Stillness,
Evolution-The Transformation of the Human Species,

Chapter Seventeen: Quantum AUM: 226
A Constant in Spiritual Traditions; AUM,
Notion of a Constant in Physics,
The Dance of Light,
Divisionless Partitioning,

Chapter Eighteen: Sonoluminescence: 232
SL,
The Unruh-Casimir Effect,
SL and The Silent Gospel,
The Body,
The Physical Form,

Chapter Nineteen: Golden Mean: 244
Fundamental Features of the Golden Mean,
Numbers,
Phi,
The Principle of Phi, the Golden Ratio,
Phase Singularity,
The Form of Recursive Energy,
Vortices,
KAM tori,
Stable Light
Dynamics of Condensation,
Guided Within

Chapter Twenty: Shroud Image Formation - Summary Conclusion: 268
One,
The Shroud Image,
The Great Completion,
The Shroud Evidence,
The Image,

Chapter Synopsis,
The Yellow Brick Road and Parallel Universes,
Review of the Process of becoming a Son of God
Final Perfection,
Perfectly Purified, The Immaculate Heart,
Loving-Kindness,
Souls Perspective,
Grace Flows from Faith in Faith Itself,
The Centering Process,
Heart Center,
Regulating Factors,
A Unifying Harmony,
Final Meditation,
Electrical Nature,
Human Potential and Human Evolution,

Chapter Twenty One: Purity of Heart: 309

Epilogue, Information Prior to Energy: 313

Bibliography: 316
Glossary found at www.silentgospel.com

About the Author

Preface

Touching and being touched

It was not until the 1980's that the interrelationship between the functions of the brain and the immune system in immunology texts began to get referenced. Connecting cellular functions, the immune system and psychology was an even greater leap. This advancement in understanding was left to the then Chief of the Section on Brain Biochemistry of the Clinical Neuroscience Branch at the National Institute of Mental Health by the name of Dr. Candace Pert, Ph.D.. Dr. Pert is credited with discovering the *role and relationship that emotions* play between the *nervous system* and the *immune system*. She demonstrated for the first time ever, the existence, role and functional attributes, of the family of long-chain amino-acid bodies, which have come to be known as neuropeptides. The physical bio-chemical link between two major physical systems (immune and nerve) and the then mental psychological aspect of emotion had been firmly established in replicable science.

These early findings led to a cascade of discoveries and a much broader understanding of the behaviors, attributes and characteristics of these chemical signals that connect, effect, and communicate between the mind and body. Dr. Pert went on to demonstrate that neuropeptides can be found literally everywhere in the body and messages carried by the neuropeptides do not necessarily travel from the brain into the rest of the body. Her team found that the transference of peptide information appeared to occur throughout the body in a virtual spontaneous bloom at *the required cell level* and that the trigger for the virtual release of biochemical units of emotion was the *thinking mind*. Dr. Pert and her team showed in replicable science that the vehicle used by the mind and body to communicate with each other is the *chemistry of emotion*. Research into these virtual blooms of neurochemistry underscored the reality that the arenas of mind-body; microbiology and neurochemistry were all operating at the most basic levels via quantum mechanics transfers. **Emotions operating within the human design were now seen as the bridge between the psycho-mental and physical processes.**

As the 90's unfolded, a broader interconnected, unified holistic view of biology was taking root into the collective Western mind; neuroscience, microbiology, physics, immunology and the study of mind and consciousness began to merge in a diaphanous blur of academia. Cross-pollination proliferated as the new communication tools such as the Internet with its search engines assisted a global network of free thinkers. The advent of faster, cheaper computers along with this global World Wide Web nourished a rapid evolution of scientific thought, along with tools to research these new areas of interest. As we came to the end of the millennium, Science was taking on the thorny topics of mind and consciousness. As of this writing, the current scientific model of recall/memory/awareness, suggests both global *quantum coherence* and *quantum entanglement* between the various electrical states of the ultra small component structures found within neural cells. Quantum physicists often attribute communication between non-physical realms and the physical realms to physical phenomena called "quantum coherence". This phenomenon is the ability of atoms to act as one spontaneously, regardless of distance.

Memories (recall) in these new models are understood to be encoded standing wave patterns of quantum-coherent oscillations, set up by changes in the fine structures of the microtubules and their constituent parts, all working in emotion-defined patterns within the substrates of the individual neurons. The stronger the emotion, the deeper and more vivid is the encoded memory within the neurons.

Imagine yourself situated at the extremely fine scale of structures found within the nerves (of the brain or other organs like the heart and or intestines). At this ultra small scale of architecture, a complex network of synapses, microtubules, dimers containing vicinal water and amino-acid chains operate in a neighborhood so close as to exert quantum effects on each other. Patterned neural activity causes a spontaneous quantum-entangled event, which if strongly anchored by powerful emotions, develops a recall via fractal resonance. The important point is that quantum coherence and its effects play an important central role in recall, mind, awareness and emotions.

What we would witness from the perspective of the 3D time-space domain are patterns of *quantum fluctuation*, diverging and collapsing spontaneously in concert with the body's signals. These signals of information-energy communication occur in five modes of transference; electrical, acoustic, chemical, neural and quantum mechanical. Massive information and energy transference spontaneously trigger a linear, coherent cascade that loop back in the form of an echo. The resulting echo causes a memory firing which feeds-back and touches the self-referencing loop on going, which allows for self-awareness. Focused attention, itself a little understood paradox of maintained coherent looping of *awareness*, is the tool used to drag to the surface the finer details of the stored quantum entangled event and resulting neural pattern, i.e. memory.

The quantum physicist would tell us that out of the choices made, probability and possibility were narrowed into a vectored standing-wave. Perspective and perception would snap a vectored localization onto the holographic illusion out of vast possibilities in the time domain producing a sense of object and structure similar to a shutter on a camera. This takes place so rapidly, in fact before any sense of the passage of time, that it seems to be spontaneous and the movie being created appears real, fluid and firm to our senses.

Yet when scientists looked for the precise location and mechanics of memory they were forced to conclude that memory is *everywhere and nowhere* and that all the actions of consciousness take place on a scale far smaller even than that of neurons. At that level of structure, the line between local and non-local, objective and virtual, depends on the qualities and degree of attention placed on the object. This is the law of that reality. These facts demanded that researchers come to the understanding that it is mind and the underlying consciousness that direct the functions and direction of the body. "I think, therefore I am", became the new motto in consciousness research. This very saying is far more insightful than one might believe as I hope you will come to see by the end of this manuscript. .

Biological Dance

Because this material supports the foundation to this manuscript it is valuable for those with interest to restate a bit of the details of this biological dance we call life.

Moment by moment within the complexity of the biological dance, two key operations are constantly occurring as one movement. One is emotional with its chemo-synaptic mechanics pulsed into being virtually; the other is mind-neural with its quantum mechanics also in play. They are fully integrated and interconnected in a yin-yang spiral looping mix. The information-energy of this moment blossoms spontaneously throughout the body's architecture via mechanics that have at their root in *quantum coherence* and *quantum entangled* processes.

On the most basic level, the neuropeptides carry the biochemical messages, which are the material manifestation of emotional information. The neuropeptide structures are **emotion-specific**; that is, each peptide molecule communicates information in a context specific to a single emotional state. Every protein has poetically its open and its closed state. Both states transmit information. Peptides are extremely small amino acid chains. When the links of amino acids surpass two hundred in length then it officially becomes a protein. In size, going from the largest to the smallest, we have proteins, polypeptides and then peptides, so as we can see these objects we are discussing are extremely small. The environmental energy soup memories and emotion molecules are formed in are always within quantum entangled spontaneously effected environments.

These chemicals and neural activities are a direct result of the *perceiving mind*. Even their state (open or closed) results from the perception of the moment. They activate the field by causing each cell to oscillate in a harmonic resonance with the emotion-specific information carried by each peptide molecule and received by each receptor site. The energetic content is encoded, stored, transported and communicated spontaneously throughout the system. The value of the energetic content is vectored by the perceiving perception and physical reactions occur. This reaction is the same micro process of harmonic resonant tuning happening on the macro level of self.

Emotion

The neuropeptides virtually activated produce a coordinated group sing-along at the cellular level, forming the environment the cell is existing within energetically and chemically, which determines the response from the DNA/RNA. A loop of info-energy occurs in the nervous systems and a fractal, holographic encoded pattern emerges precipitating a cascade event we term *emotion*. Each and every cascade event has physical consequences that affect well-being and longevity. Science tells us that each molecule is energetic-specific with the perception shifting the degree of effect of each cascade event. In short, the chemicals at the cellular level are the same, but the resulting effects are enhanced or diminished through the lens of our personalized view of the event that is taking place. Emotions are chemicals produced via quantum mechanical activity throughout the body by mind; the activity is directed by the lens of perception at that moment. Hence biology is dictated directly by perception. And perception is fluid and adaptable.

Recall

Scientists investigating the cyto-skeletons of neural cells have discovered carefully ordered internal arrays of tiny microtubules. The structure of each microtubule consists of a series of hollow chambers, each of which in turn contains thirteen columns of tubulin dimers. Messages of all kinds are believed to be propagated along each microtubule column and along the protein ridges, which connect them. Researchers in France recently discovered also that contained inside the dimer columns are tiny, monomolecular threads of water in an ordered state. This highly structured water is called vicinal water which is thought to be capable of conveying quantum-coherent oscillations for the length of the tubule, in effect, operating as an oscillating transceiver of quantum level frequencies by maintaining a permanent standing wave. The info-energy transference has been observed to take place in phased pulses operating at transfer rates well in excess of those that are possible with any known chemo-synaptic mechanics. Therefore it is likely that all events in the brain and in the body operate contemporaneously as functions of linear, sequential, chemo-synaptic functions as well as non-local field mechanics. In short, we are quantum objects that are affected by the quality and focus of our attention.

The theorem outlined within these pages has its geneses in the information that the physical architecture operates at the most primary scales in a quantum relationship with Consciousness. With this science laid as the groundwork, I ask you to imagine with me what would be possible from an individual highly trained in this knowledge; an individual with the skill to control and maintain a very specific emotional state? Conditions where mind, perception and experience would unify harmonically with that virtual cosmic sea of stillness from which all objective stuff condenses -- a sea of Light we've come to term the "Zero Point". Imagine an individual with full control of the flow of nerve impulses and full ability to maintain concentration and contemplation; a state that allows the individual to remain in unique *feeling sense awareness,* a state that some call compassionate love, even under the stress of torture. He or she would be an individual with control over objective physicality itself and from a theological perspective would be called a Saint.

Introduction

A Question of Life

The Image on the Shroud of Turin is of a tortured individual lying in the posture of death. Examining this subject in detail caused me to explore my own mortality and search for the meaning of life and of existence. This manuscript is the summation of my search to this moment in time.

We talk of *life* as an entity unto itself. Somehow going against all that is natural we separate it, distance it and speak of it in objective terms. It, *(Life)*, is out there, some mystical force that flows like a river of intelligence affecting our destiny. Yet at the same time it is the currency we all desire more of.

We've all wondered at some point in our lives how things might have been different "if only..." It appears to be a universal characteristic of being human to at one time or another ponder why things happen the way they do. We question; *why, why does that mysterious agent of life called fate enter to mix the stew of daily lives*. More confusing is that it (fate) appears to operate without any sense of justice or fairness. It flies against our notion of God and goodness. This only heightens our desire for meaning on the one hand, as it forces us to judge and discern in the other. We appear to travel this stream of awareness we call life, by attaching qualities, and attribute to things and situations. Life appears to be one judgment after another in some nebulous quest with mortality always in the wings. But is it? The great inner explorers of these core questions tell us that it's a quest for remembering self.

If one is "fortunate," there are moments in ones life of feeling in a groove, somehow synchronized with the flow of *life*. During those moments time slows or disappears from awareness and a merging happens that blurs the notion of separation. Life and the "I" experiencing merge, such moments are precious, unfortunately for most they are rare, but they hint at something truer that our normal existence.

I too felt that my fate was being manipulated by outside forces. One day, a self-serving, self-absorbed teenager; and BAM! four children and responsibilities in staggering proportion. Life it appeared had caught up with me, and the day-to-day had become a blur of parenting and family survival. I found myself laughing and sharing my children's joys as well as agonizing deeply with their pains and sorrows. Then one day they were mature adults caught in their own world of dreams and desires. I found myself forced at a point in the journey to sit back and recapitulate this stream I had traveled and found to my amazement that the virtue of compassion had magically been seeded and birthed within my heart.

I had two big epiphanies in my life. The first happened a few years after the death of my grandparents. The first occurred as I held my mother, while she took her last breath. I found myself questioning whether this was all there was to *life*, for she was only 58 years of age and had died a horrific death from pancreatic cancer. Everything appeared so clear in those moments. My life was passing; my children were growing into adults and leaving home. I believed prior to that moment that if I had a *purpose*, then my life in the end would have had *meaning*. In my attempt to define my life in the weeks to follow, I stumbled out onto a path of discovery. Little did I know or care at the time where it would take me. To my mind, both purpose and meaning were inter-linked. They were interchangeable, much the same as belief and hope are often confused with faith. I believed it would all work out and hoped for the best. What I've come to understand is that belief and hope are constructs developed by the mind in the absence of that most vital substance -- FAITH. I came to realize, that meaning is derived as a fruit of having *faith in life*. Even as I write these words, the paradox of it makes me giggle.

My first insight of this realization occurred in that sterile hospital room holding my mother as life left her form. A knowing deep in my psyche saw the perfection in it all even as the grief and loss set in.

The second epiphany happened as I cleaned out the apartment of my son who had at twenty-seven, had suddenly died on his sisters birthday. In the midst of profound grief I found myself "witnessing the mind's chatter" from a profoundly peaceful place. Out of this state of witnessing events and my other self, arose the clear outline for this manuscript.

Intimately touching mortality either creates a yearning or an avoidance of life's meaning. No one wants to look at one's own mortality but thankfully there have been a few souls with the courage and strength to delve deeply into the mystery of life and death.

Over the ages, these explorers have traversed into the emptiness of the void itself searching the meaning of life and existence. Through the grace of some higher power, some have emerged with an *experience* of Reality and Self, which certain mystical traditions term self-realization, awakening, illumination and or enlightenment. Most souls never make it to this illuminated state of remembrance; they get trapped in the dark night of despair and despondency. Caught in this trance like loop of meaningless identification, masters of inner space tell us, *is the cause of suffering* and *the onset of disease.*

These explorers of inner space assure us that, shifting perspective and identity to that part of the self able to "witness the mind's chatter", comes to experience Life as aware Presence, this eventually leads to a transcendence of suffering. These illuminated pioneers universally share with us that this aware Presence is Life Itself and the true nature of existence.

In the writing of this manuscript I found my challenge was to maintain a balance between theology, philosophy and the sciences of both the East and West. I found myself wishing for the good old days when science and religion was a unified practice. My choice was to introduce material in chapter clumps and pull in all together in the final conclusion. Another challenge was not to appear as if I am supporting any specific religion, theology and or philosophy. Lastly, to me personally it really does not matter when or by whom the Shroud was created. I cannot make this point too strongly or too often. It exists as a glorious testament to an ancient wisdom, which in my eyes is able to stand on its own. The image speaks volumes on many subjects all with importance to humanity as a whole and each of us personally. Yet because the Shroud has the tradition of being the burial sheet of Jesus of Nazareth, it becomes the most important relic of Christianity, the foundation upon which the resurrection story rests. It therefore unfortunately falls into religious and political disputation that muddies the water, distracting us from clearly understanding its real value to humanity.

Part One

The Shroud,

East Meets West

Chapter One

le Coeur de Mystère

"To dance and sing with the joy of knowing its true nature and purpose in the world?
You are here to enable the divine purpose of the universe to unfold.
That is how important you are."
Eckhart Tolle, The Power of Now.

What lies beyond comprehension is the mysterious. Schools of all types and traditions have been created over the ages to assist the inquisitive seeking mind find peace with the unexplainable. From ancient times to the present these mystery schools have existed to help those who wish to realize the truth and give meaning to life. Libraries around the world are full to the rafters with volumes written on subjects that for their time were considered to be mysterious and inexplicable. Man is a being that needs a theory or two surrounding a mystery to help the rational mind find some level of comfort in the sea of chaos it perceives itself to be drift in. Whether it is acknowledged or not, it is mystery that propels us forward in our desire to understand our universe and our relationship within it. In fact it is this very need to know that is the core force driving evolutionary movement. Our need to grasp the truth expands not only our understanding of the physical world but also the spiritual realm and the Intelligence sustaining it all.

There is that rare breed of mystery that by its very existence defines the term. With all our tools and understanding we just cannot grasp it; generally because the anomaly falls outside of our preconceived notions about how things are or should be. An interesting fact about a genuine "mystery" is that when one aspect is thought to be solved, curiously several new equally challenging mysteries rise out of the solution to take the original mystery's place. To gain insight into a genuine mystery the individual must move outside the box into abstraction and new forms of thinking. The art is to drift beyond the boundaries of current understanding, beyond the constructs that maintain the mystery in the first place. Often the best tact in unraveling these great puzzles is just to go with the facts the data presents and allow the picture to unfold.

The Shroud of Turin is truly one of these unique mysteries. It is not theoretical; it exists in a real way that allows it to be touched and studied. It has been an inexplicable anomaly residing in our midst for millennia. The greater the exploration into the image by science, the more inexplicable and distant understanding appears to be. The current name given to this sacred artifact comes from the place in which it has resided for over four hundred years, the Cathedral of St. John the Baptist in Turin, Italy.

The tradition of the Shroud has permeated Christian culture since the time of Jesus. It has remained for most of that time as an article of faith and a corner stone to the resurrection story, which is the bedrock of this now global religion.

The improbabilities of the basic facts that science has revealed, present challenges to the rational that are so profound, that our minds are stunned into awe when fully confronted with the realities. For those that have followed the story over the years, the research on the Shroud has not dampened our awe in the slightest; in fact it has become richer, as you too will soon understand.

At the very heart of the Shroud of Turin mystery are two separate but interrelated questions: what was the medium and what was the process used in the creation of this artifact? One has to do with the medium used to place an image on linen and the other has to do with the process employing that medium.

Even now, with all our scientific advances, we are unable to replicate an image on cloth that in any way would be similar to the Shroud, nor are we able to replicate any of its unique complex characteristics. This might be contrary to what is shown on television or broadcast in the global media, yet ask those with a full knowledge of the cloth and they will concur.

After studying the cloth in exhaustive detail, a group of experts brought together to study these questions, concluded that the physical body that lay within the Shroud of Turin must have radiated an extremely intense coherent light for a very short period of time, perhaps milliseconds. The word unique, if it is to apply to anything at all, surely applies to this marvelous object, the Shroud of Turin.

The Shroud

The Shroud itself is a well-preserved piece of cloth measuring 14' 3" long (4.36 meters) and is 3' 7" wide (1.1 meters), weighing approximately 5 ½ lbs. (2.45 kgs.). The "Holy Shroud" as it is also known, is fairly typical of burial linen found in antiquity, with its fibers woven in three-to-one herringbone twill of Mediterranean basin flax. It is a single piece of cloth, one half of which is the frontal image of a man and the second half is the rear image of the same man. The image, when seen from a distance, is clearly that of a man in the attitude of death and the posture prepared for burial.

What makes this Shroud important to one third of the earth's population is that it is said to be the burial shroud of Jesus and, as such, becomes the holiest relic in Christendom. The uniqueness of the Shroud comes solely from the images found on the cloth. Yes, I said images; this is because there are several objects shown on the overall Shroud image; coins and flowers to name just two. Tradition claims that the image on this cloth is the witness to the passion, love, crucifixion, torture, and ultimately the resurrection of Jesus of Nazareth. It is called the Silent Gospel by a few, for as we all know a picture is worth a thousand words. Humbly, this book is a translation of what it is telling us, what it means to us as a species, and more importantly, to us personally.

S.T.U.R.P.

Beyond the technical curiosities, reasons for such intense scrutiny of the Shroud include the broad ramifications surrounding potential authenticity. The Shroud is considered the most precious relic in all of Christendom; nevertheless, the official ownership was only granted to the Roman Catholic Church in 1983, after the 1978 S.T.U.R.P. analysis was concluded.

In 1978, over forty scientists from around the world consisting of agnostics, Jews and Christians convened for five full days of intense study of the Shroud itself. This prestigious group of scientists, known as the Shroud of Turin Research Project, or S.T.U.R.P., encompassed a broad range of disciplines ranging from forensic medicine to physics. The research and the constant expansion of information based on the data collected at that time, continues to be relevant to the present day. Research of every kind imaginable has been meticulously conducted on every aspect of the Holy Shroud. The wounds, blood and staining on the cloth alone has been exhaustively examined and studied by physicists, chemists, biologists, photographic experts, archaeologists, scriptural experts, surgeons, forensic pathologists and art experts, as well as DNA analyses.

The findings by the STURP group were clear on the material make-up of the Shroud. It was indeed the image of a crucified body from antiquity, buried in a specific manner consistent with descriptions of Jewish tradition and biblical accounts of the crucifixion of Jesus. Whether or not it is The Shroud of Jesus is in some ways irrelevant and will never truly be solved. The body of Jesus would be needed to compare blood and DNA analyses with that found on the Shroud for it to be proven positively. Yet in a court of law the evidence would point with the highest of probability that the Shroud of Turin actually is the burial shroud of Jesus. We must not, however, get caught up in this detail for it is totally irrelevant to the real information. If the Shroud came from the 1300's instead of 33AD it makes no difference to the encoded information being transmitted.

The mystery deepened as the STRUP group resolved the nature of the medium used in the creation of the image on the cloth. What had imprinted this image was very intense light. The brush of its author used a palette of light/energy in a subtle, unique method with a perspective not developed in art for another fifteen hundred years. Even with our current array of technical devices at the disposal of today's researchers, we still have not found the means of replicating this ancient methodology.

The Image

Since 1978 every imaginable modern device and technique has been employed in attempting to unravel the mystery of the creation of the image on the Shroud, including powerful NASA imaging techniques and high-powered programs working in super computers. The global brainpower of modern physics has been brought to bear on this age-old detective story. And still one central question arises; how was the image made on the shroud?

Dr. Alan D. Adler, Emeritus Professor Department of Chemistry, Western Connecticut University, in Banbury, CT. and original STURP member, wrote in a 1999 paper called, The Nature of the Body Images on the Shroud of Turin: "A large body of scientific evidence has now been accumulated on this object... ...although the mechanism of the formation of the body images remains a mystery."

In his book, New Scientific Evidence, The Mystery of the Shroud of Turin, John C. Iannone makes the following citations:

Ray Rogers, a physical Chemist of the Los Alamos Laboratory's Design Engineering division, and a S.T.U.R.P. member declared, 'I am forced to conclude that the image was formed by a burst of radiant energy – light if you like.'...Professor Alan Adler of Western Connecticut State College concluded that the Shroud images could only have been created by high-level energy, which he could not name. 'The physical body that lay on the Shroud of Turin must have radiated at a very high intensity for a very short period of time, perhaps milliseconds.' This radiant light, which Frank Tribbe in his book entitled Portrait of Jesus?, termed that the phenomenon of flash photolysis, has historical parallels in that permanent images were formed by the light and power of the atomic blast at Hiroshima. Dr. Everett James, a radiologist formerly of Vanderbilt University, calls it an 'autoadiograph emanating from the body.' He describes the process, 'It was powerful enough to project the image onto the linen from a distance of up to 4 centimeters, according to physicists John Jackson and Eric Jumper, yet gentle enough not to cause distortion in areas where there would have been direct contact as on the dorsal image where the cloth received the full weight of the body.... Additionally the image did not discriminate between registering the body surface as well as hair, blood and inanimate objects – the coins over the eyes and phylactery.' Physicist Dr. Eric Jumper argued that any diffusion process would have involved penetration of the fibers and any remotely lingering laser beam would have caused destruction.

Whatever created the image must have been some extremely high intensity, short duration burst (milliseconds) acting evenly in a coherent columniation. This caused the rapid dehydration and oxidation of the linen fibrils immediately surrounding a body. This was heat, light or other form of radiation, or a combination of the three! All the experts agree on one thing, that the energy that emanated evenly from a laid out body scorched or seared the image by some form of a coherent thermonuclear plasmatic flash. The facts concluded as improbable they may seem, that the image left to us of a tortured, blood-stained body reposing in the burial posture appears to have been created by extremely intense light emanating from the body with equality and coherency for the briefest of moments.

As scary as it is for scientists to say these things, this is the evidence of their research. If one takes these prestigious scientists at their word, the mind is found scrambling for reason even into the realms of abstract imagination on how a person would accomplish this impossible feat. Again this problem is not theoretical, for the Shroud and its images exist.

The Death of Public Interest

Before I continue, I wish to address a series of events that caused a massive exodus of public interest. Ten years after the S.T.U.R.P. groups' analysis, and five years after the Shroud was turned over to the Vatican, the Holy See chose three prestigious laboratories to perform Carbon 14 (C14) tests on one small piece of cloth taken from a corner of the Shroud. The date was July 29, 1988. The test results from all three institutions gave a calibrated calendar age range with at least 95% accuracy for the linen of the Shroud of Turin of AD 1260-1390.

It was two months later on September 28, 1988, when the New York Times ran an article with the byline: "Test Shows Shroud of Turin to be a Fraud, Scientist Hints". This article went on to explain that Carbon 14 testing made by the three labs from around the world, showed the Shroud to be created almost a millennium after the death of Jesus. The publication of this story effectively ended the public debate for many as to whether this was the burial shroud of Jesus. One branch of modern science, in its infancy at the time, had condemned the Shroud and all it was witness to.

The world's media had a field day with the story. Public opinion was effectively tweaked into thinking of the Shroud, as a whole, to be a hoax. Many took the headline as fact regardless of the other real mounting evidence to the contrary. The media's sensationalizing one piece of potentially flawed evidence used to help determine a date for the cloth, and omitting all other research data, effectively colored and dismissed the legitimacy of the Shroud in the public eye. All the other excellent evidence pointing to it as being far older was ignored. This inappropriate reporting by the media distracted attention away from the real question of how the Shroud was created in the first place. If the figure was not that of Jesus, then who might it be?

It was odd at how effective this one small piece of 'evidence' became the central point for discrediting the Shroud as a whole. The more important issue not discussed by the media was not WHO created it but HOW it was created in the first place. Due to this central mystery, and the interesting provenance of the article with its extremely fascinating anomalies, intense study continues on the object today where most of the other evidence points to the fact that the cloth was indeed the burial cloth of Jesus.

The Shroud had been effectively tainted as a fraudulent article because it was said to be that of Jesus and this one small bit of flawed data, regardless of the many other amazing facts surrounding the research, said that it could not have been. The Shroud, like Crop Circles, became associated with hoax and deception in the public eye and many looked no further. We can be thankful that not all the Academic community was swayed by the mass media blitz of the time. Most that were deeply involved knew all too well the volume of other amazing facts surrounding the Shroud as well as the potential flaws with C14 tests. As we shall later discuss, these potential flaws were in the tested material, not in the testing processes. The Shroud had been doped with potential contaminates, with the result that more recent organic carbon had been added to the piece, hence lessening the age.

Research continued with each passing year, contributing to the mounting evidence that the Shroud was in fact that of Jesus or if not he, himself, then someone with a very similar story living in the same century and area as Jesus lived and died. Though the excitement in the general public was greatly diminished, those who knew the story more intimately never stopped pressing forward. After all, the central mystery of the image was left without a satisfactory explanation. Whether it was done in 1300 or year 33 made no difference to the central mystery. To the scientist researching the Shroud it was not who or when as much as how! And this mystery was left still blowing in the winds of academic challenges. The mystery continued.

Mapping of the Shroud

The one piece of evidence I find so compelling is the story of the crucifixion and the actual map of the wounds on the Shroud. These wounds seamlessly match the biblical accounts of the wounds received by Jesus during his crucifixion. The precision of this matching would not carry as much weight if it were not for the fact that the specific crucifixion of Jesus was unique on several accounts and far from the norm at any time in history. This single piece of evidence alone, correlating early written texts with the scientific documentation, provides the strongest probability that this is indeed the burial shroud of the historical Jesus. There is, however, a proverbial mountain of evidence even better than that of the mapping of the Shroud, which I will now discuss.

Sudarium of Oviedo

The entire body of medical, artistic, forensic and botanical evidence favors the authenticity of the Shroud of Turin as the burial cloth of Jesus. As of this writing only the flawed C14 tests distracts from this premise. One small example of that evidence is the microscopic testing of a sample of dirt taken from the foot region of the burial linen by the 1978 S.T.R.U.P. team. The dirt was analyzed at the Hercules Aerospace Laboratory in Salt Lake, Utah, where experts identified crystals of travertine argonite, a relatively rare form of calcite found near the Damascus Gate in Jerusalem. It is a stretch, say researchers that a 13th century forger would have known to take the trouble to impregnate the linen with marble dust found near Golgotha in order to fool scientists six hundred years later.

Another piece of evidence rarely spoken of, supporting this conclusion, is the data connecting the Shroud with the Sudarium of Oviedo. Sudarium is Latin for "face cloth," and in Jewish burial custom a piece of cloth would be placed over the face of the dead, sparing the family further distress. From the beginning to the present this small piece of cloth has a direct, clear, unbroken provenance linking it back to early Christians of Palestine as a revered relic.

Tradition tells us that the Sudarium of Oviedo is the cloth wrapped over the head of the crucified Christ while awaiting permission from Pontius Pilate to remove the body from the cross. In addition to the forensic evidence, the significance of this specific Sudarium is that its history has been well documented and remains undisputed. It left Palestine ahead of the Persian invasion in 616 A.D. and after passing through Alexandria, Egypt, the oak chest containing it entered Spain at Cartegena, there entrusted to Leandro, bishop of Seville. In 657 it was moved to Toledo, then in 718 onto northern Spain to escape the advancing Moors. From northern Spain it continued its

The Silent Gospel

journey through time and space, well documented at each point of arrival.

After the STURP studies and Radio-Carbon Data results were returned on the Shroud, an Investigation Team from the Spanish Centre for Sindology began the first Sudarium studies in 1989. The cloth is impregnated with blood and lymph stains that match the blood type on the Shroud of Turin. The pattern and measurements of stains indicate the placement of the cloth over the face. These patterns have been extensively mapped to enable researchers to compare the markings and measurements with those of the Shroud of Turin. Dr. Alan Whanger, professor emeritus of Duke University, employed his Polarized Image Overlay Technique to study the correlation between the Shroud and the Sudarium. Dr. Whanger found 70 points of correlation on the front of the Sudarium and 50 on the back. These measurements and calculations, digitized videos and other forensic evidence indicate that the Sudarium of Oviedo covered the same head whose image is found on the Shroud of Turin.

The compositions of the stains are one part blood, type AB, and six parts pulmonary edema fluid. This fluid is significant, say researchers, because it indicates that the man died from asphyxiation, the cause of death for victims of crucifixion.

"The only reasonable conclusion," says Mark Guscin, author of The Oviedo Cloth, "is that the Sudarium of Oviedo covered the same head as that found on the Shroud of Turin." Guscin, a British scholar whose study is the only English language book on the Sudarium, is quoted as saying, "This can be uncomfortable for scientists with a predetermined viewpoint; I mean, the evidence grows that this cloth and the Shroud covered the same tortured man."

Max Frei of Switzerland did another interesting bit of telling research. Frei conducted exhaustive pollen studies on both the Shroud and the Sudarium. He found pollen from Palestine in both relics, while the Sudarium has additional pollen from Egypt and Spain that is not found on the Shroud. Conversely, pollen grains from plant species indigenous to Turkey are imbedded in the Shroud, but not the Sudarium. These finding supports the tradition associated with each relic after leaving Jerusalem.

The question that immediately comes to mind after reading this data is this: if the scientific and medical research on the Sudarium shows that it was the covering for the same man whose image is on the

Shroud of Turin, and we know that the Sudarium has been in Spain since the 600s, how then can the radio carbon dating claiming the Shroud is only from the 13th century be accurate?

But again it really is not important when it was created; the mystery remains that it exists at all. This is the le *coeur de mystère*, for even today with all our technology, we could not come close to replicating it with all its unique characteristics, much less could this have been accomplished by a man one or two thousand years ago who was supposed to be dead.

Facts on the Shroud

The STURP team concluded in 1981 that the Shroud image is that of a real human form of a scourged, crucified man. It is not the product of an artist. This opinion has not changed. The outermost fibers of the cloth are coated with a thin film of starch fractions and saccharides. In places, bits of this coating have turned straw-yellow because of a chemical change. That is how the images are recorded on the cloth plain.

~The 1988 Carbon 14 dating used invalid samples snipped from a discrete medieval repair. Furthermore, kinetics constants for the loss of vanillin from lignin indicates that the cloth is at least twice as old as the dates determines by the carbon 14 dating with faulty samples.

~ From the blood and DNA analysis a determination was made that the Shroud had covered an adult male with AB type blood. Incidentally, this blood type is typically Jewish, especially in antiquity.

~ Burial took place in the spring within 15-20 miles of Jerusalem. This is based on the images of the flower types left on the Shroud as well as the great numbers and percentages of pollen types embedded on the Shroud. The various flower images found primarily around the head would have been typical for burial at that time in Jerusalem. The type of flowers identified in the images and the large quantities of pollen appearing in high density on the Shroud are indigenous spring plants specific to the region around the city of Jerusalem, some are found no where else.

~ The wounds mapped on the image are not typical of Roman crucifixions but correspond exactly to the reported descriptions given in the Bible, of wounds inflicted on the man, Jesus, during his crucifixion.

~ The numerous types and locations of wounds are specific to the historical accounts of the crucifixion of Jesus. The historical specialists consider the odds of another person receiving the exact same treatment of punishments highly unlikely.

~ The type of linen and its manufacturing method place the cloth of the Shroud during the time of Jesus.

~

~ The Shroud has a historical provenance that goes back into distant antiquity. It is not a modern item.

~ The likely source for the chemical reaction forming the image was heat produced by a short very intense burst of energy/light. This energy appears to have emanated from the body with extreme balance and coherence, producing exact timing for an image in focus. The images on the Shroud are not only very well focused but highly resolved. Because of the distortion problems (lack of) one is lead to the conclusion that the image is done by an artist, but the chemical and other oddities prove this impossible. What stopped the chemical reaction at just the right time, everywhere on the pictures? The reaction timing is perfect in every aspect. Computerized image analysis shows no saturation plateaus or washout anywhere in the image. In simple terms, the chemical process ended late enough to form a discernable image and early enough so it was not ruined. How did the chemical reaction over come major variables such as wrinkles, the shape of the cloth, diffusion, ambient temperatures, humidity, body chemistry, and other trace impurities, etc. Yet produce a near perfect *chiaroscuro type* picture.

~Starting in the sixth century, pictures of Jesus (coins, icons, frescos and paintings) seem inspired or even copied from a single source.

~ The Shroud cloth has dimensional encoded information of the body it once held. This was demonstrated by using the VP-8 Image Analyzer, a tool developed originally by NASA to translate "light and shade, on a black-and-white photograph into relief, viewable in dimension on a monitor." This device would normally use two images to create a three dimensional relief of the area in question. In other words, the Shroud is similar in nature to a holographic photograph. Normal pictures, paintings and other images do not create dimensional image using this device.

~ There is no direct proof that the image on the Shroud is that of Jesus, for that you would need the actual body of the man. We would need a blood/DNA sample from Jesus himself in order to prove conclusively that the burial cloth is that of Jesus, but it does ask the question, if not Jesus then who might it be? Who else had the faculty to place his likeness on a burial cloth at any time in antiquity? And why would the historical accounts of the Shroud said to be that of Jesus throughout antiquity? It begs the question, why such a marvelous object with no known precedents was never again exploited? And why was it produced in negative and not a positive image? Surely a positive image would have a more powerful effect?

~ The scientists that have studied the Shroud think that the image, when it was first made, was much sharper and clearer. It is thought that when the Shroud was fresh, say the morning of the Resurrection, it was of nearly photographic quality in negative. This would have been treasured as a priceless relic of their beloved Rabbi, Prophet and Guru, especially if they met him again after as stated in the gospels. It would represent an article producing great faith within the discipleship. It would have been shared with the elect, some of whom were Greek and Roman.

~ Researchers have directly linked the image found on the Shroud to the development of religious icons of Jesus. These iconographic images all show a striking resemblance to the image of Jesus on the Shroud, which, as we have pointed out, was much clearer at that earlier time. Would not this appearance on the Shroud, therefore, be the basis for future iconography? These iconographic images can be found in the tombs of the earliest Roman Christians. Researchers using computer-modeling techniques demonstrate many similarities exhibited in all early iconography. The early Jerusalem Church, the Essenes or other Hebraic sects certainly did not have artists creating images of themselves. The notion of creating self-portraits was more a Greek or Roman concept reserved for only the highest of class. This idea certainly went against all the principles of an ascetic religious group in Judea at the time.

In conclusion, surely if there had been another person with these levels of capabilities living and dying in Jerusalem in antiquity, we would have heard about him in the histories of the times. Christianity, one of the world's largest religions, has as its underpinnings a story of just such a man; and because of the resurrection story and the faith it produced in people, it has survived and flourished to this day.

The Mystery

At the heart of the mystery of the Shroud lies the question, how was it produced? The most knowledgeable experts have postulated that they know the medium (intense light) used in producing the image but not how that medium was employed to produce such a perfect image with all its unique qualities and characteristics.

In the end, the agreed upon conclusion by the scientific researchers of the Shroud is that the image was formed by a selective scorching of the fibers by an intense, short burst of radiant light, although they are at a loss to explain how an individual would be able to duplicate that process/medium, especially a dead person in antiquity. The bottom line on the image is that after all this time, effort and money, it is still a mystery. The intention of this book is to solve the mystery by showing how this process/medium worked, a means that directly supports the scientific conclusions in full.

A body of data has arisen today from a diverse collection of scientific disciplines, which, when outlined with background, supports a specific methodology for just such a phenomena to occur; i.e. that a man dead or nearly so could radiate an intense short burst of high energy light. Light, coincidentally, that is highly coherent and laser like. Equally congruous is that it parallels a science that was understood at the dawn of antiquity, a science historically known to exist in the Middle East region. This science has been described using clouded terminology and veiled symbols by the mystical traditions of the planet for eons. Yet few realized the art to the same degree, as did the Master rabbi Yeshua.

The Silent Gospel, The Science of Divinity, constructs the processes and describes the biological path in the forming of the image on the Shroud as well as the path to immortality. This path is anchored in the rich, very ancient mystical traditions of the planet, and is supported by the current physics and sciences of the day. It is a science accessible to all in this life, if one has the genuine desire, resolve and faith to achieve it.

The very existence of the Shroud demonstrates its authenticity and the existence of an ancient wisdom and science. The Shroud, known by some as the "Fifth, or Silent Gospel", is the higher evidence left to us beyond words, showing a reality open to seeking souls who are ready to evolve by searching out the Light.

> "His disciples said to Him, 'Show us the place where you are, since it is necessary for us to seek it.'
>
> "He said to them, 'Whoever has ears, let him hear. There is light within a man of light, and he, (or "it") lights up the whole world.
>
> "If he, (or "it") does not shine he, (or "it") is darkness." Gospel of Thomas #24

What A Man Can Do

When I was a young father, I worked as an apprentice carpenter for an old Finnish master named Mattie. I assisted him in all manner of fine wood construction from cabinets to custom homes. I would be working up high on scaffolding finishing the outside of a custom home. Mattie would be below cutting the wood for me to nail or install. I would relay to him the measurements, angles and the results of his efforts. Mattie would throw the cut stock up to me and ask me how it fit. Most times my reply would be, "it's perfect" and he would reply, "are you sure it's perfect" with the emphasizes on *perfect* and I would reply, "yes, it's perfect Mattie" and he would reply always a little under his breath, with a hint of surprise, "What a man can do?" He said it with a mix of questioning, surprise and fact of statement. This repartee continued much of a year and since I heard this reply, "What a man can do?" so often, it sank deep into my marrow and sub-consciousness.

I began to contemplate during those hot Canadian summers the question and the implications of that statement. It wasn't so much that man could build the house or the tools, this was amazing, yes, but it was the idea that the piece was *perfect*, it could not have been cut or manufactured any better for the purposes required. During those laborious tasks in those quiet bucolic settings, my attention subconsciously began to drift in on the questions of man's drive for perfection and ultimately immortality. Then mysteriously somehow out of the ethers the question re-framed to become not man's drive for perfection but man's *desire to reflect divinity and all its perfection.*

Chapter Two

Placebo & Faith

"Have Faith and thee shall move mountains"

True Reality, the experienced Masters tell us, is veiled to us only by the separation we create and maintain. They explain that in *Reality* we are all one -- a singularity if you will -- and that the intra- and inter-connection exists in the timeless state of the Now. They expand by saying that this very state is the womb of all objective reality and that it is the subtle, still, intelligent energy of this womb that creates and sustains space, time, vibration and the anu (atom). This vibrantly alive Stillness is the Great Mystery, the Absolute. Regardless of race, culture or religious persuasion, they share that we are this timeless state, it is our true nature and that it is eternal and omnipresent.

The words may be tailored to their specific culture and times, but at the core, genuine realized masters impart a simple message. Individuated mind dancing in the trance of past and future possibility is what forms the illusion or veil keeping us from knowing reality in a personal, highly experiential manner. This little mirrors game that the mind constructs and maintains is termed the 'egoic self' and it is the identification with this aspect of self that acts to veil Reality from our direct experiential knowing. They would say that Awakening (to Reality) is not an attainment of something, as much as a remembrance of what has always been.

Here is the paradox; the egoic or individuated (separate) mind aspect of self constructs conceptual realities in order to maintain itself. In other words, its sole purpose is to sustain itself. The purpose for these constructions appears to be the maintaining of conceptual distance from pain and suffering caused by the original separation. These masters of Reality tell us that this very act of creating time-space is at the very core of all suffering as well as our material world. The ego's job is to maintain conceptual space, meaning distance and separation. The egoic aspect clings to the material like a baby to a teat. It lies in constant fear of losing the teat, which would mean its own annihilation. In Truth, great masters tell us our greatest fear is not in dying but the feeling of despair and pain buried deep within the ego's unique structure. A pain created by the egoic mind's very existence; despair generated in the knowing that it must be annihilated totally in order to feel the peace it craves. So the great paradox in human nature is that to end the suffering brought about by the birth of conceptual separation and the construction of the egoic little self, this aspect must surrender and release control over the placement of one's identity. I will write more on the value and purpose of the ego in the chapter on Awareness.

I write this little piece on the egoic aspect so to better understand faith. Faith is a cornerstone in the science of divinity. Without a rich understanding of faith it is difficult to fully grasp the art of immortality. Faith is a spiritual power, an energy substance that can in some ways be equated with grace. It is felt as a quality that supports life. Without a little faith it is impossible to make changes or cultivate any of the other spiritual supports like mindfulness, concentration, contemplation. Faith is not hope nor is it belief. Both of these are egoic constructs. Hope is anchored in the fear and attachment that something hoped for, something desired (by the mind) will occur in some future time. The statement, 'I have faith that everything will turn out right tomorrow', really is saying, 'I hope it will turn out the way I want it to'. Hope is dependent, attached and arises out of fear. Belief on the other hand is purely conceptual. It gives us something to hold onto as it helps to shape our perception. Belief is a pure construct of the mind, an abstraction, whereas the heartfelt sense of faith can only be experienced.

When the mother calls the baby to follow her across the street, it just runs to her. This is blind faith, which is fine for the immature; it is putting faith in another. It is generally seen as the first level of spiritual development. The disciples put their faith in Jesus their teacher and followed him till their safety was threatened.

All students that have a deep initiation with a true teacher will come to the point of egoic letting go, also called surrender, a point where they will suddenly be gripped with a terror that he or she is being threatened or is in mortal danger. This is the powerful egoic survival mechanism kicking in. A good teacher attempts to produce environments suitable to the student, allowing for a more verifiable level of faith to develop and be anchored within. It must rise as an organic, genuine outgrowth of self. You can only verify anything through direct experience; in this way you become the one knowing it. This develops a more mature level of faith, one held within oneself and not given over to another. This more mature level arises through discrimination, verified through self-inquiry within the field of loving-kindness. We need to weigh what others tell us with our own experience and our own inner truth. Mature faith arises within when a genuine balance of love for others and loving respect for oneself is found. Honest doubt can be a servant to developing mature faith, whereas despair is the absence of faith. The undercurrent of motive found in all hope and belief is the ancient foreboding silent hook of egoic fear.

The ego is trapped between the desire to maintain survival and the knowledge of physical death. You can run all you like but mortality and its agent, death, is always there, following every move. The ego is a construct of movement that interestingly desires a state of homeostasis, which is equilibrium. It will run you around and around till the time comes when you are just too darn tired to run anymore. This dilemma produces the core seed for suffering. We race forward toward the future or reminisce in the past. For most, this act continues till life puts a stop to it. This is the human condition and the only antidote wise masters tell us, is genuine faith.

Faith

Faith, like joy, arises naturally -- it cannot be forced; only hope and belief can be artificially constructed. Faith results from the degree of loving-kindness one can genuinely muster when in an exposed and vulnerable position. This aspect of being genuine, of being in integrity, will be fully developed in the later chapter on Truth.

The Aramaic word for "faith" is haimanuta. Haimanuta implies to the listener a confidence, firmness, or integrity of being in Sacred Unity. (ND Klotz pp33) It is an emotional quality that arises organically when we touch the eternal. And as we saw in the Preface, each emotion is protein specific, meaning of course harmonic specific. (See C. Pert in Preface)

So much has been said about faith that the notion is virtually corrupted in the West, especially within Christianity. The true power of faith and the adaptability of the human form can be best demonstrated by this one well-documented, extraordinary story about Mr. Wright's amazing remission described below. Medical research considers this a case of the power of mind over body; they see it as the power of belief, which they call the Placebo Effect. But if you look deeper at this phenomenon you can clearly see the words of the Master reflected.

> "And he [Jesus] said unto him, Arise, go thy way: thy faith hath made thee whole." Matthew 17:20

> (Jesus said) "...If ye have faith as a grain of mustard seed, ye shall say unto this mountain, Remove hence to yonder place; and it shall remove; and nothing shall be impossible unto you." Luke 17:19

Mr. Wright

In 1957, a cancer drug called Krebiozen had finished all its trials needed to commence testing with human subjects. It was distributed to 100 hospitals and in one of those hospitals a Dr. Bruno Klopfer headed up the study on their local cancer population. One of his patients was a man named Mr. Wright, who had read about the drug in the newspaper and had faith it would save his rapidly deteriorating life. The story below is found in the excellent book, Doctors Orders, Go Fishing by Dean Shrock PhD.

"Mr. Wright had advanced cancer with huge tumor masses the size of oranges in his neck, maxilla, groin, chest, and abdomen. He had developed resistance to all known medical treatment. His spleen and liver were greatly enlarged. His thoracic duct was obstructed, and his chest had to be drained of fluid every other day. He was on oxygen and not expected to live more then two weeks. While Mr. Wright was certain [that] the Krebiozen would save him, one of the criteria to be included in the study was that the patient have a prognosis of at least three, and preferably six months. Mr. Wright did not qualify. As much as Dr. Klopfer tried, he could not dissuade Mr. Wright's enthusiasm for this Golden Opportunity."

Dr. Klopfer thought that Mr. Wright wouldn't even live through the weekend, so he gave him the drug thinking it wouldn't be too much of a problem. On Monday, everyone who qualified for the treatment showed no change. But Mr. Wright, who had been completely bedridden, was now walking around the ward spreading "good cheer."

His tumors were now half their original size. The regression could not be accounted to any treatment outside the one injection of Krebiozen.

They continued to give the injections three times weekly as the study stipulated. Much to the joy of Mr. Wright, but to the bewilderment of the medical staff, within 10 days he was discharged from the hospital breathing normally, fully active and flying his own airplane at 12,000 feet with no discomfort.

About two months later Mr. Wright heard news reports that all of the clinical testing of Krebiozen showed no improvement in their patients. He began to lose his faith in this last hope and, "after two months of practically perfect health, he relapsed to his original state." Below is the original report on Mr. Wright by Dr. Klopfer.

"But here I saw the opportunity to double-check the drug and maybe, too, find out how the quacks can accomplish the results that they claim (and many of their claims are well substantiated). Knowing something of my patient's innate optimism by this time, I deliberately took advantage of him. This was for purely scientific reasons, in order to perform the perfect control experiment, which could answer all the perplexing questions he had brought up. Furthermore, this scheme could not harm him in any way, I felt sure, and there was nothing I knew anyway that could help him.

"When Mr. Wright had all but given up in despair with the recrudescence of his disease, in spite of the 'wonder-drug" which had worked so well at first, I decided to take the chance and play the quack. So deliberately lying, I told him not to believe what he read in the newspapers, the drug was really most promising after all. What then, he asked, was the reason for his relapse? 'Just because the substance deteriorated on standing,' I replied, 'a new super–refined, double-strength product is due to arrive tomorrow which can more than reproduce the great benefits derived from the original injections.'

"This news came as a great revelation to him, and Mr. Wright, as ill as he was, became his optimistic self again, eager to start over. By delaying a couple of days before the 'shipment' arrived, his anticipation of salvation had reached a tremendous pitch. When I announced that the new series of injections was about to begin, he was almost ecstatic and his faith was strong.

"With much fan fare, and putting on quite an act (which I deemed permissible under the circumstances), I administered the first injection of the doubly potent, fresh preparation – consisting of fresh water and nothing more. The results of the experiment were quite unbelievable to us at the time, although we must have had some suspicion of the remotely possible outcome to have even attempted it at all.

"Recovery from this second near-terminal state was even more dramatic than the first. Tumor masses melted, chest fluid vanished, he became ambulatory, and even went back to flying again. At this time he was certainly the picture of health. The water injections were continued, since they worked such wonders. He then remained symptom-free for over two months. At this time the final AMA announcement appeared in the press, 'Nationwide tests show Krebiozen to be a worthless drug in treatment of cancer.'

"Within a few days of this report, Mr. Wright was remitted to the hospital in extremis. His faith was now gone, his last hope vanished, and he succumbed in less than two days."

In 1986 Dr. Ernest Rossi, a student of Dr. Klopfer, wrote this conclusion to the case of Mr. Wright in his often-cited book, <u>The Psychobiology of Mind-body Healing</u>

"We know today, for example, that cancer growth can be controlled by the person's immune system; if you can improve the immune system, it can destroy the cancer. Obviously, Mr. Wright's immune system must have been activated by his belief in a cure. The incredible rapidity of his healing also suggest that his autonomic and endocrine systems must have been responsive to suggestion, enabling him to mobilize his blood system with such amazing efficiency to remove the toxic fluids and waste products of the fast diminishing cancer. As we shall learn later in this book, we now know a lot more about the "limbic-hypothalamic system" of the brain as the major mind-body connector modulating the biological activity of the autonomic, endocrine, and immune systems in response to mental suggestion and beliefs. In summary, Mr. Wright's experience tells us that it was his total belief in the efficacy of the worthless drug, Krebiozen that mobilized a healing placebo response by activating all these major systems of mind-body communication and healing."

To poetically paraphrase, Mr. Wright's body was bedridden and with his remaining life measured in hours not days that he was still alive at all was in itself amazing and a small miracle. After one useless injection he was out of bed walking the hospital halls in great humor. Ten days later he was out flying his own plane free of cancer and completely normal by all manner of assessment.

> "There are many things sacred in the world, but faith is the most sacred; not faith in something, but faith in itself" pp.240 <u>Sufi Teachings: The Art of Being</u> – Hazrat Inayat Khan

The medical literature is full of examples of the phenomena known as the "placebo effect". If one desired to do so, one could read a litany of case studies of dire conditions being dramatically and miraculously changed for the better, with no known cause behind the effect other then the placebo of faith.

If this were not enough we also have the mental and physical effects witnessed during extreme cases of personality disorder. Maladies appear and disappear with the arriving personality. Speaking unknown foreign language is one thing but for dramatic physical changes like disease and scarring to appear and disappear with the personality points to the power, potential and strength of some aspect of the human structure and its innate capacity.

> "Faith is a substance; if one does not possess that substance, one cannot raise it to the highest ideal which alone merits faith."

> "Faith therefore cannot be called a thought; faith is the ground itself; it is the ground from which thoughts spring up as plants."
>
> "...the perfection of faith is attained when it has risen to that ideal, that height, where it can hold itself without any support." Pp242 HK-Pp243 HK

The original Aramaic term for faith meant 'to be in integrity of being in Sacred Unity.' The direct meaning might imply to current listeners that the definition of faith is to be in attuned alignment with life. The key word in the translation is integrity. Integrity implies wholeness of self and it is this wholeness that allows sacred unity to rise within.

Jesus tells us and demonstrates many times over in the gospels that this specific alignment allows the divine, in the form of Holy Spirit or Grace, to flow through the physical; this is the source for healing on all levels. The Bible writers also say that if we allow this alignment and flow of divine energy through us to be sustained, it will strengthen us by virtue of ordering our physical systems into greater and greater unity.

The psycho-emotional aspects become unified as they resonate to this life force substance as well, resulting in confidence and inner firmness felt as creative resolve. The resonant quality, when focused towards wellness of the physical -- in this case salvation from the cancer -- reorganizes the physical template back into wholeness and integrity. When the focus is to channel this cohering substance or quality to another, as Jesus often selflessly demonstrated in the gospels, this act of bringing coherence into the other results in healing. The level of extreme alignment in the story of Mr. Wright literally will not allow for non-aligned objects or structures to remain within the field of resonant influence. It is literally a reorganization of atomic structures from a quantum level. But as the story also shows that if one aligns with despair, then illness and death soon surely follow.

Life has brought me into contact with Mr. Wright types of scenarios. I've witnessed the beauty, power, potential and possibilities that reside within humans. You can see it in day-to-day life if you look closely, but when you personally witness extreme cases like Mr. Wright's, you start to wonder what the limits might be to that potential. Remissions of all types are well documented, spontaneous or not, they are still all so amazing. My own mother had pancreatic cancer and was told by her doctors that she had six months to live, and six months later to the week she passed over.

Why is it that some people rapidly succumb to illness whereas another taps the deep well of the heart, finding courage and faith that profoundly changes their perspective and reality? The collective power of the human body and all its systems remaining intact, yet able to evolve and change at rapid rates, astounds the mind's ability to comprehend. I cannot imagine my own grandfather in his teens being placed in a new car with radio, CD, and cell phone on a Los Angeles freeway with everyone traveling 80 miles per hour, bumper to bumper. It boggles the mind the way we've adapted and grown in such a short time. Raw amazement and awe transform anyone that truly looks at biology and the diversity and abilities inherent in humans. The creative power to reproduce a hundred trillion cells from a zygote or clone from a slice of DNA humbles the investigative mind. The creative beauty inherent in the ability to develop an idea or make new tools alone can overwhelm reason.

As Humanity cascades into the twenty-first century, creativity is synergistically spiraling at exponential rates. We are adding new information and tools at a dizzying pace. We will double all the known information within the following year or so. The concept of new is taking on richer and deeper meaning with each passing day. There is an old Sufi saying that poetically goes something like this, 'If you have the question then already within you have the answer.' Oddly, in science this appears to be the case, for if the intelligence to form the question exists then so does the consciousness to explore an answer to the question.

We as a species have become skilled at exploring questions outside the self but when it comes to exploring inner qualitative space we are more timid. The heart quality of courage is a good example: courage to be true to oneself or the courage to place others above the wellbeing of oneself. To run into harm's way for a loved one is one thing but to do it for people unknown, with no personal ties, immediately evokes awe and deep feelings from a depth rarely touched. It is man rising above the status of his animal nature. Witnessing it, even if it is on television, touches those deep feelings within us, and we are moved to honor these few people as being very special.

My sense is that man will begin to place more and more of his attention on developing and exploring the inner senses and this will be in direct ratio to our exploration of outer space. We have taken the exploration of the outer reality to the borders of extinction; if we are to survive as a species, however, the communicative inner senses will need attention. The Fifth or Silent Gospel was created for this time. The silent information embedded within the Shroud, if allowed, will touch our inner truth, move our awareness and shift our perception of ourselves as well as the very nature of reality. The embedded information within the Shroud as it begins to speak to you, connects you with the Eternal, allowing the presence of faith and great integrity.

Communication

The creative push to perfection that we call evolution is centered on communication. The old Darwinian 'survival of the fittest' model of evolution is fading; survival now appears to be based on the capacity for communication. This new vision of evolution and survival is not based on individuals who are developing but living systems interlinked into a coherent whole. Like cells in an organism that take on different tasks for the whole, different populations enfold information not only for themselves, but for all other organisms, expanding the consciousness of the whole, while at the same time becoming more and more aware of this collective consciousness. From this new model we are all cells in the human structure. It is this structure of consciousness that will evolve -- which is to say, expand to a greater capacity and expression of connectedness and communication.

Communication is a two-way street. The flow of information and the energy to carry that information must go both ways. Communication is a prerequisite for life and consciousness. Consciousness means literally, con scire, to know with, or to know together.

> "I think that self-awareness comes about through Mutual Awareness.
>
> "I think the reason that we are conscious is because we are inter-conscious in relationship to other people. Consciousness is shared. And I don't think an individual human being, without language, and without relationship to other people or any other thing, would be

conscious. I think that consciousness has to be understood in relationship, not as an isolated thing."

Rupert Sheldrake

We are, from a physics perspective, electromagnetic beings in movement. These movements of energy are communications. Electromagnetic signals of different frequencies are involved in communication within and between organisms, and between organisms and the environment. Organic life is comprised of many coherent oscillating platforms all working and communicating to maintain itself as a single coherent oscillating matrix of systems acting as one coherent platform.

The coherent platform acting in resonance is a prerequisite for universal communication. Thus, it seems that the essence of the living state is to build up and extend the coherent spatial-temporal platform for communication. Expanded collections of coherent platforms reflect the evolutionary state of consciousness creating and holding them in a standing wave field. The body form of any life form is a direct reflection of its collective consciousness. Form follows the resonance of the consciousness.

Living systems are thus neither subjects alone, nor objects isolated, but both subjects and objects in a mutually communicating universe of meaning. We are both wave and particle and neither. The depth of any consciousness revolves around the qualitative universe and the quality of the connectedness forming it. In other words, it is not just how clean the connections of communications are, but also the quality imparted in the embedded information-energy. Qualitative implies emotion, a sense of feeling. At the core of all senses are the two central polarities of love and fear. The quality of the info-energy connection refers to how supportive it is; does the embedded carrier wave act to support and sustain connectivity or does it form interference waves that distort coherence?

A human is a complex design with a depth that few on this spinning blue gem fully realize. Humans have awareness and the consciousness that they are aware. This makes this species unique. They have the ability to make choices on what receives their attention and what does not. Humanity is endowed with abilities to loop awareness inward to primal levels. They can follow their heartbeat or their breath rhythm inward into alive-stillness, to the universal heartbeat.

In my studies of human potentiality, I was immediately drawn to religion and theology and from thence into the mystical wings of those same major religions. I investigated the spiritual and geometric aspects of life. I researched the words and lives of those uniquely realized individuals who have transcended the world of form, who laid the foundations for our philosophy, religions and mystical traditions. During my quest I noticed constant references to the heart: the sacred heart and the immaculate heart. Over time I came to realize that the heart was a key and the portal to our highest potential and possibly to our salvation as a species.

Lebhon

The Aramaic word lebhon, as in the Beatitude; "'Blessed are the pure in Heart, for they shall see God.' KJV translates heart, as "any center from which life radiates- a sense of expansion plus generative power: vitality, desire, affection, courage, and audacity all rolled into one." (Prayer of the Cosmos, Neil Douglas Klotz)

How one purifies the heart in order to know God is summed up by Jesus when asked by his disciples,

"Teacher, which is the greatest commandment in the law?"

Jesus replied: "Love the Lord your God with all your heart and with all your soul and with all your mind. This is the first and greatest commandment. And the second is like it: love your neighbor as yourself. All the laws and prophets hang on these two commandments."

New Testament, Matthew 22:36-40

In these few lines are outlined the precise process and method for the ultimate attunement, one that allows one to realize that he too is a Son of God. Jesus tells the reader not to love the Jewish or Christian god but your God. He speaks clearly of the integrity of all three aspects of self: heart, soul, and mind. To create this integrity one must first recognize these three aspects and then unify them under the quality of love. Jesus points out that this alignment begins with creating unity of your heart, then your soul and your mind with the love you have for yourself and others. Jesus tells us that the greater your love is for your self, the greater your love is for others, and most importantly, the greater will be the unity between this trinity of aspects comprising the self. Jesus tells us that when your love of others is no longer differentiated from your love of self, then full integrity is achieved.

Out of these commandments came The Golden Rule, "Do unto others as you would have them do unto you." This simple commonsense rule is at the heart of true Christianity as well as all the other major religious traditions. To demonstrate the power and vast potential of this simple commandment, the image was left on the Shroud as testament to the glory and power of Faith and Wisdom. In the Greek translation this is known as Pistis Sophia or Faith-Wisdom. These two attributes are age-old cornerstones in the attainment of Truth. When this attainment is mastered the Mystery emerges and no veil exists between Truth and Self. The doors to the infinite open wide, allowing form to mirror awareness, while all aspects of self unite with an omnipresent and eternal identity. The psychological and physical bodies march in unified step through life allowing a deepening of the connection and the experience called Reality.

The Shroud's very existence is a silent communication left by a master of Reality. A puzzle to engender faith and spur on evolutionary movement enabling the very universe to unfold.

My goal in the following chapters is to connect the known ancient mystical sciences, that when perfected by a man results in a brief intense release of energy from the body, to the teachings and life of Jesus. Then correlate the possibilities/probabilities that Jesus or someone of his era had means and opportunities to learn these sciences. This completed we'll look at the conditions that allow for such a radical occurrence to happen in the sciences of East and West.

Chapter Three

The Rainbow, Wisdom or Golden Body 'Ja'-lus in Tibetan

The goal is purity of heart, which is the freedom within which God's love can operate freely from the resistance of mind

Buried within the ancient wisdom texts of Tibet, China, and India, there exists accounts of individuals that have used and transformed their physical bodies in the most radical of manners. Adepts of skill have demonstrated control of the physical systems in ways that completely defies logic and physics. Yet within many of these same traditions spiritual realization or transcendence is recognized not by physical feat but by the manifestation of luminosity during life known as saintly radiance. Researcher and author Michael Murphy recounts in his epic book, <u>The Future of the Body</u>, stories of "luminosities" occurring around holy personages during times of deep spiritual immersion. He concludes that, "luminosities are described with enough consistency from culture to culture to suggest that they actually happen."

There are levels of experiencing in all things, and this is true with Illumination as well. The most venerated leave a body that remains in a state of incorruptibility and free from decay for varying amounts of time after death. An even higher level of attainment is thought to be achieved, when the adept leaves little, if any, of his body behind at all, rather, transforming it into luminous, radiant light upon the arrival of physical death. These extraordinary levels of Realization demand recognition from those left witnessing the phenomena. After these final extraordinary events, students feel compelled to immediately begin sharing the information their Master imparted during life with more zeal and passion. These events either continue or begin new spiritual lineages. The transmission of information and practices in a direct unbroken lineage of person to person is necessary for the sake of accuracy and clarity in preserving the steps required for attainment. As in the times of Jesus, this process of the Masters' full realization of

Truth, and the students carrying on their Masters' message or practices continues in the present.

Ramalinga Swamiga

Ramalinga Swamigal, the Saint of Vadalur, Tamil Nadu in southern India is a modern day saint and one of the few great souls to have dissolved his body completely. His story is not only well documented but he left us over forty thousand verses describing his experiences. On January 30, 1874 at the age of 50, Ramalinga wrote and released a short statement directing his disciples. It ended with "...I am in this body now and after awhile I shall enter into all the bodies of His creation. Close the door and lock it outside. The room, if ordered to be opened, will be void." Then he shut himself in his room. Later that same night a brilliant flash of violet light suddenly emanated from his room. When it was opened it was found to be empty. These events were chronicled and investigated by the Chief British administrative officer of the South Arcot District along with other subordinates. They concluded that Ramalinga was a great soul who had vanished into thin air.

In 1878 the Manual of the South Arcot District was published. In it the Collector, Mr. J.H. Garstin, describes the disappearance of Ramalinga. He stated that, "In 1874, Ramalinga Swami entered into a room at Mettukuppam and asked his devotees to lock it outside. He did not come out at all. His disciples believe that he has merged with God."

Ramalinga's key principle was compassion to all living beings. He taught that the love of God, or God's grace, will flow into the form of the compassionate being. To receive God's grace, one should become kindness incarnate and firmly establish in oneself feelings of unity and fellowship. He entreated devotee's to pray silently, filled with the love of God, to meditate upon the Supreme Grace Light seated in one's heart and enter into ecstasy. Ramalinga described several successive transformations. The first of these being the transformation of the mortal human body into "Suddha deham" or "perfect body", achieved by universal spiritual communion and devotion to God. Second was the transformation of the "Suddha deham" into the "Pranava Deham" or "Body of Grace and Light." And thirdly was the transformation into the "Gnana deham" or "Body of Wisdom" -- the body of God Supreme. According to Ramalinga the Pranava deham can be visually seen but cannot be touched. Adepts with this level of realization appear much younger and youthful than their age.

Dzogpa Chenpo

It is interesting and no coincidence how similar Ramilinga's key principles to holy life are to that of Jesus. Stories of luminosity or saintly radiance are common among Christian saints, Sufis, Taoist sages, Hindu yogis, Buddhist mystics and indigenous shamans. We are not talking about bio-luminosity here as in a Lightning Bug that we caught and saved in jars as children, although that subject is of interest and points to the reality of radiating light when the right chemical exchange occurs. We are instead talking about radiance emanating from the physical body like light from a light bulb. To understand this process we turn to the rationalist Buddhist of Tibet and the practice of Dzogpa Chenpo.

In the Himalayan regions, the early indigenous religion was that of the Bön. Bön pre-existed the creation of both the sovereign territories, later to become the country of Tibet as well as of Buddhism. When Padma Sambhava, an Indian tantric sage, brought Buddhism from India to Tibet in the 8th Century AD he found the richly tilled ground of the Bönpo. It was here that he married the Buddha's teachings in this land, laying an excellent and enduring foundation. When he left in a Rainbow body at the end of his time there, a new lineage of Buddhist teachings was created. This was the start of what has become the Nyingma tradition and is the foundation of Tibetan Buddhism as we have come to know it.

At the heart of the Nyingma tradition is the practice of Dzogchen. Nyingma alludes to an ancient school, but this is simply because it is the oldest of the four schools of Tibetan Buddhism (Nyingma, Kagyu, Sakya, and Gelugpa). The Nyingma teachings are uniquely categorized in nine yanas, or vehicles. The main practices are emphasized in the three inner tantras of Maha Yoga, Anu Yoga, and Ati Yoga. Ati Yoga is also known as the Great Perfection, Dzogpa Chenpo, or simply as Dzog chen/Dzogchen. The Dzogchen teachings have been passed down in an unbroken line from teacher to student from the Primordial Buddha Samatabhadra to the present day. Dzogchen is known as The Great Completion or Great Perfection, transcending ritual and symbol. Dzogchen practitioners who have attained ultimate insight (wisdom) and compassion, a phase in which pure and total presence is stabilized (Trek-chod), are then allowed to practice To-gal.

To-gal is the final practice of Dzogchen. This final practice enables the master yogi or yogini to dissolve his or her physical body into the essence of the elements at the time of death. The master disappears into a body of light becoming the wisdom body, the same term used by Ramalinga. This term is called 'Ja'-lus or The Rainbow Body, in Tibetan. The final process of dissolution of the body happens over varying amounts of time ranging from a short period to many days. During this process the body shrinks dramatically eventually down to only bits of hair, toe-finger nails, and possible nasal septum left behind. Some saints such as the great Milarepa (1050-1123) and Padmasambhava dissolved entirely into light, leaving no relics behind at all. The culmination of one's life into the rainbow body is widely recognized as a sign of extreme sanctity in Tibetan Buddhism and among the Bönpo. Reports of this level of transmutation are rare, but still they occur and have been chronicled far into antiquity. Interestingly, the Bön, laid historical claim to a lineage of Dzogchen that pre-dates the entry of Buddhism into Tibet.

The rainbow or wisdom body is also the central aim of Indian Buddhist tantricism known as Vajrayana that the Taoists call the golden body. Another term is Soruba Samidhi, the golden body, a state of God-realization in which Divinity descends and transforms the spiritual, intellectual, mental, vital and physical bodies. It is considered physical immortality or the highest perfection.

Mipham Rinpoche (1846-1912), one of the greatest scholars and masters of Tibet, wrote, "Crowning the banner of the complete teaching of Buddha is the beautiful ornament of the clear light teachings of Dzogpa Chenpo." His Holiness Dilgo Khyentse Rinpoche further explains, "Dzogchen is a state, the primordial state, that state of total awakening that is the heart-essence of all Buddha's and all spiritual paths, and the summit of an individual's spiritual evolution. "

At the heart and the root of the practice of Dzogpa Chenpo is pure loving-kindness. This is clearly highlighted in the short excerpts from Meditation the Dzogchen (Dzog Chen) Way, Advice from His Holiness Penor Rinpoche. H.H. Penor Rinpoche is the Supreme Head of the Nyingma School. His excerpts on the subject were transmitted November 12, 1999, and translated by Khenpo Tsewang Gyatso Rinpoche. His Holiness Penor Rinpoche is considered one of the foremost masters in the Buddhist Tradition of Tibet. He is the embodiment of the profound wisdom and limitless compassion, which are the hallmarks of this tradition.

> "This is the root of all the dharma practices: generating the Bodhicitta [loving-kindness]. If one can really generate genuine Bodhicitta within one's mind, then it is very easy to move nearer to ultimate liberation....
>
> "...If one practices the Bodhicitta, that kind of pure intention to really benefit all other sentient beings, and then the samatha meditation practices to establish one's mind in full concentration, then of course there will be the Great Perfection ("Dzogchen") meditations.
>
> "But if one cannot cultivate the Bodhicitta within one's mind, the path to enlightenment is already broken. Without Bodhicitta, there is no real path. Bodhicitta is that which is without any partiality. The pure intention of Bodhicitta, is the thought to benefit all sentient beings without any exception.
>
> "...So the most important points are to have faith and devotion in the dharma, then meditating and contemplating on Bodhicitta and compassion."

Khenpo A. Chung

In recent years, reports coming out of Tibet describe the attainment of the rainbow body by a Gelugpa monk (different school of Buddhism), named Khenpo A Chung, who lived and died in eastern Kham region of Tibet. Three of his teachers are still alive in nearby villages, and his attendant, Lobsang Nyen Thag, lives in a nearby gonpa (spiritual center). Other witnesses that attest to the events surrounding the Khenpo's manifestation of the rainbow body are now living in India. Below are two independent versions of the same story. The first is found in the best selling book by Sogyal Rinpoche called, <u>Tibetan Book of Living & Dying,</u> Rider Pub., Sogyal Rinpoche Ch.10 - p167-169)

The Rainbow Body

"Throughout the advanced practices of Dzogchen, accomplished practitioners can bring their lives to an extraordinary and triumphant end. As they die, they enable their body to be reabsorbed back into the light essence of the elements that created it, and consequently their material body dissolves into light and disappears completely.

"This process is known as the "rainbow body" or "body of light", because the dissolution is often accompanied by spontaneous manifestations of light and rainbows. The ancient Tantras of Dzogchen, and the writings of the great masters, distinguish different categories of this amazing, otherworldly phenomenon, for at one time, if at least not normal, it was reasonably frequent.

"...This may be very difficult for us now to believe, but the factual history of Dzogchen lineage is full of examples of individuals who attained rainbow light body, and as Dudjom Rinpoche often used to point out, this is not just ancient history. Of the many examples, I would like to choose one of the most recent, and one of with which I have a personal connection. In 1952 there was a famous instance of the rainbow body in the East of Tibet, witnessed by many people. The man who attained it, Sonam Namgyal, was the father of my tutor and the beginning of this book.

"He was a very simple, humble person, who made his way as an itinerant stone carver, carving mantras and sacred texts. Some say he had been a hunter in his youth, and had received a teaching from a great master. No one really knew he was a practitioner; he was truly called a "hidden yogin."

"...he then fell ill, or seemed to, but became strangely, increasingly happy. When his illness got worse, his family called in masters and doctors. His son told him he should remember, 'Everything is illusion, but I am confident that all is well."

"Just before his death at seventy-nine, he said 'All I ask is that when I die, don't move my body for a week.' When he died his family wrapped his body and invited Lamas and monks to come and practice for him. They placed the body in a small room in the house, and they could not help noticing that although he had been a tall person, they had no trouble getting it in, as if he were becoming smaller. At the same time, an extraordinary display of rainbow-coloured light was seen all around the house. When they looked into the room on the sixth day, they saw that the body was getting smaller and smaller. On the eight day after his death, the morning in which the funeral had been arranged, the undertakers arrived to collect the body. When they undid its coverings, they found nothing inside but his nails and hair.

"My masters Jamyang Khyentse asked for these be brought to him, and verified that this was a case of the rainbow body."

Here is the same story as told by Fr. Francis Tiso, a Catholic vicar, researching the Rainbow Body phenomena first hand.

"My father was a hunter in his youth. Later he became very devoutly religious and practiced a lot. We didn't know that he was such an accomplished Dzogpa Chempo meditator. He was very secretive about his meditation. For most of his life my father spent his time carving images, mantras, and scriptures in stones in many places. He was very humble and no one ever expected him to be such a special person, which is as it should be for a true yogi.

"Once I was in a retreat. My brother came to me and said: 'Father is slightly sick. I don't see anything serious, but he says he is going to die.'

"Then after a couple of days, on the evening of the seventh day of the fourth month of the Water-dragon year (1952), father died at the age of 79. A lama had advised my brother that they should take special care of their father's body when he died but my relatives didn't understand what that meant.

"So, soon after his death they arranged the body in the same way as for an ordinary person. But they began noticing rainbow lights and rainbow tents around their place, and the body started to reduce in size. Then they realized that their father had attained enlightenment in the ultimate nature through Dzogpa Chenpo meditation and that his gross body was dissolving in what is popularly known as 'Dissolution into Rainbow Body'.

"After a couple of days (I can't remember how many days he told me), his mortal body was dissolved. I hurriedly concluded my retreat and went home. Then everything had gone and only the twenty nails of his body were left behind on the spot where his body was being kept. We collected these remains and except for a few little pieces that we kept for ourselves, we offered all the nails and hair to Jamyang Khyenste Chovkyi Lotro, as he wished to have them. Everybody in the valley was talking about my father's death. If a famous Lama died in this manner, it wouldn't be a surprise, but when a humble lay person displayed such a great accomplishment, it amazed us all."

Paramahansa Yogananda

These stories, as well as the volumes of others buried within the sacred texts, attest to a little understood phenomenon by the West; and because of their locations they are not documented in a way as to satisfy Western science. In the same year as the death of Sonam Namgyal, however, one well-documented, fully collaborated case of a body remaining in a state, perfectly uncorrupted and free from all decay, occurred in Los Angeles, California. It is the well detailed case of Paramahansa Yogananda , a Hindu swami that entered mahasamadhi (conscious death) on March 7,1952 in Los Angeles, California. Because his passing over occurred in Los Angeles, California, Mr. Harry T. Rowe, the Chief Mortuary Director for Forest Lawn Memorial-Park had the duty to record the death and its causes. In his notarized letter to the organization Yogananda created, The Self-Realization Fellowship, Rowe wrote;

"…No physical disintegration was visible in his body even twenty days after death…This state of perfect preservation of the body is, so far as we know from mortuary annals, an unparalleled one…. At the time of receiving Yogananda's body, the Mortuary personnel expected to observe, through the glass lid of the casket, the usual progressive signs of bodily decay. Our astonishment increased as day followed day without bringing any visible change in the body under observation. Yogananda's body was in apparently a phenomenal state of immutability… No odor of decay emanated from his body at any time…. The physical appearance of Yogananda on March 27th, just before the bronze cover of the casket was put in position, was the same as it had been on March 7th. He looked on March 27th as fresh and unsavaged by decay as he had looked the night of his death. On March 27th there was no reason to say that his body had suffered any visible physical disintegration at all. For these reasons we state again that the case of Paramahansa Yogananda is unique in our experience."

This excerpt can be found at the end of <u>Autobiography of a Yogi</u>, which is Paramahansa Yogananda's story as told by him. Yogananda tells the story in his book on page 56 about a saint named Gandha Baba and his abilities to manifest things:

"The vibrations in turn are regulated by Prana 'Lifetrons', subtle life forces of finer than atomic energies intelligently charged with the five distinctive sensory idea substances.

"Gandha Baba, attuning himself with the pranic force, by certain yoga practices was able to guide the 'lifetrons' to rearrange their vibratory structure and to objectify the desired result. His perfume, fruit, and other miracles were actually materialization of mundane vibrations, and were not inner sensations hypnotically produced."

Then again he stated, "Awake in God, true saints effect changes in this dream world by means of a will harmoniously attuned to the Creative Cosmic Dreamer."

Master Zi Sheng Wang

The first time I heard the term rainbow body used by a student of Dzogchen was in Oakland, California. I was attending a healing and transmission by a Tibetan Qigong Master by the name of Master Zi Sheng Wang. Master Wang was Chinese born and had been Tibetan trained. At the time he had been doing Qigong for nearly 60 years and was a student of Khenpo Munsel Rinpoche, a highly respected Tibetan Buddhist lineage holder of the Nyingma tradition. Khenpo Munsel

Rinpoche, whose Dharma name was Chr Cheng Jia Zuo, and was the 11th lineage holder descended from Padmasambhava, the recognized founder of Tibetan Buddhism.

In 1998 the International Chinese Medicine Congress honored Master Wang as the Most Outstanding Qigong Master of the Year, as well as one of China's foremost energy healers. This recognition alone should speak volumes as to Master Wang's level of attainment. As the morning healing session began he shared his story with us in brief. He concluded his abbreviated biography by saying that when he finished his work in the West, he was going back to Tibet where he would leave this existence in a Rainbow Body. His demeanor in imparting this information to us was very matter of fact, allowing him to easily segue into the healing session without having to address the subject at all.

Master Wang is the founder and president of the San Francisco based International Tibetan Qigong Association, author of the book, The Path of Dzogchen. He has begun several community projects attempting to better the lives of the local community.

Milarepa

The life of Milarepa, one of the most beloved saints of Tibet, is an example that serves to bolster great encouragement to all that seek freedom. He demonstrated how an average person involved in destructive behavior and wrong living can rise to enlightenment within a lifetime. He was born around 1050 of the Common Era. When he was approximately seven or ten years of age his father died. At this time his father's brother began to exploit his mother and Milarepa's sister and himself. In 1068 Milarepa went to study black magic in Central Tibet and by1070, he is credited with casting a deadly magic spell killing twenty-five relatives. The uncle and aunt at the root of his anger, however, did not die. We are told in the story that for a period of nine years Milarepa sent hailstorms against the crops of the uncle's villagers as a means of revenge. He is said to have practiced black magic until 1088 when he experienced the need for repentance and initiated the study of Rdzogs Chen, without, however, good results. He then sought out Marpa the Translator, disciple of the Indian Guru Naropa (1089/94) under whom he did severe penance, making a three-year solitary retreat, 1094-97. He practiced Vajrayana meditation in the caves of Tibet and Nepal, returning to his village in 1097 where he met his sister Peta after a long separation. In 1100 he went on retreat at La phyis

Gang, where he attained enlightenment. Between 1100 and 1123 he trained disciples and composed a great many Dharma songs, and is credited as one of the founders of the Kagyu Order. He died, probably in 1123, leaving no relics; Buddhist tradition has that his body disappeared into a rainbow of light.

The ultimate realization of Milarepa's life and the enormous shift in consciousness this average man achieved during his life's journey has made him one of the most beloved examples within Tibetan Buddhism.

Sri Aurobindo

Another highly evolved/attained individual was Sri Aurobindo. On December 4, 1950, in the presence of Mother (his chief disciple) and a few disciples, Sri Aurobindo realized the state of being called mahasamadhi at the time of his leaving his physical body. A golden hue shone about his body, taking on a new luster described by the Mother as "a luminous mantle of bluish golden hue around him."

As the story goes, the body remained perfectly intact with this golden hue persisting for a period of four days after he had died. Numerous accounts claimed the truth of this phenomena. On December 9th, 100 hours later, the body began to show the first signs of decay and was interred.

> "The spiritual life finds its most potent expression in the man who lives the ordinary life of men in the strength of Yoga... It is by such a union of the inner life and the outer that mankind will eventually be lifted up and become mighty and divine."
>
> Sri Aurobindo, 1950

Loung Pordaeng

In Samui, Thailand, in a specially constructed temple, its most famous resident, the highly venerated monk named Loung Pordaeng (also Loung Por Ruam) sits in display for all to see. When he died at the age of 79 on May 6, 1973 more than 30 years ago, he was sitting in a meditation posture, a position his body still holds today. Remarkably, after all these years his body remains in remarkably good condition with few signs of decay, an astonishing achievement in a very hot and humid jungle climate with monsoons part of the year!

Allan Koay a writer for The Star Koh Samui, of Thailand was one of twenty journalists from Malaysia, Singapore, Thailand, Taiwan and Hong Kong that accompanied the National Geographic Channel, Mummy Road Show, as they examined this remarkable monk. Koay wrote that the head abbot explained: "Before Loung Pordaeng passed away, he mentioned in his notes to his junior monks that if his body decays after death, they can cremate it. But if it doesn't, it was up to the juniors and the committee whether they want to cremate it or keep it as proof to others that this is one of the great achievements of deep meditation. ….And they all agreed that it should be announced as evidence."

Rumor has it that many people have caught sight of Loung Pordaeng's spirit walking the grounds of the temple, as well as boarding the boat to the mainland and carrying out a monk's daily chore of begging for good. The head abbot neither confirmed nor disproved these claims. "In Buddhism, it is believed that once a person dies, sometimes the spirit might come back and make a visit," he explained, "and if anyone is on the same frequency, he or she can tune in and see it. I have heard about these sightings all the time, but I haven't seen Loung Pordaeng's spirit myself."

Two leading scientists for the National Geographic's television program 'The Mummy Road Show', Ronald Beckett an endoscopy expert, and Gerald Conlogue a paleo-imaging specialist, checked this venerated monk for signs of natural preservation. Koay wrote that, "What they (this team) found not only amazed them, but also changed the way they viewed life as well." They were astonished that the body had not been mummified in any way that they could tell and that it remained whole even in a hot, wet climate after so many years. They found all the organs intact and only 20 to 30% smaller than in a living body; even the intestines were still intact, a part of the body that usually decays rapidly! These scientists, after a thorough examination of Loung Pordaeng's body, had no explanation for the lack of decay or the remarkable state of preservation.

This Buddhist Saint is said to have "possessed the ability to meditate for up to 15 days without food or water, and to have predicted the time of his own death accurately. He also knew that his body would be preserved after his death and wanted it displayed as proof of the power of meditation and to inspire Buddhists everywhere." Loung Pordaeng experienced Purity of Heart and in deep meditation merged with the infinite Stillness, transmuting all the elements of the physical body.

Purity of heart is attained through resonant entrainment occurring from genuine Bodhicitta (loving-kindness) and compassion with that strong magnetic power, Love, which connects all the particles of the universe together. This is the practice of the total remembrance of Love, both outwardly and inwardly. It produces a harmony performed in the center of the heart, and as the heart transfers its knowledge, which is not the knowledge of reason, to all the body, it purifies the entire human being with its every beat. This fans the fire of Illumination and burns the curtains of illusion allowing Grace to light the shadows of mind. Simply said in scientific terminology, this natural process is a harmonic fractal attunement of all the various coherent oscillating platforms comprising the physical, with the fundamental Great Mystery of Love.

A trained master yogi can "attune himself with the pranic force by certain yoga practices" enabling the yogi "to guide the 'lifetrons'(smallest particles) to rearrange their vibratory structure and to objectify the desired result".

But the completely aligned soul does not attempt to waste time on objectifying his powers, rather the true master allows a complete merging with the infinite Awareness. This specific phased superposition of electromagnetic and sympathetic resonant alignment allows for unique biological processes to occur within structures of the physical template; this wash of idealized fractal-embedded-frequencies, attuned to the compassionate womb of Pure Potentiality, massage the entire body and all it systems. This results in a massive unifying of the electromagnetic spectrum via resonance.

As the ground state is achieved, the higher and higher waveforms of the spectrum fall into resonant coherent entrainment. This pure harmonious balance is achieved soon after as all the various energy-forms oscillate in resonance with the timeless. A high-energy, highly coherent sonic wave washes the entire body. Milliseconds later a massive phase transition occurs due to perfect mirroring, included is an intense flash resulting from the phased superluminal implosive tunneling. This is enabled by the wholly constructive heterodyning nature of the nested geometric energies within an invariant matrix.

When the wash of recursive-scale-invariant waves implode inevitably toward light speed, a sonoluminescence occurs within the oxygen/gas filled fluids. This process cumulates in the emission of a very high, intense light for a millisecond. In the case of the Shroud, this light scorches the cloth leaving a negative image of the cells that emitted them.

To truly understand sonoluminescence and how it pertains to biology, a primer on resonance and coherence is required to build a firm foundation. First, however, we will look at the man Jesus and his teachings to see if in anyway they correlate to this ancient science, and if there was any possibility that he might have had access to these mystical sciences.

Note:

Padma Sambhava also known as Guru Rinpoche was an Indian tantric sage who brought Buddhism from India to Tibet in the 8th Century AD. He had been invited from India by the Tibetan King Trisong Deutsen. Padma Sambhava ("The Lotus Born" Guru) went on with the help of the King, to convert the entire country. He is the patriarch of the Nyingmapa lineage. Padma Sambhava's main disciple was the Tibetan queen who became his consort, the Dakini Yeshe Tsogyal, the first female lineage holder in Tibet.

Special Note: H.E. Chagdud Tulku Rinpoche

After this chapter when most of the book was complete, an individual who had given great inspiration to me passed away. H.E. Chagdud Tulku Rinpoche was born in Tibet in 1930 and on November 17, 2002 he attained paranirvana. He was of the Nyingmapa lineage and as his death shows, a true master of reality.

> "In front of family and friends", his wife of twenty-three years writes, "After his last breath, Rinpoche remained seated in a state of meditation for more than five days, with no signs of physical deterioration whatsoever, then was flown from Brazil to Nepal."

The Rinpoche's teaching always rested on these key points: bodhichitta, impermanence, and the dream like illusion of existence.

Chapter Four

The Guru Jesus

"Where your treasure is, there will your heart be also"
(Matthew 6:21)

It is impossible to separate the Shroud of Turin from the man Jesus of Nazareth; the two are intimately linked throughout the echoes of time. The facts are clear from a scientific perspective and if read with no bias tells us that the Shroud exists; it was formed by a man using a brief burst of intense light in the Spring somewhere near Jerusalem deep in antiquity.

To understand the biological process in the creation of the Shroud and the Science of Divinity that allows the processes to unfold, it's helpful to look at the man Jesus of Nazareth and the teachings He left to the world. In taking this tack it is my hope that it will allow the process to unfold organically, become less abstract and more personal. The Silent Gospel left to us in the image on the Shroud speaks volumes to the vastness of human potential and the infinite possibilities dormant awaiting the actualized self; tying the processes directly to the practices and understandings that Jesus during His life professed opens to us the possibility of personalizing the knowing left in the Silence of the Shroud. Later in the book we will see that these practices are not specific to any one religion or sect, in fact the opposite is true, for it is a deeply personal experience of touching and being touched simultaneously by the Eternal.

In the chapter on Truth, we will see that Truth is Truth no matter what cloak of terminology or symbolism it wears, and that it is only the levels or depth of experience with the Sacred that changes and that this change is only held in perspective, not in Reality. I understand how this can sound confusing and almost contradictory, but my intent is to be accurate. Words, like images or symbols, can only point to or at, Truth; they are tools used in an attempted to conceptualize, in this case something that encompasses and animates all life. My using the man associated in tradition with the Shroud just made sense to me, but one must understand, I am not writing this to support any religious dogma. From my perception, Truth lies at the core of all religions. If a man or woman were to be as deeply rooted in wisdom and love as Jesus, they too would exhibit the same level of communion with the Divine. His or her own belief is all that stands in the way of realizing this on-going communion. I've come to realize that there is a place within each heart where the Eternal resides and awaits compassionately to be embraced.

The Man Jesus

And he said, "Whoever discovers the interpretation of these sayings will not taste death."

The Gospel of Thomas # 1.

These powerfully truthful words of Jesus were recorded in the Gospel of Thomas. One of the twelve closest disciples of Jesus, Thomas most likely wrote the sayings down to help himself recall the teachings of his Master. He later shared them with other truth seeking souls during his ministry. This ancient Gospel of Thomas consisting of 114 sayings of Jesus is one of the oldest documents found to date with the words of Jesus. It is simply a list of the Sayings of Jesus with no additional commentary. The version found was a copy of an original that most historians believe was created shortly after the crucifixion of Jesus. When you read this text, or for that matter any of the gospels, it is abundantly clear that the man Jesus (Yeshua) was exceptional. And it was revered by his disciples as a Master teacher-healer. In the end, this reverence developed into fearless-devotional-love abundant in faith.

In Jesus' native tongue of Aramaic, he was known as Yeshua, a form usually spelled Joshua, meaning Yah, The One Nameless Being or the Sacred Life and shua, will save, preserve or restore you. The Greek-English form of Yeshua later evolved into Jesus. From the time of His ministry onward His disciples came to call Him Yeshua bar Alaha, literally translated as Jesus Son of God. We shall see shortly that in the end it was this addition of bar Alaha that brought about His crucifixion.

Even today the practice of being given a name associated with a high ideal or aspiration is common. This custom is especially true among mystical sects regardless of the culture. It is believed that the vibrational atmosphere associated with the breath-sound of speaking a name significantly influences the molding of the person's character and fate. The Word was seen to have mystical powers of transformation and alignment. As such, one can understand that aligning a Jewish son with the energy of Joshua was as popular then, if not more so, than it is today. There were other young men at the time of Jesus with the name Yeshua/Joshua; this is why He is referred to as Jesus of Nazareth.

Mary was probably around 15 years of age at the time Jesus was born. Most historians place the birth of Yeshua around March 1 in the year 7 or 6 BC. In 4 BC Augustus Caesar issued a decree that everyone in Israel should be registered. [Luke 2:1] Upon the arrival of the three Wise Men, they warned Joseph that Herod planned to harm the young child, Yeshua. Joseph fled Bethlehem with Mary and the child, exchanging the land of Judah for the culturally integrated and religiously tolerant and fertile lands of Egypt. Soon after leaving Judah, Joseph learned of Herod's orders to kill all the young male children less than two years of age. This was a confirmation that the danger was real.

According to the story, Joseph and his young family traveled extensively in the lands of Egypt. The locations and general times are well documented in the ancient records. Many of the sites where they settled for a time became sacred to the early Christian Coptic sects and are to this very day places of pilgrimage. The Copts believe the journey through Egypt took three years, while Muslims believe it took seven. An excellent version of the story is related in <u>Be Thou There: The Holy Family's Journey in Egypt</u>, edited by Gawdat Gabra and published by The American University in Cairo Press. The actual time spent was likely between three to seven years. Josephus (the Jewish historian) wrote in great detail on the death of King Herod the Great, March 13, 4BC. Herod's kingdom was divided among his sons, Herod Antipas tetarach of Galilee, and Herod Archelaus Tetrarch of Judea, Samaria, and Idumaea. Because Herod Archelaus was the new ruler of Judea and had an even more ruthless reputation for cruelty than his father, Joseph continued his self-imposed exile, ending up eventually in Nazareth. At any rate we know that the young boy was back in Judea sitting in the Temple, listened to, as well as instructing the teachers present sometime after 3 AD.

Joseph and his family moved extensively throughout the ancient world, including various cities and great distances. In each of these towns and cities there would have been teachers of religions representing a great variety of philosophies and associated mystery schools. During their time away from their native land the young child, Yeshua, would have been introduced to many of the religious and spiritual beliefs of the region. These would have included not only Jewish, Egyptian and Greek, but also other more exotic belief systems such as the Buddhist and Hindu philosophies. Brother Wayne Teasdale writes in his book, The Mystic Heart, "It is well known that Buddhist and Hindu monastic communities existed in Alexandria, Egypt, in the first century before Christ." Sometime before Yeshua's tenth birthday, Joseph received guidance in a dream that it was safe to return to Israel. He and his family, therefore, made the long difficult journey back to the town called Nazareth.

Cross Pollination

One hundred years before the birth of Jesus, Egypt was already a well-established center of higher learning, offering a culture within which monastic institutions thrived. The mystical sects of the Indian sub-continent, as well as other preexisting mystical sects, cross-pollinated each other along the fertile lands of the Nile River. The Nile then, as it is now, was a highway for trade and commerce. It is now well known by historians and archeologists that many gods and forms of worship co-existed in Egypt at that time. The gods of Mesopotamia, Canaan, Syria, Phoenicia, and of the Jews were worshipped contiguous to the Egyptian gods of Luxor, Memphis and Alexandria.

It is also known that ancient mariners from India traded exotic cargo with Egypt in the times of Roman Rule. Cargo from areas such as Java, Vietnam, Thailand, Sri Lanka, and India made their way via India to the thriving port city of Berenike on the Red Sea near the border with Sudan. It was the chief port for the import of goods not only for Egypt, but also for all of Roman held territories. It was the sea entry for goods from the Far East into the Mediterranean regions. The cargo was shipped across the Indian Ocean, north through the Red Sea to Berenike, located about 160 miles east of today's Aswan Dam at the headwaters of the river Nile in Egypt, and then sent overland to where it would be shipped down the Nile to Alexandria and the Mediterranean. In Aswan on the island of Elephantine archeological remains inform us that a Jewish community thrived in the sixth century BC. It was extremely close to the huge temple of Khnum, again showing the tolerance and potential for cross-pollination of religious ideas. This tolerance for other religions is similar to the cross-pollination of the early Jewish/Christian sects with the existing Greek/Latin/Roman pagan practices that gave birth to the new flower of the Roman Church and their Orthodox counterparts.

Religious Environment During Jesus' Time

Centuries before Jesus and the Essenes, masters and schools fertile with profound ideas on human potential and mystical teachings existed. Members of these religious and philosophical sects traveled and traded their goods as well as their knowledge and beliefs. In those days, conversations around the water cooler involving science, politics, agriculture and the weather were all religious in nature. It was common to debate the merits of one god versus another, especially when traveling into a new country or region. Knowing and respecting the local deity would have been very important at that time.

Our tendency is to forget the time scales of religious and moral development. We tend to see things in isolation when in fact they are built on the foundations of diverse histories of various races, cultures and mystical traditions. It is said that we stand on the shoulders of those that came before us.

What follows is a brief list and timeline in the development of the concepts of God, Reality and human potential present in the regions of trade surrounding the Jewish nation of the first century. All of these traditions over time cross-pollinated each other, affecting the evolution from then to now. Our current concepts of our self and our relationship to God and existence come out of these great traditions. Truth was in existence and shared in mystery schools for millennia before Jesus was born. He emerged into a region ripe with the cross-pollinating trade winds of empire.

~ The Rig Veda, one of the earliest written teachings on the potential of man; circa 3700 – 1500 BCE. The oldest writings known to humanity are the Vedas, the revealed scriptures of Sanatana Dharma (Hinduism). The earliest dating of the Vedas date back to perhaps 3800 B.C.E. when this oral tradition was first put into written form.

~ The Upanishads, the basis for Hindu beliefs, are a collection, a corpus of spiritual-mystic-yogic treatises written from circa 1400 – 800 BCE.

~ The Mysteries of Osiris and Dionysus, Many of the teachings from these mystery schools are present in Christianity and identical to the historical account of the life, death and resurrection of Jesus. Osiris was a God man found in pyramid texts as early as 2,500 BCE and according to Forlong, the worship of Osiris included the presentation of sacred cakes, called Mest, along with a sacred wine cup. Dionysus was a similar story in almost every way. Dionysus is first mentioned in Greece in Linear B tablets from roughly 1,200 BC. Herodotus describes initiation into the mysteries of Dionysus in the fifth century BC. The worship of Dionysus was popular in Hellenistic times (after 332 BC) and extended from Italy to Greece and into Egypt and the Middle East (Palestine). The Mysteries of Dionysus included initiation by bathing – baptism, a sacred meal, a myth about the death and resurrection of the god Salvation, and the souls of the followers would drink from the cool spring of eternal life. Dionysus was identified with the lamb, and called King of Kings, Only Begotten Son, Savior, Redeemer, Sin bearer, Anointed One, the Alpha and Omega.

~ Amenhotep IV-better known as Akhenaten, a name he took early in his reign meaning, "He Who is of Service to Aten", was part of the 18th Dynasty of Egypt 1352-1336 BCE. He is recognized as starting the first monotheistic cult in Western religious development. He proclaimed that worship of the Aten or One Supreme God was to take pre-eminent status in Egyptian religion.

~ Zoroastrianism-Zoroaster, Greek for the prophet Zarathustra or Zarthost is also referred to by the name Zoroaster in Western texts. He was believed to have lived during 600 B.C. in Persia, which is the region covered by modern-day Iran and Iraq. Current estimates have revised this date to anywhere between 1500 B.C. and 1000 B.C., or even earlier. This makes Zoroastrianism one of the oldest monotheist world religions. Zoroaster was a Persian or Kurdish teacher who taught about the lasting struggle between the forces of good and evil. The good was symbolized as the light. The concept of angels was appended from the Kurdish Cult of the Angels (Yazdanism); 1000 BCE. The Kurdish Kings eventually conquered Egypt and became the lineage of Pharos ruling Egypt years after the Exodus.

~ Pythagoras, 581-497 BCE, a Greek philosopher who traveled to the Mystery schools of Egypt, India, the Chalde and Jerusalem. Returning to Greece he established a spiritual/scientific brotherhood based on the wisdom and knowledge from these Mystery schools. His contribution to the science of harmonics and their application to all aspects of life remain true to this day.

~ Siddhartha Guatama, the historical Buddha, considered the Founder of Buddhism; India circa 563 BCE.

~ Plato, 427-347 B.C.E., philosopher and father of sacred geometry, the core shapes honor his name, "platonic" solids.

~ The major teachings of Taoism, the Way, arose in China, circa 300 BCE.

Trade

The lands around Nazareth, where the boy Jesus grew into adulthood, were hubs for trade and commerce on some of the truly great trade routes of the day. Nazareth is near the Sea of Galilee and it is around this large body of water that the two main trading routes from Egypt converged on their way to the main hub of Damascus. These two key trade routes brought products, yes, but also new ideas and technologies to the people who lived there. Travelers and traders from many different cultures, along with their belief systems, passed through, stopping to trade on these common ancient highways of commerce. We need to remember that in that day and age vocal sharing was nearly the only means of communication. There were no newspapers, book venders, radio, television or Internet. During the young life of Jesus, there was always an open active exchange of ideas, stories, news and philosophies along with the trading of goods in the markets. The Middle East was a place where the North African cultures along with the European and Mediterranean cultures, mixed with the Far Eastern cultures. It was the melting pot of the day. It is not so far fetched to think that the boy Jesus, raised near Galilee, was exposed to this wealth of ancient knowledge and wisdom. The record clearly shows that by the tender age of approximately 12, he was sharing this wealth of understanding in debates with the Temple priests and others that would listen.

Higher Education

It was common practice, according to the Jewish historian of the times Josephus Flavius, that young men would travel to different sects as one came of age to experience the diverse philosophies and educational styles. The Pharisees, Sadducees, Essenes, and Zealots were the major Jewish parties/sects of the day, each with their own centers of learning, each with a unique slant on things. It was like going away to various private schools to get a well-rounded education. At that time, religion and science were not separated as they are today. Astronomy, Astrology, Mathematics, Numerology, Geometry, Healing/Botany/Medicine, and Architecture were all taught and seen through the lens of the specific religious sect doing the teaching. You could not separate the disciplines at all from religion. In the days of Jesus you could learn about all these areas of religion/science and at the same time test your beliefs to see which sect/system felt right for the individual to follow into manhood. This was the norm according to Josephus and most young men took a little from several different sects just to cover all the bases. Josephus himself partook in three different sects before settling on the one he favored. Jesus appears, from his language and knowledge, to have done something similar. He might not have stopped his education by studying only the main Jewish sects of the times, more likely he would have been influenced by other ideas with which he came into contact, either, over the years of travel, or in the markets. By the very nature of His radical views and the departures He took from the establishment line, it appears that He must have, at some point, obtained some powerful external influences.

From all historical accounts left to us the young Jesus was, at the very least, introduced to the ideas and practices of the aesthetic sect known as the Essenes. This sect called themselves The Sons of Light. Josephus Flavius, a historian of the times, referred to them as the Essenes. Some believe the meaning for the word Essene arises from the Hebrew/Aramaic word Osin, meaning doers (of the works and will of God). (Kenneth Hanson, <u>Words of Light, The Dead Sea Scrolls, The Untold Story</u>) Josephus writes in his accounts that he himself had first hand experience with this ascetic mystical sect that held firmly to the ancient orthodox traditions and wisdom of the Jews. In order to connect with the heartbeat or rhythm of the universe, a daily practice was a sunrise prayer and heart meditation that slowed the heart and cleared the mind. Information detailing this meditation is found in the Dead Sea Scroll that is today called the Meditation Scroll.

The Sons of Light had members scattered throughout the region, however one of their main communities appears to have been located two miles inland from the Dead Sea at a location today known as Qumran. It is in this very area that a vast ancient library of texts was recovered that has come to be known collectively as the Dead Sea Scrolls. Most of these documents are dated to a few hundred years BCE. Some of them had to do with the rules for the sect, some with the mystical practices of this aesthetic order, and yet others were the original Old Testament bible stories. Archeological research generally connects the Dead Sea Scrolls, the settlement at Qumran, and the Essenes/Sons of Light. These texts were a daily source of teaching and inspiration to the elect who were the chosen members of the sect. Entry into this sect was not granted without a long initiation period. Slowly, after years of study, one would be brought closer to the inner core of the sect and the higher mystical teachings. These documents would be studied and discussed daily, and often looked to for reason, comfort and guidance.

When we look at the words attributed to Jesus we often see a man that was at the very least introduced if not fully educated by the Essene sect, even if it was for a short period of time -- similar to Josephus' experience. Jesus' words in the Bible were often matched with pieces found in the Dead Sea Scrolls. This does not mean that he was a member of the Essenes during his ministry, on the contrary he appears in many of his teachings to oppose many of the current day Jewish sects, including those of the Essenes. Jesus was, if anything, a courageous reformer who fearlessly pointed out the hypocrisy found within the Law and practices of the spiritual leaders and the sects they led. He openly defied Jewish law with regards to purity laws, working on the Sabbath, support of women, and the inclusion of gentiles into Jewish practices. The biggest departure might have been His teaching to love your fellow man, and your enemy with all you could genuinely muster. To the heavily taxed Jews in a Roman held Jerusalem, he must have sounded at times not just different, but at times insane.

Epiphany

After a mystical epiphany at the hand of Spirit, Jesus was led to travel to the Jordan River and receive his ritual purification and initiation from John the Baptist (his cousin). What occurred then is best left directly to the words from the various gospels.

"And it came to pass in those days, Jesus came from Nazareth of Galilee, and was baptized by John at the Jordan;

The Silent Gospel

"and immediately coming up from the water, he saw the heavens dividing, and the Spirit as a dove coming down upon him;

"and a voice came out of the heavens, 'Thou art My Son -- the Beloved, in whom I did delight.'"

Mark 1:9-11 Young's Literal Translation (YLT) version:

Luke 4:1 continues the story, saying, 'I, Jesus, full of the Holy Spirit, returned from the Jordan and was led by the Spirit in the desert.' The King James Version of Matthew 4:1-11, finishes the story with the passages that have come to be known as The Temptation of Jesus:

1. Then Jesus was led by the Spirit into the desert to be tempted by the devil.

2. After fasting for forty days and forty nights, he was hungry.

3. The tempter came to him and said, If you are the Son of God, tell these stones to become bread.

4. Jesus answered, It is written: 'Man does not live on bread alone, but on every word that comes from the mouth of God.'

5. Then the devil took him to the holy city and had him stand on the highest point of the temple.

6. If you are the Son of God, he said, throw yourself down. For it is written: 'He will command his angels concerning you, and they will lift you up in their hands, so that you will not strike your foot against a stone.'

7. Jesus answered him, It is also written: 'Do not put the Lord your God to the test.'

8. Again, the devil took him to a very high mountain and showed him all the kingdoms of the world and their splendor.

9. All this I will give you, he said, if you will bow down and worship me.

10. Jesus said to him, Away from me, Satan! For it is written: 'Worship the Lord your God, and serve him only.'

11. Then the devil left him, and angels came and attended him.

Jesus then returned to his homeland of Galilee and Nazareth radiant with the power of the spirit. News about him spread throughout the whole countryside, as Luke writes, on his way back to Nazareth he taught in their synagogues along the way, and everyone praised him. (Luke 4:15)

Luke 4:16-44 goes onto say:

16. He went to Nazareth, where he had been brought up, and on the Sabbath day he went into the synagogue, as was his custom. And he stood up to read.

17. The scroll of the prophet Isaiah was handed to him. Unrolling it, he found the place where it is written:

18. The Spirit of the Lord is on me, because he has anointed me to preach good news to the poor. He has sent me to proclaim freedom for the prisoners and recovery of sight for the blind, to release the oppressed,

19. to proclaim the year of the Lord's favor.

20. Then he rolled up the scroll, gave it back to the attendant and sat down. The eyes of everyone in the synagogue were fastened on him,

21. and he began by saying to them, Today this scripture is fulfilled in your hearing.

22. All spoke well of him and were amazed at the gracious words that came from his lips. Isn't this Joseph's son? they asked.

23. Jesus said to them, Surely you will quote this proverb to me: 'Physician, heal yourself! Do here in your home town what we have heard that you did in Capernaum.'

24. I tell you the Truth, he continued, no prophet is accepted in his hometown.

25. I assure you that there were many widows in Israel in Elijah's time, when the sky was shut for three and a half years and there was a severe famine throughout the land.

The Silent Gospel

26. Yet Elijah was not sent to any of them, but to a widow in Zarephath in the region of Sidon.
27. And there were many in Israel with leprosy in the time of Elisha the prophet, yet not one of them was cleansed; only Naaman the Syrian.
28. All the people in the synagogue were furious when they heard this.
29. They got up, drove him out of the town, and took him to the brow of the hill on which the town was built, in order to throw him down the cliff.
30. But he walked right through the crowd and went on his way.
31. Then he went down to Capernaum, a town in Galilee, and on the Sabbath began to teach the people.
32. They were amazed at his teaching, because his message had authority.
33. In the synagogue there was a man possessed by a demon, an evil spirit. He cried out at the top of his voice,
34. Ha! What do you want with us, Jesus of Nazareth? Have you come to destroy us? I know who you are; the Holy One of God!
35. Be quiet! Jesus said sternly. Come out of him! Then the demon threw the man down before them all and came out without injuring him.
36. All the people were amazed and said to each other, What is this teaching? With authority and power he gives orders to evil spirits and they come out!
37. And the news about him spread throughout the surrounding area.

(Then Jesus Heals Many)

38. Jesus left the synagogue and went to the home of Simon. Now Simon's mother-in-law was suffering from a high fever, and they asked Jesus to help her.

39. So he bent over her and rebuked the fever, and it left her. She got up at once and began to wait on them.

40. When the sun was setting, the people brought to Jesus all who had various kinds of sickness, and laying his hands on each one, he healed them.

41. Moreover, demons came out of many people, shouting, You are the Son of God! But he rebuked them and would not allow them to speak, because they knew he was the Christ.

42. At daybreak Jesus went out to a solitary place. The people were looking for him and when they came to where he was, they tried to keep him from leaving them.

43. But he said, I must preach the good news of the kingdom of God to the other towns also, because that is why I was sent.

44. And he kept on preaching in the synagogues of Judea.

From this time on His reputation was that of a Great Teacher, Healer and possibly even a prophet. This was the start of Jesus' own small short-lived sub-sect, (not that he did not draw at times very large crowds). It was most often the simple, common man that Jesus called to make up the core of his disciples for those three years. But as evident by the establishment's fear of him during that short time, his reputation as a teacher-healer must have grown very rapidly. It was this very rapid rise in popularity that was the threat. Indeed, so great was this threat that the leaders of the Temple had him arrested in the quiet of night and following their own pronouncement of judgment of him, sent him to Pilate to be killed.

Pilate, however, even after his short time with Jesus had not found fault with him even under great pressure to do so. Pilate also appears to have developed a respect or possible fear of Jesus, for over and over he comes back to the priests saying that he can find no fault with this man. But the Jewish leadership made it clear to Pilate their wishes to have Jesus not only killed but crucified and made an example. Why, because as John 19: 7 says, "he made himself the Son of God", and as such, he needed to be made an example to all others looking to become a Son of God, because then you do not need priests! Here is an abridged version of the events according to John's gospel. In

The Silent Gospel

the gospel according to St. John, Annas had sent him bound unto Caiaphas the high priest.

> 18:31 Then said Pilate unto them, Take ye him, and judge him according to your law. The Jews therefore said unto him, It is not lawful for us to put any man to death:
>
> 18:38 Pilate saith unto him, What is truth? And when he had said this, he went out again unto the Jews, and saith unto them, I find in him no fault at all.
>
> 19:4 Pilate therefore went forth again, and saith unto them, Behold, I bring him forth to you, that ye may know that I find no fault in him.
>
> 19:5 Then came Jesus forth, wearing the crown of thorns, and the purple robe. And Pilate saith unto them, Behold the man!
>
> 19:6 When the chief priests therefore and officers saw him, they cried out, saying, Crucify him, crucify him. Pilate saith unto them, Take ye him, and crucify him: for I find no fault in him.
>
> 19:7 The Jews answered him, We have a law, and by our law he ought to die, because he made himself the Son of God.
>
> 19:8 When Pilate therefore heard that saying, he was the more afraid;

(He then brought Jesus in again and spoke with him in an attempt to find a way to release him.)

> 19:12 And from thenceforth Pilate sought to release him: but the Jews cried out, saying, If thou let this man go, thou art not Caesar's friend: whosoever maketh himself a king speaketh against Caesar.

At this point, if Pilate wished to keep peace among the Hebrews and the Temple at this most unstable of times, he had no choice left but to condemn Jesus to be crucified. Still Pilate did the unusual act of having a plaque carved in wood to be placed in a prominent location on the cross. This plaque was in the form of a title written in Hebrew, Latin and Greek for maximum effect.

It read: JESUS OF NAZARETH THE KING OF THE JEWS.

John continues in Chapter 19:

19:20   This title then read many of the Jews: for the place where Jesus was crucified was nigh to the city: and it was written in Hebrew, and Greek, and Latin.

19:21   Then said the chief priests of the Jews to Pilate, Write not, The King of the Jews; but that he said, I am King of the Jews.

19:22   Pilate answered, What I have written I have written.

The man, Jesus, aware and present to the events unfolding held firm to be witness to the Truth and as such was not strung with rope onto a cross as was tradition but was nailed so that he could not use his mystical powers to escape.

After the crucifixion, Mary Magdalene went to the sepulcher and saw that the stone had been removed from in front of the tomb. According to John 20:16, she sat weeping there until a man appeared who she believed was the gardener. She asked him where they had taken Jesus body. Then Jesus saith unto her, Mary. She turned herself, and saith unto him, Rabboni; which is to say, Master.

The Word

There is a saying in the Gospel of Thomas, Number 2, which admonishes, "Let him who seek, not cease seeking until he finds, and when he finds, he will be troubled, and when he has been troubled, he will marvel and he will reign over it All."

These words were recorded before Christianity had been formalized. It was not until 325 CE that the Roman Emperor Constantine ordered the council of bishops and theologians to gather in Nicaea, now in Turkey, and to reach a common agreement to act as a foundation for institutional Roman Christianity. In this process, however, some areas of Jesus' life and teachings were glossed over or omitted while others were embellished and even, in some instances, fabricated for political reasons.

One thing is clear, that despite political manipulations and institutional dogma, very few individuals have had the impact of Yeshua bar Alaha. There can be little doubt of this man's magnetism, charisma and personal powers. An entire movement was created from his teachings and life.

This new offshoot of the Hebrew Jewish lineage was vigorous and inspired with new ideas and concepts not only on living, but more importantly, on the way we perceive our potential and ourselves. The ideas were at first shared with a few of his disciples, and then to increasingly larger audiences whose hearts resonated to the Truth within his message. Most people who acknowledged him as their teacher saw him as a savor or messiah from the bondage of Rome. However, he taught and pointed to a higher level of freedom and the self-induced bondage that arises from ignorance. There is a metaphor used in Zen Buddhism that helps us to understand the disparity of viewpoints regarding Jesus in those times: A finger points to the moon: although the finger points to the moon, the finger and the moon belong to two different worlds.

Jesus expanded our vision of our selves and our relationship with Spirit, achieving this within an oppressed land and culture in a very brief period of time. He enlarged our concept of God and the power of love and compassion. He accomplished his work within thirty-three years of life, even though, according to current biblical scholars, he never wrote a single letter of script. To those around him he was teacher and master, but it was not until the resurrection and ascension that his disciples developed the courage and conviction born of pure faith. From that point on they followed the teachings and wishes of Yeshua bar Alaha, living with complete faith in their Master, even when tortured and threatened with death.

It was from this well of deep faith within his disciples' that this new sect sprouted and grew strong. These disciples were normal working men and women and it is clear that their teacher too was a man born of a woman the same as you and me. This is not to take away from His greatness in anyway; rather in my mind it adds to it. A mortal man, born of a woman, can aspire and reach immortality gives greater hope and promise that other humans everywhere can also enjoy the promise of knowing heaven and God intimately.

Background

Jesus was born in a time and place where the known world was in a state of movement and change, and he would have been exposed to many products, ideas and beliefs rather than being isolated in a cultural backwater. The known world was fecund with philosophical and spiritual thought before and during the time of Jesus on earth. Christianity, of course, as of yet was not one of them.

His homeland was under Roman control and it was the language of Rome and of Greece within which commerce and trading were conducted. Greek was the English of its day and as such the main trading language. If you wished others of a different language to grasp your ideas you wrote it in Greek. However, the day-to-day language of the people living in Judea was Aramaic, which was the common language of the people, as it was for Jesus. He would have quickly learned to read and speak Hebrew, the language of his religion, and then Greek for trade, but his day-to-day conversation was the sacred and ancient tongue of Aramaic.

Unlike Greek and Latin, the Aramaic language offers a much broader, more fluid and poetic interpretation of words. Whole ideas and concepts may be encapsulated within a word or phrase, challenging the listener, or reader, to select the meaning according to his understanding and consciousness. The church fathers in the early days of traditional Christianity attempted to put the Aramaic accounts of Jesus into the language of scholars which was Greek and interpret these accounts according to the cultural linguistic context of their times and culture. This process diluted heavily the context of the words and their symbolism.

Neil Douglas-Klotz (NDK) writes in his excellent book, <u>The Hidden Gospel</u>,

> "A single word can have in Aramaic or Hebrew often many different meanings ...For instance, the Aramaic word shema (as well as its Semitic root ShM, or shem) can mean light, sound, name, or atmosphere. If we consider the admonition of Jesus to pray 'with or in my shem' (usually translated 'in my name'), which meaning is intended? According to Middle Eastern tradition, in the words of the sacred scriptures or the words of a prophet all possible meanings may be

present. One needs then to look at a given statement several different ways. In addition, Aramaic and Hebrew lend themselves to rich and poetic wordplay, like inner rhyming of vowels, repetition of consonant sounds, and parallel phrasing. These devices further increase the possible translations and interpretations of a given statement."

The word "light" is often used in biblical and scriptural texts. What depth and richness arises from this more expanded understanding of shema/shem, "light". Taking the time to fleshing it out offers profound new insight into the sayings of the Jewish man, mystic and guru, Yeshua bar Alaha.

"In the beginning God created the heaven and the earth."

"And the earth was without form, and void; and darkness was upon the face of the deep. And the Spirit of God moved upon the face of the waters. And God said, Let there be light: and there was light.

"And God saw the light, that it was good: and God divided the light from the darkness."

Chapter 1:1-4: of Genesis

The root word for heaven in Aramaic is Semaya and comes from the same root, Shem (light), with the added syllable – aya indicating "without limits". The concept of light, sound, vibration and atmosphere without limits would thus be visualized by the disciple, when placed in the context of the times and culture.

By drawing upon the broader interpretation of the Aramaic words, this familiar opening to Genesis could now be read as:

"When God created space and matter and matter was without form, void; Love moved upon the water and light existed, then Divine Mind created polarity to separate himself from that which he had created."

Neil D Klotz

Another word often used in the Bible is "holy" which describes a quality coming from the Divine. It combines the roots of two Semitic words: KD, meaning the point or pivot upon which everything turns, and Ash, meaning the image of a circle unfolding from a point with power and heat. This becomes the Hebrew word qadash, which is commonly translated as holy. Through the centuries the concept of qadash became the Old English word halig, meaning: that which is sacred, spiritually pure, and deserving of respect and awe. This word, holy (halig), referred to a specific Light, Divine Light, that of, or coming from God, the "Light of God". All natural things were seen to be filled with the Light of God and thereby sacred or holy. Many, if not all, native earth-based matriarchal traditions held that all life contains the spirit of the cosmic Mother-Father God, and is therefore sacred, to be held with honor and respect.

Being blessed or graced means receiving that special kind of light/energy, containing within it Love, Grace, Presence or Holy Spirit, which is complete, fully coherent and whole. The quality of that energy, of that light, when felt in the heart, radiated as pure LOVE rising into Agape, Ecstasy or Bliss. So "Holy, Holy, Holy" could be interpreted as, "Loving, Loving, Loving". From this interpretation one can rationalize that Love is an energy equal to the Light of God. Being filled with the Holy Spirit was to be in ecstasy, agape, filled with pure Love. And how would we know such a person? We return once again to the Fifth Beatitude we read in the KJV, Matthew 5:7, "Blessed are the merciful; for they shall obtain mercy." When these words are rephrased to include more of the Aramaic content, the verse could be stated as, "Filled with the Loving Light are those that birth from their inner heart, (point of pivot) compassion."

Jesus is therefore telling us clearly that those genuinely compassionate persons are those with knowledge birthed from experience gained from communion with God. "You shall know them by their fruits." This change in perception allows us to see a direct correlation between the words of Jesus with the ancient mystical sciences of the Indian sub-continent. This small change in perception allows us to see with greater ease the man Jesus as Yeshua bar Alaha, a Son of God, a Self-Realized Saint, Rabboni or Awakened Master.

According to the mystical Hindu traditions being the Son of God is our birthright and rightful inheritance. It is the goal of all gifted with the breath of life; furthermore these traditions provide a science of training called the yogic sciences, which it is said can enable anyone

The Silent Gospel

with the necessary motivation of desire and resolve to realize this inheritance.

All throughout the teachings of Jesus we find methods to assist us to Love God and develop compassion, methods that preexisted and paralleled ancient practices of the Indian sub-continent. The concepts Jesus presents may not have come directly from India but his lessons and example bear a direct resemblance to those of the Buddha and the forest Rishis before him. Paramahansa Yogananda, one of the truly modern day saints of Eastern philosophy, has said,

> "Prophets of all lands and ages have succeeded in their God-quest. Entering a state of true illumination these Saints have realized the Supreme Reality behind all names and become the scriptures of the world. These, although outwardly differing by reason of the variegated cloaks of words, are all expressions - some open and clear, others hidden or symbolic- of the same basic truths of Spirit."

Truth is Truth whether known by some exotic sage or by you or me; it is all the same in Truth. Jesus taught this Truth from a place of knowing that could only have been gained through direct experience. He had enough wisdom to deeply impress this understanding on his disciples who subsequently past it onto those that followed. He gave us the first great law in Mark 12:30: "Love God with all your heart", and the second in Mark 12:31, "Love your neighbor as you would have them love you".

It was simple then and it is clear now, the Law is to Love God with all your heart and to be compassionate. This statement is the universal law of all Illuminated Beings. It is the path and goal for the attainment of the Awakened, Realized state of Natural Light. It is the path to Nirvana, Agape, Ecstatic communion and the Golden Body of the Taoists.

> "…Yet the actual feeling of this joy is experienced not in the head but in the heart." …<u>The Divine Romance</u> by Paramahansa Yogananda.

The Transfiguration

The Bible states in John 1-5: "This is the message we have heard from him and declare to you: God is light; in him there is no darkness at all."

If we take this phrase literally, applying the deeper meaning of shem, Jesus is telling John that the Intelligence of the Universe that animates all life is that Pure Awareness of God is free from all ignorance.

It is taught throughout the major mystical traditions of the world that men and women can directly experience this Pure Radiant Awareness. Descriptions of this mystical experience are one of Divinity as Love and Lover; hence this field is called the Beloved. Maintaining this connection of fully integrated integrity with Truth allows the self of the individual to merge into one with the 'Be-loved'. It is said that at this point the heart is liberated from ignorance and it knows beyond question the truth of its existence. Sri Yukteswar writes in his book <u>The Holy Science</u>,

> "In this state, all the necessities having been attained and the ultimate aim effected, (end of ignorance) the heart becomes perfectly purified and instead of merely reflecting the spiritual light, actively manifests the same. Man, being thus consecrated or anointed by the Holy Spirit, becomes Christ, the anointed Savior. Entering the kingdom of Spiritual Light, he becomes the Son of God."

It is clear from the accounts of Jesus by his disciples that he was one who had experienced this state of unity with God. The Eastern sciences describe this mystical state of being in great detail. One of the fruits the yogic sciences describe is visibly seen coming from the body of a Son of God.

Witnesses to this radiance emanating from Jesus prior to the crucifixion were recorded in both Luke and Matthew in the King James Version (KJV) of the Bible. Christians throughout the ages call this awe-filled event, "The Transfiguration." Luke describes this experience in Chapter 9:28-29:

> "And it came to pass about an eight days after these sayings, he took Peter, John and James with him and went up onto a mountain to pray. And as he prayed,

the fashion of his countenance was altered and his raiment was white and glistening."

In another version of Luke, the same event is translated,

> "And it came to pass, about eight days after Jesus said this, he took Peter, John and James with him and went up onto a mountain to pray. As he was praying, the appearance of his face changed, and his clothes became as bright as a flash of lightning."

Matthew 17:2 states:

> "There he was transfigured before them. His face shone like the sun, and his clothes became as white as the light."

The point of quoting these verses and sharing the Man/Guru perspective of Jesus is to show that long before Jesus was crucified, he demonstrated an ability to perform amazing miracles and emanate strong visible light from his body, and that he did this in front of small and large groups of witnesses. This action alone demonstrates his sainthood and places him clearly in the category of a highly Self-Realized Master.

Jesus was exceptional, however, even beyond other healers and sages of his time. The rapid escalation of His reputation and following, as well as the manner in which He was crucified, attest to this. When viewed from the historical perspective, as well as from documented reports, it is easy to see that this man exhibited all the traits of an extraordinary level of experience in communing with the Divine. The life of Yeshua bar Alaha closely resembles many of the great Illuminated saints of the Indian subcontinent. The reason this is important, at least seeing the possibility of this type of connection, will become clear as we get to the core of the process.

It has now been well documented that these same cultures of the East traded heavily with the Middle East by several land routes and at least one major sea route at the port of Berenike, Egypt, on the Red Sea near the border with Sudan. Berenike was a strategic location to the Romans and it was well documented that goods were carried to the Nile River, where smaller boats waited to transport the cargo north to Alexandria. Cargo is then known to have moved from Alexandria across the Mediterranean to a dozen major Roman ports and hundreds of minor ones. This port pre-existed the Roman rule in the area. My point is that where trade and commerce flowed so did scientific and religious ideas.

The actions of Jesus during his life and the counsel he gave to his disciples at the end of his physical time here on Earth – "to go out and be with people, heal the sick and teach them about Eternal Life" -- was to also guide them likewise onto the Path of Compassion. He sent them over the known world to share his teachings, end suffering and help to heal those they met. The Buddhist bodhisattva ideal of selfless service in order to relieve suffering and bring liberation to others before themselves was officially introduced in the West.

All the disciples immediately followed this Buddhist ideal of selflessness, regardless of the real personal danger and hardship it was sure to bring. Turn the other cheek and the term 'those that live by the sword die by the sword' became a new mode of expression. The disciples, due to the direct experience with their risen Master, held faith born of a knowing that was fixed firmly in their heart.

Yeshua appears to echo the teaching of the East directly when He says in Luke 11:34-35, 'When thine eye is single, thy whole body also is fully of light… Take heed therefore that the light which is in thee be not darkness.'

It is clear that Jesus was this compassionate Being in life and, as the resurrection stories tell us and the Shroud shows so clearly, he maintained this outward love for all, even through torture and so-called death. Even Pilate was moved to fear by Jesus' dedication to Truth.

Jesus taught that we all are united, that heaven is here if you have the eyes to see it and the ears to hear it. Jesus used his life as a model for radical understanding of Truth, and in a final gesture of Love left us the Silent Gospel as a physical proof of a higher reality and physics we are now just coming to understand.

> "With kindness, with love and compassion, with this feeling that is the essence of brotherhood, sisterhood, one will have inner peace. This compassion feeling is the basis of inner peace."
>
> His Holiness the Dali Lama.

"Jesus said: "I" is the light (of Awareness) that shines upon all things. "I" is the All from which everything emanates and to which everything returns."

Gospel of Thomas

Chapter Five

Resurrection

Luke 24 –31: And their eyes were opened, and they knew him; and he vanished out of their sight.

It is impossible for me to fully feed the rational mind on this subject without touching the heart of the Shroud tradition, the resurrection. The simple definition of resurrection refers to the process of rising from the dead. But in the times of Jesus, the dead could also mean without vibrancy, to be ignorant of Spiritual Truth, or a reference to those without spiritual grace. Resurrection was a healing born of faith; a rebirth generated by the vibrancy of the Holy Spirit. Resurrection during the times of Jesus was seen as ascension of body and or spirit to the house of the Father. It was likened to a pilgrimage to a time and place where spirit/light/breath descended and filled the body.

Translated by the Greeks we received the concept of going to Heaven. Full and complete resurrection was to enter the kingdom of Spiritual Light, where one becomes the *Son of God*. Resurrection therefore was seen as the experience of merging completely with the radiant Absolute. Known by different names in different cultural traditions, the process and results nevertheless are explained in similar terms. Terms like Awakening and Enlightenment, or Illumination were equally interchangeable. It had a general meaning of referring to a process with a peak experience of becoming a *Son of God*. An experience occurring near or at the time of death where a radical phase transition of the physical form occurs into one of pure, brilliant, radiant light.

Each of the biblical writers has their own version of this story but the core story is the same. Here I use the complete King James Version of the Resurrection story according to the Gospel of Luke. I found that reading the Resurrection story in all its versions helped place the Shroud information into a direct and personal context, it fleshes out the raw bones of sterile facts of academia. Furthermore, embedded

The Silent Gospel

within the story are important clues that enforce both tradition and the scientific reality of the use of light in the creation of the image. Each version of this event is a bit different in focusing on specific details, but the overall story is the same. My comments are in brackets and I've made bold the areas of special interest within the text. In the end, all the pieces of this puzzle fall into clear focus out of which came the image on a cloth and give a richer meaning to the Silent Gospel.

Luke: 24:

1. Now upon the first day of the week, very early in the morning, they came unto the sepulchre, bringing the spices which they had prepared, and certain others with them. (There were a few that came and witnessed this, it is not the story of one persons)

2. And they found the stone rolled away from the sepulchre.

3. And they entered in, and found not the body of the Lord Jesus.

4. And it came to pass, as they were much perplexed thereabout, behold, two men stood by them in shining garments: (Clothed in radiant light.)

5. And as they were afraid, and bowed down their faces to the earth, they said unto them, Why seek ye the living among the dead? (The Living were considered any ascended, self-realized being, the dead were consider all the rest.)

6. He is not here, but is risen: remember how he spake unto you when he was yet in Galilee, (Risen is a reference to those of the Living.)

7. Saying, The Son of man must be delivered into the hands of sinful men, and be crucified, and the third day rise again. (Rise Again, as the Transfiguration event already showed, this was not the first time)

8. And they remembered his words,

9. And returned from the sepulchre, and told all these things unto the eleven, and to all the rest.

10. It was Mary Magdalene, and Joanna, and Mary the mother of James, and other women that were with them, which told these things unto the apostles. (Mary was also the same mother of Jesus.)

11 And their words seemed to them as idle tales, and they believed them not.
12 Then arose Peter, and ran unto the sepulchre; and stooping down, he beheld the linen clothes laid by themselves, and departed, wondering in himself at that which was come to pass. (He held the burial clothes that had placed around the body of Jesus. The Shroud and the Sudarium)
13 And, behold, two of them went that same day to a village called Emmaus, which was from Jerusalem about threescore furlongs. (which two? Cleopas /Simon)
14 And they talked together of all these things which had happened.
15 And it came to pass, that, while they communed together and reasoned, Jesus himself drew near, and went with them.
16 But their eyes were holden that they should not know him.
17 And he said unto them, What manner of communications are these that ye have one to another, as ye walk, and are sad?
18 And the one of them, whose name was Cleopas, answering said unto him, Art thou only a stranger in Jerusalem, and hast not known the things which are come to pass therein these days?
19 And he said unto them, What things? And they said unto him, Concerning Jesus of Nazareth, which was a prophet mighty in deed and word before God and all the people:
20 And how the chief priests and our rulers delivered him to be condemned to death, and have crucified him.
21 But we trusted that it had been he which should have redeemed Israel: and beside all this, to day is the third day since these things were done. (They considered him to be their King and material savior.)
22 Yea, and certain women also of our company made us astonished, which were early at the sepulchre;
23 And when they found not his body, they came, saying, that they had also seen a vision of angels, which said that he was alive.

24 And certain of them which were with us went to the sepulchre, and found it even so as the women had said: but him they saw not.

25 Then he said unto them, O fools, and slow of heart to believe all that the prophets have spoken: (Remember the other meanings for heart.)

26 Ought not Christ to have suffered these things, and to enter into his glory?

27 And beginning at Moses and all the prophets, he expounded unto them in all the scriptures the things concerning himself.

28 And they drew nigh unto the village, whither they went: and he made as though he would have gone further.

29 But they constrained him, saying, Abide with us: for it is toward evening, and the day is far spent. And he went in to tarry with them.

30 And it came to pass, as he sat at meat with them, he took bread, and blessed it, and brake, and gave to them.

31 And their eyes were opened, and they knew him; and he vanished out of their sight. (This is a normal description of a fully awakened Master's power and adds weight to his body vibrating at a frequency not able to be seen by our normal eyes.)

32 And they said one to another, Did not our heart burn within us, while he talked with us by the way, and while he opened to us the scriptures? (This refers to the flame of ARDOR love develops in the heart.)

33 And they rose up the same hour, and returned to Jerusalem, and found the eleven gathered together, and them that were with them,

34 Saying, The Lord is risen indeed, and hath appeared to Simon.

35 And they told what things were done in the way, and how he was known of them in breaking of bread.

36 And as they thus spake, Jesus himself stood in the midst of them, and saith unto them, Peace be unto you. (Jesus manifests physically again in their midst.)

37	But they were terrified and affrighted, and supposed that they had seen a spirit.
38	And he said unto them, Why are ye troubled? and why do thoughts arise in your hearts?
39	Behold my hands and my feet, that it is I myself: handle me, and see; for a spirit hath not flesh and bones, as ye see me have. (He proves that he is there physically to them showing the scars of his crucifixion.)
40	And when he had thus spoken, he shewed them his hands and his feet.
41	And while they yet believed not for joy, and wondered, he said unto them, Have ye here any meat?
42	And they gave him a piece of a broiled fish, and of an honeycomb.
43	And he took it, and did eat before them.
44	And he said unto them, These are the words which I spake unto you, while I was yet with you, that all things must be fulfilled, which were written in the law of Moses, and in the prophets, and in the psalms, concerning me.
45	Then opened he their understanding, that they might understand the scriptures,
46	And said unto them, Thus it is written, and thus it behooved Christ to suffer, and to rise from the dead the third day,
47	And that repentance and remission of sins should be preached in his name among all nations, beginning at Jerusalem.
48	And ye are witnesses of these things. (This was a pretty good crowd that was witness to His presence.)
49	And, behold, I send the promise of my Father upon you: but tarry ye in the city of Jerusalem, until ye be endued with power from on high.
50	And he led them out as far as to Bethany, and he lifted up his hands, and blessed them.
51	And it came to pass, while he blessed them, he was parted from them, and carried up into heaven. (Blessings is the giving of the Light/Love of God)

The Silent Gospel 81

52 And they worshiped him, and returned to Jerusalem with great joy: (This is the joy of awakening to Truth)

53 And were continually in the temple, praising and blessing God. Amen. (The Temple is the body and heart as Jesus taught, and Amen is the same word as Aum or Om as it's known in the West.)

Summary: The Story is:

- A man was crucified in a very specific and unique way.

- The details and method of the crucifixion and burial are detailed and they were unique in many accounts from the normal methods employed by the Romans of that time and place.

- He was a special case. Even the high priests of Jerusalem feared His presence to the point they needed his death. He was considered a prophet that was "mighty in deed and word before God and all the people:" one that some considered to be the "redeemed Israel." IS-RA-EL translates, I the one great light (RA) of (EL), God.

- He was tortured and murdered because of His beliefs, His strength of faith and because he was a revolutionary threat on several levels: social, political and religious.

- This man was taken down from the cross before he was actually dead as evident of the blood and water that flooded from the wound inflicted to insure death by the Roman soldier placed there to guard the crucifixion. He was still bleeding when placed in the cloth, for even though he was first thoroughly cleaned for burial, a great number of bloodstains are present on the Shroud. I am not saying that He did not die and was reborn after but at the time he was taken down from the cross and placed in the tomb, he had not completed the process of dying. This is clear in the texts.

- This Man was taken down, quickly prepared for burial and then placed in a rock tomb by his beloved disciples, including Mary his companion and Mary his Mother.

- When they, (the woman and others), returned to the body to add spices and perform prayers and rituals over the body, they were met by two Angels, which in Aramaic can mean messengers, that were dressed in garments of light; just as Jesus is described in this same manner later in the same text. He was also described in this manner prior to the crucifixion at the event known as the Transfiguration.

My personal thought on these messengers who were dressed in garments of light are two-fold although they are not central to the story or the thesis. First, that they were Angels of a sort, they were Self-realized Masters of an associated brotherhood from his early training, or members of the Therapeutic sect of healers that through some ancient knowledge performed ritual and service resulting with the rising of Jesus to the land of the Living.

The land of the dead was considered the world of normal life. The land of the living is the home of fully Illuminated Masters – heaven here on earth if you like. This state is well described in Eastern philosophy, so I have no need to go into detail here, but in brief, Masters living in the Land of the Living can and do at time operate in and on several dimensional levels of existence. (see superconductors)

There is a collection of five ancient texts known as the Askew Codex. The Askew codex was bought by the British Museum in 1795, having been previously acquired by a Dr. Askew from an unknown source. It is more commonly known by the name inscribed upon it's binding, "Piste Sophiea Cotice". Some suggest a more appropriate name might be "Books of the Savior".

The Pistis Sophia is a translation and commentary of a special collection of ancient Gnostic Coptic manuscripts, derived from preserved Egyptian-Coptic Christian Codices originating from the historic period of the early Church. The document is pre-"official religion" of the Roman Empire circa 325 C.E. The Pistis Sophia literature was one of many books withdrawn from the new condensed Bible texts yet it remains an inner teaching of the Coptic and African Christian mystical communities. The words Pistis Sophia are Greek, translated as "Faith Wisdom", and represent a teaching given to the Disciples of Christ Jesus AFTER his resurrection. The actual manuscripts were dated from 150 to 300 C.E. This extensive and expansive teaching, however, is claimed by the writers of the text to have been given for a period of eleven years after the resurrection. In essence, according to the original writers, these are some of the post-

Gospel teachings of Christ after He took on His Light or Wisdom Body.

Significant for modern times, these are teachings revealed not only to Jesus' male disciples, but also to his female disciples! Pistis Sophia in its fuller context represents not only the Wisdom of the Divine Father and the teachings of the Divine Son, but the Divine quality of the Holy Spirit through the Mind of the Godhead personified as a "divine feminine" extension and embodiment. The Holy Spirit is exemplified in actual female forms of the Divine Mother, the Celestial Mother, the Virgin of Virgins, the mother of all Buddha's, or Mary the Mother and Mary Magdalene the wife/consort. The insertion of the feminine creative principle is an important aspect to fully allow respectively, as well as understanding the geometries of total inclusion. These codices demonstrate that these early Christian sects not only knew of these but also remained an inner teaching of the Coptic and African Christian mystical communities a few hundred years after the Crucifixion.

The conclusions from the various bible texts regarding these events are all clear: Jesus was buried and came back from near and expected death miraculously. Everyone was very surprised to say the least. He then met or showed himself to/with certain members of his disciple community to share more on their jobs to come and His future.

He had somehow transfigured his body into the kingdom of Spiritual Light, a process long understood and written about in the Eastern philosophies. Remember the lines in Luke 9-29 that say, "…the appearance of his face changed, and his clothes became as bright as a flash of lightning." Additionally, Matthew 17:2 states: "There he was transfigured before them. His face shone like the sun, and his clothes became as white as the light." This incident was before the crucifixion, Matthew continues, "even his Clothes became as bright as a flash of lightning". This same process must have happened again according to my hypothesis at the time of the creation of the Image on the Shroud. It may have been even brighter, if only for the briefest of moments. I will give my understandings of the methods and science for a man to accomplish this in the following pages but Jesus gave the way clearly when He replied to the question in, Matthew 22:36-40,

"Teacher, which is the greatest commandment in the law?" Jesus replied:

"Love the Lord your God with all your heart and with all your soul and with all your mind. This is the first and greatest commandment. And the second is like it: love your neighbor as yourself. All the laws and prophets hang on these two commandments."

If we analyze these two primary commandments, Jesus' understanding for the attainment of Divinity is revealed. The key word in the above phase is 'your'. It makes the statement immediately personal and intimate. Jesus is telling us that the process is between you and your various aspects of self. He is sharing with us that attainment is accomplished when a specific form of qualitative unity is achieved among the three key components of self, namely the heart, egoic mind and soul. Energetically, the entire being loves and this state produces a unique level of harmonic coherency between all these three parts. He is telling the listener that unity of self must be achieved before Unity with the Divine occurs. The secret to accomplishing this unity is given in the second commandment; love your neighbor as yourself. So you must love yourself first because as the rationale goes, you cannot give others what you do not have to give. This is why Sri Yukteswar said; "Hence the culture of this love, the heavenly gift, is the principal requisite for the attainment of the holy salvation; it is impossible for man to advance a step toward the same without it."

So the questions Jesus leaves us with regarding the science of divinity are these: what is it to love ones self, and what does that initially feel like so that one knows if it is genuine?

Chapter Six

Have Heart

"Blessed are the pure in Heart for they shall see God." (St Mathew 5:8)

"The body is the instrument of the mind."

&

"The mind is an instrument of the heart."

"{Downward} meditation draws all strength to the center of one's being, to the heart, and from there it radiates to all parts of the body and mind."

"Meditation has a great advantage over suggestion for it not only keeps the heart in rhythm, it places the center of life-force there."

Hazrat Inayat Khan

At the core of all mystical traditions lie forms of meditation, contemplation, and other psycho-physiologic practices that aid the transforming of the heart. Jesus Christ said over 2000 years ago that, "…before kingdoms change, the hearts of people must change." My explorations into the heart have shown that the above quotes from Hazrat Inayat Khan are literally accurate. I can entice and dance with the rational in these pages, touch the intuitive with these words, but to know these statements in reality one must explore his or her own heart. Puran Bair says it well in this quote, "…you can truly experience what it is to listen to your heart. Its guidance is different from logic, and its concern is not self-centered."

I, like so many of the young people growing up in the 1950's and 60's, was taught in school that the heart was a simple organ that had the function of pumping blood which carried nutrients and oxygen to the cells. It was just an organ like any other. I was educated to believe that the brain was the key organ for survival and directed the functions of our body including the heart. I was led to the belief that the brain was the key organ for awareness and the seat of consciousness itself.

As I matured I noticed that poets and the lyrics of songs spoke differently about the heart. The heart was a place of deep emotion with the ability to connect, touch, transcend, or be broken. Being raised a Catholic, another anomaly to the standard concept of the heart that was always visible in my daily life, was the image of the Sacred Heart of Jesus and the Immaculate Heart of Mary. These two images were encoded with deep meaning in me and I began intuitively to associate the meaning of Jesus pointing to his heart with the words in popular songs of the times. I think it was in my junior year in high school that I came to the realization that for mystics and poets alike the heart held some magical almost mystical central place at the core of our very being. These two vastly different concepts appeared to oppose each other yet they both held strength and value.

Unrecognized by my conscious awareness, the seeds of exploration had sprouted within me. I subconsciously looked for meaning to marry these two concepts. I heard whispers that you could be brain-dead but still maintain life, and that the heart needed no external source for it to beat. Logic told me there was more to the picture than I had originally been taught. I turned to those that reason said would have the answers to my questions. I turned to those that were said to have heart. It dawned on me in those early days that heart referred to a quality, yet there was more, much more. The deeper I looked into the subject of heart, the more profound the subject became, as you too will soon see.

Heart of the Matter

"People of the Divine have cast the desires of the two worlds out of their hearts; thus their hearts beat only for the Divine."
Hazrat Mir Ghotbeddin Mohammad Angha

We use terms of the heart to describe varying dispositions that all point to the core of our being. A person may be cold hearted, a leader with heart, he may have won her heart, or never lost heart. If one's innermost feelings, or inclinations are understood about another, one might say he knew it in his heart, or that he's a man after my own heart.

Terms of the heart refer to a quality below the radar of conscious mind and raging emotions. So I ask you to take heart, have a strong heart and with the heart felt courage take a brief look with me at the master regulator of the body, the human heart, for it is this organ that lies at the core of all the psychological, physiological and spiritual components involved in the science of divinity. And it is the first thing Jesus tells us with which to love our God.

Emotion and feeling are two of the main characteristics we've given to the heart. This is not unusual when we remember that the definition and term for heart in English comes from early Aramaic leba, which is seen as the center of courage, intelligence and feelings. Leba is the pith, marrow, center or best part of anything, it is linked to mind. Neil Douglas-Klotz, who is a scholar of the Aramaic language, details this information in his excellent book, The Hidden Gospel. The Chinese have a similar concept of heart called shen (soul), thought of as the seat of universal consciousness or true mind. As a matter of fact, most cultures have this concept somewhere buried deep at their core. Even our word core originates from the French word coeur, meaning heart.

The general feeling and meanings of Leba are true on many levels that can be intellectualized. When we focus on just the scientific, medical and electro-magnetic aspects of the heart, it becomes clear that the heart is a dynamo acting as director, conductor and symphony, organizing info-energy for the rest of the body and the body-state as a whole. The human physical form is now understood to be electric in nature and the center for translating and regulating that energy is now known to be the heart. Not that other parts don't play a role; of course they all play a role and some more significant than others, but the heart is seen as the master oscillator for the body as a whole. What this means is central to understanding the bigger picture. An oscillator regulates rhythm like a crystal does within a watch. The heart, like any mechanical oscillator, regulates the flow and rhythm of electro-magnetic information within the greater system. The heart's powerful electro-magnetic music washes every cell in the body with each and every beat and can be measured many feet out from the physical shell of the body. Other parts of the body may add to the song playing in the heart similar to an instrument in an orchestra. The new sound adds to the overall symphony either in a harmonious or discordant way.

One single beat of the heart, if viewed for its electrical and magnetic properties, is a full symphony of frequencies playing a classical composition. The healthier the heart, the greater availability it has to more complex and melodious compositions. Then, in the next beat, it plays again with subtle or not so subtle changes. If listened to over a period of time the song of the healthy heart appears to dance with its unique rhythm, one that is in step with breath and neural activity. This process of creating an array of complex, spectral harmonious frequencies washing through the cells of your body with information and energy begins early in fetal development and continues until death. The information-energy produced in the heart is a collection of data from many of the important centers of the body; as well it also appears that influences come from beyond the physical body matrix. This notion extends beyond the environmental envelope in which our physical bodies live, the heart is believed to be the connection to the higher self, atman or soul.

Aims of the Heart

Neil Douglas Klotz writes in his interpretations that the Aramaic word for, "Heart, leba, comes from the root that means passion, courage, audacity, and vitality, literally it refers to the center, or best part of one's life". In the old root of the word, the picture given to us is that of an interior generative action that creates, expanding out from the center or coeur of our being.

The word lebhon, which is a derivative of the word leba, meaning heart, as in the 6th Beatitude, Matthew 5:8, King James Version (KJV) says, "Blessed are the pure in Heart, for they shall see God." Heart can be interpreted, Neil Douglas Klotz says in <u>Prayers of the Cosmos</u>, "as any center from which life radiates – a sense of expansion plus generative power: vitality, desire, affection, courage, and audacity all rolled into one."

Aramaic mystics during the times that Jesus linked purity of heart and salvation, as did the Egyptians a thousand years before, with the courage, even the audacity driven of deep desire, to touch the center of the life-giving vitality and truth of the heart, as well as realizing its aims. The Egyptians felt that the heart needed to be pure and as light as a feather to enter the afterworld of the Gods. The feather that one was balanced against was Maat, meaning Truth.

"The heart has its reasons, which reason knows nothing of"

Blaise Pascal

One can search the words of realized saints from all religious persuasions and find similar references to the above quotation by Pascal. If the heart has its own intelligence, as written and highlighted beautifully by this quote from Pascal and the one before from Bair, in the first paragraph of this chapter, then what are the concerns and aims of the heart? For the answer to this I defer to the Master Sri Yukteswar in his book <u>The Holy Science</u>, because of its simplicity and clarity. "The Heart's immediate aim is the cessation of all suffering to effect the possibility of the ultimate goal." He continues:

> "Man naturally feels great necessity for Existence, Consciousness, and Bliss. These are the three real necessities of the human heart and have nothing to do with anything outside the Self. They are essential properties of his own nature."

> "… All the necessities of the Heart – Existence, Consciousness, and Bliss – having been attained, ignorance – the mother of evils, becomes emaciated and consequently all troubles of this material world, which are the sources of all sorts of sufferings, cease forever. Thus the ultimate aim of the heart is affected."

> "In this state, all the necessities having been attained and the ultimate aim effected, the heart becomes perfectly purified and instead of merely reflecting the spiritual light, actively manifests the same. Man, being thus consecrated or anointed by the Holy Spirit, becomes Christ, the anointed Savior. Entering the kingdom of Spiritual Light, he becomes the Son of God."

> "In this state man comprehends his self as a fragment of the Universal Holy Spirit, and, abandoning the vain idea of his separate existence, unifies himself with the Eternal spirit; that is, becomes one and the same with God the Father.

> "This Unification of Self with God is Kaivalya, which is the Ultimate Object of all created beings."

Within this short summary by Sri Yukteswar are four important points to be highlighted.

- The aim is the cessation of all suffering for the purpose of being able to possibly effect the ultimate goal, which he clearly states as Unification of Self with God.
- When the necessities of heart are attained, all troubles of this material world cease forever.
- When the heart becomes perfectly purified man actively manifests spiritual light.
- When completing these aims of the heart, man enters the kingdom of Spiritual Light and becomes a Son of God. This is the Kingdom that Jesus spoke of and the one that Christians have come to know as heaven. Hell is simply the ignorant state of being hooked on the karmic wheel of cause and effect where most of us reside.

The Center of Self

One of the most interesting and telling perspectives of the heart arises out of the mystical Muslim sects that have become known as Sufi. From a Sufi perspective the heart lies in between the carnal ego-mind self and the psyche-soul aspect of self. Because of its location between these two powerful forces, it is always in a state of being pulled and tugged on. The ego-self is anchored in time, which is mind in past or future, and the soul dances in a non-local timeless domain of the Now. Only when the ego surrenders its self, which means aligning with the soul's desires, can a true harmony arise within the heart and hence the body. This alignment, or surrender, is affected by allowing, which is a state of non-judgment. Out of this alignment arises a natural harmony from which peace arises. If the silence or Now state is nurtured, a natural joy arises out of the peace, the necessities of the heart are experienced, and the aim of the heart's existence is affected.

The question then becomes, by what procedures does the heart acquire the balance and harmony of these two strong forces?

There are many individuated procedures that have been developed for acquiring the necessities of the Heart, most of which deal with psychological and or physical obstructions. But one thing is clear, each procedure attempts to create the proper environment for the birthing of a deep non-self-centered natural form of love, which Sri Yukteswar says "is the principal requisite" for the process and the procedure for attainment of this holy state. He writes, "This Holy Sound Pranava Sabda manifests spontaneously through culture of Sraddha, the energetic tendency of the heart's natural love; Virya, moral courage; Smriti, true conception; and Samadhi, true concentration."

The first requirement is the allowance of the culture of Sraddha to develop within the heart. Sri Yukteswar continues,

> "The Virtue of Love, the Heart's natural love is the principal requisite to attain a holy life. When this love, the heavenly gift of Nature, appears in the heart, it removes all causes of excitation from the system and cools it down to a perfectly normal state; and, invigorating the vital powers, expels all foreign matters-the germs of diseases-by natural ways (perspiration and so forth). It thereby makes man perfectly healthy in body and mind, and enables him to understand properly the guidance of Nature.
>
> "When this love becomes developed in man it makes him able to understand the real position of his own Self as well as of others surrounding him.
>
> With help of this developed love, man becomes fortunate in gaining the Godlike Company of the divine personages and is saved forever. Without this love, man cannot live in a natural way, neither can he keep company the fit person for his own welfare; he becomes often excited by the foreign matters into his system through mistakes in consequence he suffers in the body and mind. He can never find any peace whatever, and his life becomes a burden. Hence the culture of this love, the heavenly gift, is the principal requisite for the attainment of the holy salvation; it is impossible for man to advance a step toward the same without it."

Moral Courage is the will to be honest, to have integrity, another way of saying to be totally truthful to one's self. This at the core is being self-loving or self-compassionate. I will share more on this in the following chapters.

True Conception refers to the ability to change places with the object of concentration. You become that object and you see the world including yourself from its point of view.

True Concentration is achieved by focusing the mind to a point where only the object of concentration remains. When you feel the heart's natural love and focus on it, making it the object of your deep concentration, magnanimity grows stronger in the heart. Here again Sri Yukteswar on the Holy Science, "When magnanimity comes into the heart this makes man fit for the practice of Asana Pranayama (control over prana, involuntary nerve electricities), and Pratyahara (changing the direction of the voluntary nerve currents inward). These practices enable man to satisfy his heart by enjoying the objects of the senses as intended for Garhasthyasrama (domestic) life."

Magnanimity is the noble state of having generosity of spirit. Sai Baba explains it in this quote; "If our heart contain Truth and our conduct is conditioned by Love, then Peace which is within, is available to us." Voluntary control of the involuntary nerve electricity of the body is a result of these yogic sciences. I've recently witnessed this level of ability firsthand in a wonderful yogi named Mr. Kawakami. This yogi has subjected himself to all sorts of testing by the scientific and medical establishments to show both the pitfalls of their philosophies and the benefits of yogic practice. He has demonstrated many amazing abilities that defy rational logic to large scientific audiences. Relevant to the science in the creation of the Shroud are his abilities to control the heart rate, the flow of blood, and record no scientific signs of stress or pain when there should naturally be some as a result of inflicted physical mutilation. Mr. Kawakami is a living man, one of many having not only this yogic knowledge, but also has mastered aspects of it. He can subject his body to be skewered like a kabob yet not bleed and have all manner of instrumentation confirm that he is in no pain or even being affected by his self-inflicted torture.

The knowledge of the true potential of the human physical systems and the effect of awareness, attention, attitude, and or mind can have on those systems allows for the control of what we like to call the automatic nervous system and thereby all that it governs. This control of the involuntary nerve electricities, as Sri Yukteswar calls it, and the ability to voluntarily change the direction of nerve currents, "leads to control over death and allows for the body to operate in the vigor of new birth each day." What is important for us to understand is that it is not just Sri Yukteswar who makes these claims, rather it is the basis of an ancient science, neither purely metaphysical nor abstract, but sciences with rigors like any other good science. This pure science has a procedure and a step-by-step development leading to a specific outcome.

In Sri Yukteswar's words, "... Fixing attention firmly on any object thus conceived, when man becomes identified with it as if he were devoid of his individual nature, he attains the state of *Samadhi* or true concentration by which one experiences the Aum vibration that reveals God. ...the soul is baptized in Bhakti Yoga (devotion). This is the state of Divinity."

When man directs all his organs of sense toward their common center, the sensorium or Sushumnadwara, the door of the internal world, he perceives his God-sent luminous body of Radha or John the Baptist, and hears the peculiar "knocking" sound, Pranava Sabda, the word of God. "Thus perceiving, man naturally believes in the existence of the true Spiritual Light, and, withdrawing his self from the outer world, concentration of the self is called Samyama." By this "concentration of self on the sensorium, man becomes baptized or absorbed in the holy stream of the Divine Sound.

> "... In this state man repents; that is turning away from this gross material creation of Darkness, Maya, he climbs back toward his divinity, the Eternal Father, whence he had fallen, and passing through the sensorium, the door, enters into an internal world is the second birth of man. In this state man becomes Devata, a Divine Being."

Info-Energy - Not Just an Mechanical Pump

To grasp the handle controlling the involuntary nerve activities of the body, the first principle to understand are that energy and information are linked, differing only by the chosen mode of perception. In reality these two concepts support and maintain each other. Gary Schwartz, Ph.D. and Linda Russek, Ph.D. write of this in their brave book, <u>The Living Energy Universe,</u>

> "There are two fundamental non-material concepts used throughout the sciences: information and energy. Information refers to pattern, form, structure.

Energy refers to force and power, the capacity to do work and overcome resistance.

"Energy does the work of information. Information has energy, and energy has information. Information without energy is 'powerless'; energy without information is 'purposeless'."

It is now understood that the center for the info-energy dance of the human body is in the cardiac matrix. When exploring the physiological mechanisms, by which the heart communicates information and energy with the brain and body, scientists found measurable proof that the heart communicates with the brain and the rest of the body in four biological ways.

- Neurologically (through the transmission of nerve impulses)
- Biochemically (through hormones and neurotransmitters),
- Biophysically (through acoustic/pressure waves).
- Energetically (through electromagnetic field interactions).

These are each info-energy transference systems. Through these biological, info-energy transference, communication systems, the heart has a significant influence on the function of our brains and all of our bodily systems. The heart is the master rhythm regulator, organizer and conductor of the physical ongoing symphony. When a heart beats it does not just pump blood and nutrients to the cells, there is information and energy to produce change that is sent out in a radio-like echo signal to all the cells and beyond. This information signal radiates out in a 360-degree configuration that can be measured accurately several feet away from the body. Remember, communication is a two-way street; the flow of information and the energy to carry that information must go both ways and that communication is a prerequisite for life and consciousness. The main process and vehicle for that transference is through resonance, which I will cover in depth later in this book.

An overview of the process goes something like this: the cardiac complex produces the electromagnetic energy for a domino process to occur in time with each electrochemical cascading

The Silent Gospel

explosion, as well as the informational content as to what that process or change might be. The heart is the center of an eternal dance of balance and counter-balances. One small example of this type of balancing act is pH values of the various internal systems. Each system, and the body as a whole, requires very specific pH values for optimum operations. The letters pH stands for percentage of Hydrogen, with the scale going from acid to alkaline. For instance, if the percentage shifts too far from the norm in the blood, an immediate breakdown in the operations of the system occurs, with illness and death to the entire organism right behind. This is just one example of the type of critical balance that the heart matrix attempts to maintain. The heart matrix communicates directly with many of the key organizing and regulating systems of the body.

One of the tools of the heart matrix includes the information and energy of the acoustic pressure waves produced by the actions of all the various cellular and system liquids, as well as the movement and pressures of the blood. Cells have liquid crystal properties, especially the cardiac cell matrix and are very sensitive to pressure; even slight pressure produces piezoelectric activity, which is energy-encoded information. This characteristic is emphasized in the case of liquid crystals. The slightest pressures have dramatic effects; and the makeup surrounding every cell indicates liquid crystal design. Yet every info-energy communication transference mode touches each cell in some way with every beat heart. These specialized cells in the heart producing the prime electrochemical cascade of heart muscle tissue, is collectively known as the beat. This liquid crystal characteristic of cells that results in piezoelectric activity, occurs internally at all locations as the massage of the pressure wave cascades by. The action of wave touching wave producing other waves each with their unique properties, causes a specific reaction especially in the body's glands.

Other tools in the toolbox of the heart are nerve impulses that carry information as well as hormones and other chemicals produced directly by the heart itself. Yes, the heart also functions as a gland producing proteins and hormones, all cascading out from it, humming their unique music to the cells. These cascading modes of communication in turn produce other proteins and hormones, which effect changes. The inter-play of energies at a molecular/cellular level sends a cascade throughout the body of nerve impulses and corresponding chemicals in the form of peptides, polypeptides and proteins. These ultra small proteins vibrate info-energy to the cells designed to receive them. The DNA/RNA responds by producing other small proteins that are humming. The change in the quality of energy charge felt, as humming, is energy in motion or simply E-motion. In other words, emotion is a collective energy response to communication events that have already occurred internally. The current model sees the heart at the center of a dynamic, interactive network that includes the brain, nervous, respiration and hormonal systems, as fundamental components from which emotional experience emerges.

The relationships between emotion and health have long been recognized so there is no need to go into a discussion of this relationship at this time. What I have intended to show in the simplest of ways is the relationship between the immune system with the heart.

Fifth Way

There is a fifth more important primal mode of info-energy transference communication system, however, that is not so easily measured. This fifth mode is of a quantum mechanical nature. Ions, photons, electrons and other subatomic wave/particles share information and energy in and out of a realm beyond the limits of time-space. We are all, according to today's physics, nothing more than complex quantum objects, electromagnetic phenomena, and/or holographic phenomena of consciousness, or a bit of all three, take your pick. No matter how you slice it, all these communication, energy information transference systems allow for easy modulation by the subtlest of energy, especially that of attention, which is observation by another name.

When these biological, communication, info-energy transference systems are in harmony, when an ordered phase discipline is operating, then electrical coherence is reflected in the spectral emissions coming from the cardiac complex. Creating this harmony is a learned skill, which anyone with desire and resolve can accomplish.

Heart Facts

- The main function of the heart is to pump blood containing oxygen and nutrients to the body. The blood is first pumped to the lungs to pick up oxygen and then to the rest of the body.

The Silent Gospel 97

    Blood flows inside the heart in an orderly fashion, first going to the right atrium, then to the right ventricle, then to the lungs and finally to the left atrium and left ventricle.

- The heart beats almost like a clock, averaging about 60 to 100 times per minute, (average) continuously from birth to death. This occurs whether you are asleep or awake, conscious or unconscious.
- Your heart beats nonstop over 100,000 times in 24 hours. 80 beats per minute times 24 hours are 115,200 beats per day. Many people have higher beats per minute than 80BPM.
- The heart is a biological oscillator. It is the main and strongest known oscillator of the body. Oscillators regulate the rhythm of an object or system. Oscillators can be mechanical or organic, and include anything that produces a rhythmic pattern of energy or movement.
- Biological oscillators fall into synch like dancers to a rhythm.
- Heart cells will pulse in synch on a microscope slide.
- The heart is the strongest known biological oscillator in mammals.
- The heart will entrain the other oscillating systems in the body and can entrain other hearts and bodies, even over substantial distances if sufficiently powerful, which is to say magnetic. Magnetic people are said to be charismatic.
- The rule is that the strongest oscillating field exerts the greatest influence over other oscillators within its field of effect. This effect, when it creates synchronization, is called entrainment. When entrainment is highly ordered it is understood to be coherent. The field for the human heart goes well beyond the physical structure of cells, so the field generated by the heart touches and influences every cell in the body with each beat.
- The electrical field of the heart is 40 to 60 times stronger than the electrical field of the brain. This percentage depends upon the degree of passion, excitement or physical activity. Electrical fields have a magnetic field. Generally, the stronger the electrical field, the stronger the magnetic field. Electrical fields are measured in Cycles Per Second (CPS) or Hertz (Hz) that can also be described as frequency. Frequency refers to the frequency of the oscillations or cycles of energy in time. Gauss is the measurement of magnetism. Gauss is a centimeter–gram–second unit of magnetic flux density. In other words, gauss is a

- measurement for the degree of weight or pressure within a second of time exhibited by a mass or field.
- The magnetic field of the heart is up to 5,000 times stronger than the magnetic field of the brain. This is a significant amount.
- Because of these facts and others, the heart is the central player in setting the frequency signatures of all bodily systems -- from that of the brain all the way down to the shape of the DNA.
- Within the heart is a separate "little brain" and nervous system connecting the heart directly to the Neocortex. This is the new brain within the brain structure.
- The Immune System, Hormonal Balance and the aging process are all directed by a peptide, which is a small chain of amino acids, called ANF, an emotion bearing information molecule, produced in the upper chambers of the heart with each loving contraction. This hormone appears to help rid and balance the body from the harmful hormones created under stressful, fear based emotional states.
- The heart is Autogenic. This means it does not require a signal from the brain to beat. The impulse to contraction is not dependent on external nervous stimuli, but arises in the heart muscle itself. A small bit of specialized tissue called the sinoauricular node, embedded in the wall of the right auricle, is responsible for initiating the heartbeat. This is not dependent on ANY external stimulus. This means that no other part of the physical body controls this function.
- Your blood vessels alone laid out end to end would stretch 60,000 miles. A lot of miles for such a pump the size of your fist.
- The heart pumps two gallons of blood per minute through 250,000 miles of vascular system in the average adult. The equatorial circumference of the earth is 24,902.4 miles. Therefore, the vascular system is 10 times the circumference of the Earth. It is estimated that a given portion of the blood completes its course of circulation in approximately 30 seconds. To this day it is not understood how the heart is able to push/pull with the insanely high-calculated pressures required to send the blood around the complete circuit.
- Your heart pumps 2,000 – 4,300 gallons of blood throughout your body every day.

The Silent Gospel

- With every electrical change of the heart, emotional neuropeptides, which are emotion molecules according to Cadence Pert in her book <u>Molecules of Emotion</u>, cascade throughout and from all parts of the body.
- The heart is hardwired to the brain, left and right lungs, intestines, and Autonomic Nervous System (ANS). The ANS is comprised of the Parasympathetic System and the Sympathetic Nervous System. One branch speeds up the systems of the body and the other slows down physical systems. Through skilled training Yogi's can control the autonomic nerve response systems and the functions these systems control. They can control the flow of blood and the heart rate with breath and will.
- The heart's energy field permeates every cell of the body and can be measured at any point in, on or near the body.
- The heart's electrical field can be measured up to ten feet away from the body and when two bodies communicate; the heart rhythms of one individual can be witnessed to affect the other.

In Prof. Winfree's remarkable 1987 book (2) <u>When Time Breaks Down: The Three-Dimensional Dynamics of Electrochemical Waves and Cardiac Arrhythmias</u>, a work discussing the breakdown of rhythmic biological timekeeping, clues are discovered about timelessness in a wide variety of circumstances but mainly in fibrillating hearts and rotating waves of chemical excitation. In the wide diversity of contexts, the same paradoxical entity occurs. "... It's a motionless, timeless organizing center called a phase singularity. This is a place where an otherwise pervasive rhythm fades into ambiguity - like the South Pole, where the 24 time zones converge and the Sun merely circles along the horizon." In other words, within the heart's field is a timelessness, a stillness that he terms a singularity.

- Heart disease is the number one killer of adults in America.
- Over 57 million Americans have one or more types of cardiovascular disease.
- 41.8% of all deaths in the United States are caused by cardiovascular disease. That is 1 out of every 2.4 deaths.
- On average, someone dies of cardiovascular disease every 33 seconds in the United States.
- According to the National Center for Health Statistics, life expectancy in the United States would increase by almost 10

years if all forms of major cardiovascular disease were eliminated.
- We understand that there is a loop of entrainment that directly connects heart to brain function and through sharing of info-energy the physical, emotional stability and health are sustained or compromised. Loving-kindness and other positive emotions produce an excellent cardiac environment for physical functions like the immune system to operate and flourish. This creates the environment for improved immune response, reduction of stress chemicals in the blood, improved digestive function, increased rate of healing, slower rate of aging, opening of awareness to deeper fields of information, and a sense of inner calm. When we experience feelings of loving kindness, even for a few minutes, the body benefits for hours afterwards.
- Coherence in the electrical field of the heart entrains the brain and all other oscillating systems in the body.
- When we are in a state of calm, peace, love or appreciation, the energy wave-forms are smooth and coherent. This tends to bring other oscillators into entrainment. Head, heart and gut are literally in synch. Research has shown that this state corresponds to increased clarity, intuitive awareness, buoyancy and inner peace.

"The fourth energy center is the Heart chakra or Anahatam. Literally means 'unstruck or unbeaten' like the transcendental sound, which is constant, just as the heart beats constantly. It is located in the spinal column, directly behind the center of the chest, at the heart level. It is connected physiologically with the heart plexus of nerves. It is depicted as a twelve-petalled lotus, green in color with a six-pointed star and is inscribed with the letter ya. It is associated with creative power, unconditional love and compassion, and the ability to overcome fate. In the writings of the Siddhas, anahata is said to be where one's thoughts and desires are fulfilled. With its awakening, one becomes a master over the situations of life. One no longer depends upon fate to determine one's conscious will." [1]

The Open Heart

An ultra Orthodox sect at the time of Jesus, the Essenes, did a

---

[1] Babaji and the 18 Siddha Kriya Yoga Tradition, M. Govindan, M.A., Kriya Yoga Publishing

Heart Meditation synchronized with the dawning of the sun as a part of their daily practice. Forms of this Heart Meditation have been carried forward to this very day and reflect a deep knowledge of the above information. I repeat once again, that if Jesus was not an Essene he was nevertheless educated in their beliefs and practices as evident from his words.

I personally have come to believe, like the early Sufi text states, that "the Heart is the seat of God when opened, but a tomb when closed". This can never be known by the rational mind, it can only be experience by the knowing heart. The question that arises is, "What is an open heart?" and "How is the opening achieved?" The great Sufi teacher Hazrat Inayat Khan writes in his book <u>Sufi Teachings: The Art of Being</u> (Pp. 157) "The Sufi, therefore, takes the path of being nothing instead of being something. It is this feeling of nothingness which turns the human heart into an empty cup into which the wine of immortality is poured. It is this state of bliss which every truth-seeking soul yearns to attain."

The key comment in this passage is this "feeling of nothingness". This can be a frightening concept for the personal self to deal with, similar to dealing with the fact of death, but it is a feeling, and therefore physical and associated with life. I mentioned earlier the Egyptians belief that the heart needed to be as light as a feather. Being nothing would allow the heart the freedom to be as light as a feather. The gift of logic allows the loop of consciousness to return to the idea of this state of nothingness communicating its quality to the physical, allowing the conscious personal self the opportunity to feel and experience it. It is a transmission or transference of a state within the qualitative universe. Communication is a two-way flow like liquid going down a straw and air going up, if you hold your finger on one end of the straw nothing moves. The opening of this communication channel takes an alignment of the heart that some call attunement or at-one-ment. At-one-ment is a physical, phased alignment that produces a unique form of sustained coherence, a balance of self. The state of nothingness, simply said, is a state of selflessness which, when felt in movement is called compassion. Compassion is supportive-allowing in action. It is both the womb and heart of all objects.

Sacred or Purified Heart

I have offered just a few of the amazing facts about the heart. Reading some of the current popular books on the heart will significantly add even greater depth to the list of properties associated with the human heart. Even more amazing attributes of the heart can be read in most of the ancient cultural religious texts. They all whisper the value, power, and beauty arising out of the sacred or purified heart.

The one image I love the most is the one of Jesus with a red heart sitting on the center of His chest. He is in the mudra (hand posture) of blessing or sharing; this is the right hand palm out facing the viewer, and the other hand points to the flaming heart in the center of His chest. This image alone explains to the initiated all that is needed.

To receive love, one must share or give love openly, and if one does this with all his heart, mind and soul, his heart will burn with grace -- the Light of God. At that moment the heart is perfectly open and totally purified. It acts and conducts activity by Love. A Peaceful heart is the by-product. The Prophet Mohamed said; "Consult your heart and hear the secret ordnance of God, discovered by the inward knowledge of the heart which is faith and divinity."

The Science of Divinity is biological and to fully attain this knowledge, it is taught that the soul requires a body. Why else would God create it? It is the mirror that allows the eternal Self to self-reflect, create and polish to perfection in order to return and see itself as it truly is: no scars, faults or problems, no separation, pain or suffering, beyond joy, ecstasy and concept. It is objectless attunement to the Nature Light of Emptiness.

There is no process of eradication of sin in the purification of the heart; rather it is an organic attunement to honesty, truth and love held in faith. It is a genuine submission that opens the door of potential, possibility, and the eternal; an attunement to the beauty of life as it is, to the glory and mystery that it truly is, without judgment, operating moment to moment from the vastness of pure awareness. Saints of all culture have come to this state through technique, prayer, meditation, or the grace of God. Oddly, even this state of communion has degrees or levels of experience. As evident by the Shroud and the Resurrection story, Jesus attained one of the highest levels of direct experience, a mystery that will be made clear in the following chapters.

The heart includes a dimension of subconscious faculties for knowing reality immediately and qualitatively. This faculty we've termed Heart Intelligence. It is a sense beyond the radar capacities of reason and logic. The heart is home for the intuitive, a sense beyond the grasp of the egoic mind which is reliant on the five outer senses, and for the electromagnetic spectrum anchored in the timeless, unbound by distances or intellect. This Wisdom holds our deepest knowing and our true tendency or nature. If healthy, the heart's knowing will carry you back to realizing your true nature. Sharpening the faculty of discernment is part of the initial process in purifying the heart. You will often see this word, 'allowing' coming to the front of the process. The Sufis use the word submission, the Hindus use surrender, for Christians it is faith, but a correct Western translation might simply be understood as 'authentic allowing'. This authentic allowing is being present to *what is,* in the moment and finding in your heart the courage to be with the moment and know it is appropriate for that moment. I say authentic because it must not be merely the outcome of a conceptual action or moral obligation. It is a state that rises honestly as one heals the heart.

> "The heart may be sensitive or insensitive, awake or asleep, healthy or sick, whole or broken, open or closed. In other words, its perceptive ability will depend on its capacity and condition."
> Llewellyn Vanghan-Lee

The heart is like a mirror ready to reflect, the soot of raging emotions and the acids of destructive attitudes soil the knowing and capacity of the heart. We can easily confuse the egoic desires, opinions, social conditioning, and fears with the *knowing of the heart.* In the name of following our hearts, we are often only following the desires and fears of the ego mind trapped in the trance of separation. The heart is a prize for which both spirit and the world compete. These two powerful forces pull with the strength of their collective qualities. The heart will assume the qualities of whatever attracts it. Attraction to the limiting qualities of the past and future only results at best in a limited reflection of the divine reality. When the goal is total union, only total purity will do.

How can we know whether we are following the desires of the little self or the guidance of the heart in the world of today? The heart does not operate through concepts, propositions or assumptions, it senses and attracts through the qualitative aspects of the universe. The pull of the heart, when healthy, awakens the healing forces of humbleness, gratitude, appreciation and love. When authentic and spontaneous, these spiritual qualities arise from heartful living. As Jesus implied, this is accomplished by being truthful to one's Self and listening to the call of the Divine echoing within the Cave of the heart. It is a response to the inner guidance of Love and Wisdom. This guidance may appear to be irrational and even counter to one's own apparent self-interests. That is its beauty and power. It develops a quality of compassion that does not come cheap. It submits faithfully, spontaneously and joyfully to the requirements of the moment. When purity is reached it knows no fear and always joyfully submits to the Absolute, for Reality is then known. Great teachers tell us that the complete healing of the soul is possible through the soul's contact with Wholeness through the heart.

This is why Jesus in his commandment to the disciples placed it first. "Love **Your** God, With ALL **Your** Heart, Soul and Mind." The heart is King, if the country goes into ruin the king too will die. Sufis feel that control of the heart Charkra, or himma, is a prerequisite for controlling one's destiny.

Chapter Seven

Truth

"Pilate therefore said unto him, Art thou a king then? Jesus answered, 'Thou sayest that I am a king. To this end was I born, and for this cause came I into the world, that I should bear witness unto the Truth.
Every one that is of the Truth heareth my voice.'"
18:37 John

These too are the words of Jesus according to John 4:24 KJV:
"God is a Spirit: and they that worship him must worship him in spirit and in truth."

There is a primal question; one that appears to echo the infinite and like a shepherd drives humanity forward into the unknown of future. That question is four simple words, as much a part of humanity as is our DNA, What Is The Truth? Interestingly, the emphasis is always on the word The, referring of course to the ultimate. The thirst for The ultimate truth is the movement at the heart of all exploration, the Holy Grail of desire – the seed of passion and wonder. Truth is the mother of paradox that conceived and consummated all science and study. It fuelled humanity's primordial quest out of darkness, a quest for meaning and purpose, and in some magical way is intimately linked with all questioning. The ancient pursuit, the Grail of Truth, goes beyond myth and the mystical realms; it is life's evolutionary force at work and the ultimate aim of the heart.

As we all know, truth can be and often is extremely personal, relative in every way to the awareness of the observer. Yet the major mystical traditions assert the existence of an experiential state allowing one to glimpse and even merge with 'Truth' with a capital 'T'. Whatever the name given culturally for that state, the various ways of describing the inexplicable all sound similar, if not identical, in nature. According to the great sages Truth is the Absolute and when experienced in the heart is pure Love felt as Joy. Yet when we read or listen to these descriptions, some deep inner part of us resonates validity and in our hearts we experience this yearning to go home.

Truth, some say, is the knowledge based on experience that I am not separate from the whole. Truth, it might also be said, is to know one's true nature. Eckhart Tolle speaking on page 90 in The Power of Now, highlights clearly the challenges of writing or speaking about anything, but especially something so challenging as the subject of Truth.

> "A word is no more then a means to an end. It's an abstraction. Not unlike a signpost, it points beyond itself. The word honey isn't honey. You can study and talk about honey for as long as you like, but you won't really know it until you taste it. After you taste it, the word becomes less important to you."

Fortuitously, there are a few souls that have tasted Truth. Ramana Maharshi is one such soul who clearly delineates the subject of realizing Truth when he says, "There are no stages in Realization or degrees of Liberation. There are no levels of Reality; there are only levels of experience for the individual." Ramana's statement profoundly shows us both the nature and paradox of Truth, which is Reality.

The notion of Truth/Reality/Awareness being whole and absolute, with only the interpreted experience of that state changing, is extremely insightful and useful in sustaining our ability to understand the Science of Divinity -- the Science behind the creation of the Shroud. What happens to the physiology of self when one has the experience of being totally aligned in heart, soul and mind, in a coherent state of total truth? By changing the experienced relationship, we change perception, and in doing so change our individuated awareness, which loops back changing the experience. This individuated awareness is our sense of self. Awareness achieved through experience is what hones the loop between the little "I" to the expanded "I". Through direct experience, Awareness allows reality to become personal, thereby developing a richer sense of self. But this is not The Self, it is just a sense of self, and it is this sense of self that allows for the looping/mirroring of Awareness within Itself. At the same time it is also what allows us to have our unique experience of the Awareness of Self, which masters tell us we are. This is why Ramana's quote above is so important. The development of this sense of self is the original, divisionless division that bifurcates without dividing. It is the fractal holographic light game that gives rise to the sense of the individuated self, which in turn gives birth to the illusion of relative truth moving in time, a requirement for awareness to become aware of itself.

Herein lies the conundrum, the riddle within a riddle. Great-awakened sages tell us that this very quest for knowledge and truth is what keeps us separated from The Truth. The quest they say brings one to the place where one simply tires of the struggle, where one surrenders to life and at that moment life reveals Truth and Reality.

Signposts of Truth

Over the centuries awakened souls have given birth to many disciplines that are littered with the signposts that consistently point to the realm of Truth. Truth is a cornerstone of spiritual life itself. Even the words of Jesus himself, as in the quote at the opening of this chapter where he is speaking to Pilate just prior to the crucifixion, reflect this conviction that he should bear witness unto the truth, even in the face of mortal death. But the signposts of truth can mean many things to many people. And since the purpose here is to determine the biological processes in the formation of the Shroud, we should go back to see what the word meant to Pilate when uttered by Jesus.

If you and I were alive and standing in the judgment hall with Jesus and Pilate, the Aramaic meaning of the words of Jesus as quoted by John at the beginning of this chapter would have inferred to you and me the following meaning: "I am here to be that harmonious breath that arises from one who is in harmony with All Life, and is what is required to fully surrender to God."

We would have felt the integrity and strength of Jesus at that moment, as did Pilate; we would have felt the peace in Jesus' voice and witnessed the great importance he placed on remaining in a state of integrity even when facing an agonizing death. We would have been humbled and shaken by the truth of it, as was Pilate. It was so powerful that over and over again Pilate, in fear of the man, tells the Jews that he can find no fault in Jesus.

Truth, in the common Aramaic form, meant to act in keeping with universal harmony. It was from this alignment that the secondary meanings of vigor and strength were derived and, according to Neil Douglas-Klotz in the Hidden Gospel, it liberates and opens possibilities.

Jesus was telling Pilate that he was not born to be somebody -- especially not a king; but rather born to be a witness to Truth, and that only those souls realized in Truth would understand. Add to this pronouncement his words in John 4:24 KJV, "God is a Spirit: and they that worship him must worship him in spirit and in truth," and the relationship Jesus gave to spirit and truth become evident.

The word in Aramaic for spirit also meant 'breath'. These two concepts were always linked in the minds of the listeners in Jesus' time. It was impossible to separate the two word concepts that would have implied at that time a harmonious spirit, or radiant energy infusing and creating harmonious breath. To align with Truth was a means of aligning with Spirit. Spirit, when related directly to God (with a capital G), refers to a specific Ultimate Power or potentially-infused Intelligent, Harmonious Light. We would only see the effects of this Holy or Sacred Intelligence; hence this is how we can understand the Holy Spirit or Holy Ghost. Miracles and the mystical occurred when this harmony entered into one's self.

The term worship, when spoken in the original Aramaic, most likely referred to bowing oneself before another, a form of submission, honoring or surrendering. So Jesus might be saying in John 4:24 something like this: "God is the Intelligent Harmonious Light that breathes Life. They that honor Life must surrender to that Intelligence in a complete and genuine manner. In-so-doing that harmonious breath and direction will be produced from within." Add to this interpretation two clear statements from the Coptic Gospel of Thomas, below, and the base psychological prerequisite for affecting the aim of the heart -- which is to be perfectly purified – is attained.

"His disciples questioned Him and said to Him, 'Do you want us to fast? How shall we pray? Shall we give alms? What diet shall we observe?'

"Jesus said, 'Do not tell lies, and do not do what you hate, for all things are plain in the sight of Heaven. For nothing hidden will not become manifest, and nothing covered will remain without being uncovered.'

> "Jesus said to them, 'If you fast, you will give rise to sin for yourselves; and if you pray, you will be condemned; and if you give alms, you will do harm to your spirits. When you go into any land and walk about in the districts, if they receive you, eat what they will set before you, and heal the sick among them. For what goes into your mouth will not defile you, but that which issues from your mouth - it is that which will defile you.'"

Gospel of Thomas No.6 and No.15

In this way, Jesus instructed his disciples, telling them that the most important thing they can do for attainment is to be truthful, genuine and honest to their inner truth essence. BE TRUTHFUL if you wish to know Truth!

"Think good, do good, speak the truth."
>   Zarathustra

Psychological Factors

What does being truthful really mean? To fully understand the biological process of Divinity and the physics that generated the Shroud, one cannot separate the psychological factors involved. It has long been understood that there is a direct connection between illness and your mental emotional state. The effects on your body when your emotional state goes downhill is well documented in volumes of medical journals, but the inverse affects of what occurs during sustained levels of positive emotional states are only now beginning to be investigated. What would happen if a person could live in a perpetual genuine state of natural harmony that would arise from the loving-kindness birthed from always being genuine with one's essence? What would occur in the biology if one loved Life with all his or her heart, soul and mind?

Indicators to comprehend these affects are the words used by Masters to describe the process of coming to Truth. These words are Alignment, Attunement, At-one-ment, Harmony, Balance and Resonance; these all reflect some form of energetic ordering, some degree of organic, biological, harmonic fractal coherency. The emotional result of this unique form of organic ordering of the parts of the self, ranges from various levels of experiencing vigor, clarity, strength, peace, joy, love, bliss, agape and ecstasy.

If one listens to and reads the signposts given by those of experience, truth, even relative or conditional truth, appears to align one's being with The Truth, The Reality. They are in resonance with each other if only for one beat of the heart. Full alignment requires a highly tuned sense of discernment born of quiet moments spent sensing and refining the finer vibrations. Being true to oneself is also a cornerstone of maintaining emotional integrity resulting in physical wellness. So in the final analysis, the concept of vigor and strength arises from an ability to honestly live one's relative personal truth.

His Holiness the Fourteenth Dalai Lama says in, <u>Compassion and the Individual</u>, "…According to my personal experience, mental stability and physical well-being are directly related."

Components of Integrity

In the Gospel of John: 20 we find the following:

16   Jesus saith unto her, Mary. She turned herself, and saith unto him, Rabboni; which is to say, Master.

17   Jesus saith unto her, Touch me not; for I am not yet ascended to my Father: but go to my brethren, and say unto them, I ascend unto my Father, and your Father; and to my God, and your God.

18   Mary Magdalene came and told the disciples that she had seen the Lord, and that he had spoken these things unto her.

To obtain the divine inheritance that Jesus exemplified in the sepulcher to Mary Magdalene in John chapter 20: verse 16, 17 and 18, the lonely and uncertain path of self-discovery must be traveled directly through personal honesty. If through grace and desire one is able to refine this attunement, Truth reveals itself from the veils created by mind. The logic goes like this: one needs to cultivate truth in order to know Truth. Truth in behavior is honesty, and honesty is experienced as complete integrity of being in loving-kindness. This in turn produces the clarity and strength to see through the illusion of mind to the true nature of all objective reality. After all, does not integrity mean an integrated whole? If so, then what are the parts that require harmonizing?

I've found it easiest to think in terms of physical parts and systems in terms of energy. Think of the body with all its sub-components as various energies that are able to play harmoniously with each other, very much like a grand symphony. The symphony has many different instruments all playing in vastly different ranges, yet somehow, with the help of the conductor, maintains a harmonious rhythm or interplay that produces the song, which is you. One sitting and listening hears one song yet it's comprised of many different frequencies coming from many different instruments. The same is true for the body. Within the mind-body system something similar is attempting to occur every moment of life. What is getting integrated on a base conceptual level are our thoughts, words and physical actions, with the motive which acts as a carrier wave for the energies of our thoughts, words and actions. When all these energies are in phased harmony with our true essence, our entire being is fully in a state of coherent integrity. The core essence, that some mystics call a 'fragrance', is by some paradox, unique to each person and remains so until there is absolutely no sense of self-witnessing at all. They would say that yes, we might be roses coming from the one rose of creation, but still we are unique while in three-dimensional time-space. This is obvious by simply looking at the vast degree of different nature exhibits.

It might be easiest to understand this paradox by seeing the uniqueness of each person's total makeup. Not only physiques are unique but also the cellular makeup of the DNA/Gene matrix combined with the individuated experience of life we carry into Truth. From our basic scientific understandings of how size and shape affects the harmonic resonance, to the quantum nature of perception and awareness, it all adds up to a unique quantum/physical resonant dance, equaling a uniquely individuated base resonance in three-dimensional space. This individuated aspect arises from the soul or quantum information level and is an extremely subtle energy because of its ultra base, long low rhythm. This ultra-long wave relationship in resonance is, I believe, what maintains the physical in a coherent form; however, more will be discussed on that later.

The understanding of energetic phased alignment of all oscillations that comprise the other physical parts/systems with this core rhythm (the fundamental), maintaining a sense of self in existence is required for full integrity. When one feels a sense of this harmony-state, it is called peace.

Chapter Eight

Heart Intelligence

Faith and love both develop in the heart: the House of Eternal knowledge. As the Prophet Mohamed said: "Consult your heart and hear the secret ordnance of God, discovered by the inward knowledge of the heart which is faith and divinity."

"That we are at all is the great mystery. The unknown force animating us, present in all that is blooming and fading, is our deepest felt sense, and, strangely, the feeling we most often overlook. Like breathing, this aliveness—this passionate presence—is taken for granted, and we pay attention instead to an endless stream of thoughts.

"Yet, as our attention comes to rest more in pure presence, a natural intelligence emerges. This intelligence bypasses our genetic gifts, IQ, age, cultural conditioning, and education. We might call it an intelligence of the heart."

Catherine Ingram

The idea of intelligence that is innate to the heart goes back in time to the first written histories of man. Poets, bards, sages, shamans and mystics have spoken plainly about the intelligence of the heart throughout the reaches of time. You find the heart's attributes in poem, song, and when reading the sacred text of those uniquely experienced illuminated souls. Hinduism, Sufism, Buddhism, Kashmeerian Shivaism, and the teachings of Jesus all hint that the heart is the House of Eternal knowledge or the place of real knowing and this knowledge reveals itself in the words of Mohamed as faith and divinity. But words do little good in the search for truth, for the mind is unable to grasp these words with any real meaning until a direct experience illuminates their wisdom and ultimate truth.

Zen Buddhism uses the metaphor of a finger pointing to the moon: although the finger points to the moon, the finger and the moon belong to two different worlds.

We will once again refer back to the scientific view of heart science to see if there is a thread to support Mohamed or Catherine Ingram's quotes.

Science of the Heart

A traditional medical view describes the heart as a hollow muscular organ of vertebrate animals operating as a force pump that maintains the circulation of 4,300 gallons of nutrient rich blood a day by its rhythmic contraction. A small bit of specialized tissue called the Sino auricular node, embedded in the wall of the right auricle, is responsible for initiating the heartbeat. This electrochemical cascade is comprised of a vast range of frequencies producing a torus-shaped waveform that expands out many feet past the edge of the physical body.

At the close of the last millennium new technologies and devises allowed medical sciences to focus on bio-energy research with greater detail. Because heart disease is such a large cash cow, funding was channeled to the support of individuals and institutions that focused in on the core of psychophysiology of the cardiac matrix. The new devices allowed the study in finer specificity to be conducted on this massive electromagnetic waveform. Large streams of studies and data flowed into academia creating diversity of disciplines. Somewhere out of these new disciplines came a term that was new for the scientific community; it was called Heart Intelligence. Like all new ideas, it evolved rapidly from simple origins.

In those early days, Heart Intelligence referred to an independent wisdom inherent to the heart. The support for this idea came originally from the deduction of two core facts: the first fact is that up to 65 percent of heart muscle tissue is embedded with neural cells similar to those found in the brain; the second is the autogenic nature of the heart. Autogenic means it does not require a signal from the brain or any other external source to beat. Simply, the impulse for contraction is not dependent on external nervous stimuli, but arises in the heart muscle itself. That no other part of the physical body controls this function is hard to grasp and intuitively this fact alone immediately places it at the core of the physical matrix. Please understand, this does not mean that other outside forces do not affect it, for they do, it simply means that no external source provides the trigger that initiates all its many functions.

Later we discovered that it produced hormones (chemicals) thus acting like a gland. We also learned that it produces sound pressure waves that wash every cell, affecting piezoelectric activity in the liquid crystal matrix of the cell. It also initiates and organizes neural activity and is the master oscillator for the entire physical body. When we take all these facts into account, the heart is seen as a master conductor and dynamo for information/energy communications regulating the functions of the physical structure. So the natural question that arises is; what is the intelligence that is operating here? for if it needs no outside source to operate, the intelligence must be innate.

Because of these bare facts, as well as a litany of others that we have discussed in Chapter 6 – Have Heart, researchers in the cardio/bio-energetic sciences began to ask unique questions. As the tools and computers evolved so did the quality and diversity of the research. One of the new areas of research was termed Heart Rate Variability (HRV). I will go into this subject in more depth in the chapter dedicated specifically to this subject. This one area of research alone gave us a completely new vision of the function of physical rhythms and their importance in wellness. For now, however, HRV refers to the magnitude of the fluctuation in the number of times your heart beats per minute in conjunction with respiration. HRV became the grail in heart medicine and with good reason for it was a statistical solution to virtually all chronic disease, including aging. This field was so rich with information and potential that it fractured into smaller specialized areas researching the flood of new global data much too soon. Out of these new fields of study came a new definition for Heart Intelligence.

Wave Theory

Dr. Irving Dardik, a vascular surgeon and Founding Chairman of the United States Olympic Sports Medicine Council, wrote an article in "Cycles Magazine" (CYCLES Vol.46, No 3,1996) "UNIVERSAL CYCLES: The Origin of Disease and Health Heart Waves; The Single Solution to Heart Rate Variability and Ischemic Preconditioning". As a vascular surgeon and the founding Chairman of the United States Olympic Sports Medicine Council, Dardik had the unique opportunity to consider the behavior of the heart in both worst-case circumstances of acute distress and intervention in the operating room and in best-case circumstances of sports performance and fitness training on the playing field. By stepping outside of the constraints of each specialty, he was able to discover "a completely new understanding of how the heart behaves as a wave".

This new perspective on the heart's functioning explained how the seemingly complex, disparate information of the body's behaviors, molecular biology, and genes is organized into a single coherent picture. He called this the Wave Theory. The theory's implications were vast. It solved conceptually a few medical mysteries, as well as explaining the underlying origin of chronic disease. Interestingly, at the same time it provided for the means of prevention and reversal of those diseases. Dardik's Wave Theory provided the means for optimizing health, performance, and longevity.

Dr. Dardik wrote in that same article that the, "Heart Wave is the body's master wave" and that "it reflects and organizes the degree of synchronization of all behavioral waves from those of the whole organism through molecular biological and genetic oscillations. As all hierarchical levels wave within one another as a continuum (super-loop), the organization of the organism as a whole is simultaneously a top/down (outside/in), bottom/up (inside/out) phenomenon."

This information was revolutionary on every level. A super-looping, recursive, self-referencing organism is an organism with intelligence and consciousness. Add to this the Autogenic nature of the heart and you get a picture that is hard to ignore. Maybe the brain was not the most important organ after all!

Not to delve too deeply into this discussion at this point, it is enough here to say that researchers studying the frequency components of the cardiac waveform started to see that slices of the frequency components related to other functions going on in the body, or that those same external functions were somehow reflected in and or modulating the cardiac waveform. These researchers began to attribute specific ranges of the cardiac waveform with other functions or systems of the body.

Researchers began to notice that the waveform of the heart developed a harmonious coherency when sustained ordered breath and/or deeply felt positive emotions were present. They noticed phased harmony present in the two major branches of the Autonomic Nervous System (ANS). Correlations were seen with relaxed ordered breath, positively felt emotions and neural balancing, with coherency within the cardiac energetic frequency signature. This coherent signature was tagged with the term Heart Intelligence. Money for training became available to qualified people who would develop the skills for creating this coherent signature. The reasons were clear and well grounded in medical science: learn the skill to create the signature, and wellness-immune functions will be optimized.

Heart Intelligence was rationalized as being a synergy of intellectual (rational thought), intuitive, and emotional components. In short, Heart Intelligence was a reflective signature of some internal agreement that produced coherent harmony in the music playing within the body as seen from the heart's perspective.

This synergy of physical function reflected in the heart did not tell us anything about its intelligence, it simply pointed to the reality of the intelligence existing. If this energetic agreement was between the intellectual, intuitive and emotional components, there must be another component organizing it all. Since the heart was now thought of as the master regulator, the intelligence governing the organizing was termed Heart Intelligence. A characteristic of this Heart Intelligence is its spontaneous and non-localized quantum nature. Spiritual teachers call this organizing synergy the 'witnessing aspect', others naming it the soul, while the Greeks have called it the psyche. This aspect of the Heart Intelligence is the root of psychology -- the study of why we do the things we do.

Synergy

Coherent Synergy reflects a balance between these two powerful forces of spirit and the world. It manifests when the informational connected synergy between the trinity aspects of self is present. It also reflects harmonious connectedness and communication for the organism as a whole; in HRV research it is phased-harmony between the big players operating in the body. From my research into this subject, I discovered that specific internal cardiac-coherent synergy reflects the informational connection to soul or non-local self-wisdom. These open connective mirror-like communications are self-referencing and recursive in a fractal environment. The result, Dr. Dardik explains as, "...all hierarchical levels wave within one another as a continuum (super-loop), the organization of the organism as a whole is simultaneously a top/down (outside/in), bottom/up (inside/out) phenomenon."

The Heart Intelligence signature can be produced artificially through creating and or recalling positive emotions and sustaining specific regulated breath. It is produced naturally via a genuine state of being with truth. Over and over again I've witnessed this signature of Heart Intelligence when the individual is simply being honest with him or herself in a genuine heartfelt way. "I must call my daughter to let her know I'm coming." The individual would at that moment for the first time in an hour suddenly produce scale invariant internal cardiac coherency. This connective knowing can manifest through intuition, knowing and yearning, or all three, producing a synergy of the intellect, intuition and emotions. As in the example above the individual knew even while engaged in this other very personal activity that he-she should all of a sudden call/connect with a loved one. This suggests the value of aligning these functions with Heart wisdom rather than bringing them together in some artificial form of synergy.

Another clue to Heart Intelligence points to the knowledge derived from the electrical information being broadcast from the heart and picked up as voltage on the surface of the skin. The coherent signature is an electrical signature reflecting harmonious (coherent) activity between various systems and their functions. Coherency is the inverse of dissonance and highly chaotic activity. This chaotic activity is a normal feature called variability and is a feature of mind creating disturbances in the field. Mind, as we recall, originates all emotional neurochemistry and the cascade to balance and normalize. Electrical coherency reflects phased harmony, in this case between the mind, intuition and emotional components.

Aligning with the knowing of the heart wisdom can produce very powerful synergy in these functions. In other words, functions in synergy reflect a communication that has already occurred at a quantum level. It may seem very subtle but it is critical to a full understanding of the data to which this research is pointing. Heart Intelligence is a system synergistic balance that commenced spontaneously via virtual modes of transference. Understanding this makes real the mystical realm. In a very uncomfortable way it merges soul, biology, spirituality and science. It points to a science that the ancient and current mystics understood and used. It is the path of the 'one heart', and it is the key to longevity.

> "Man's word is Spirit in man. Spoken words are sounds occasioned by the vibrations of thought; thoughts are vibrations sent forth by the ego or by the soul. Every word you utter should be potent with soul vibration." (Yogananda Scientific Healing Affirmations)

Soul-infused words are recognized as truth, honesty and integrity; they have the power to move mountains when spoken with genuine loving-kindness. As this music of truth develops and anchors in your heart, selfless service with an attitude of gratitude and kindness, pours in opening the heart. The geometry of the waveform allows the heart energies to expand in a constructive connective mode, thus enabling one's awareness to contain a larger view of the whole. With this knowledge comes motivation not only to do what makes us feel good, but also what makes others feel good. In this way empathy becomes the force manifesting the Golden Rule: 'Do unto others as you would have them do unto you'. The physical state of sustained Compassion is the fruit of living that Rule.

Developing a strong connection to Heart Intelligence requires a true discernment of integrity and awareness in the feedback loop. This means bringing attention to the voices and desires spoken in your heart. When you do so, you generate a truthful alignment of intention, words and behavior with the emotional state called compassion, as you cannot give or know loving-kindness until you have first given it to yourself.

> "The body does not die because you believe in death. The body exists, or seems to, because you believe in death. Body and death are part of the same illusion, created by the egoic mode of consciousness, which has

no awareness of the Source of life and sees itself as separate and constantly under treat. So it creates the illusion that you are a body, a dense, physical vehicle that is constantly under treat. To perceive your self as a vulnerable body that was born and a little later dies – that's the illusion. You want to keep one side of the illusion and get rid of the other, but that is impossible. Either you keep all of it or you relinquish all of it.

"However you cannot escape from the body, nor do you have to. The body is an incredible misperception of your true nature. But your true nature is concealed somewhere within that illusion, not outside it, so the body is still the only point of access to it."

The Power of Now, Eckhart Tolle

Jesus referred to this knowing so eloquently voiced above by Eckhart Tolle when he spoke of this synergistic balance of heart, mind and soul in love.

Chapter Nine

Intent & Compassion

"The first outburst of everything God does," the 13 century German Christian mystic, Meister Eckhart says, "is compassion"

To grasp and make personal the meaning lying hidden within the Silent Gospel, we are drawn to its intent. What was the motive in its creation? Whenever we do anything, no matter how unconscious that action might be, underlying that action is intent. When you go out in the morning to go to work and you get into your car, you are intending to drive safely to work. And whether you're conscious of it or not there is a quality associated with that energy motivating the action. So to understand honesty and intent we are drawn to explore first the qualitative universe.

Most of us use the greater portion of our attention on the outer five senses, however, these attributes deal with traits that feed the egoic mind. They comprise the primary basis for the rational mind and the ground of your perception. The egoic mind is addicted to this constant stimulus; it feeds the intellect like a hungry monster, but the intellect can never experience joy, faith or love to name just a few qualities we value, it can only understand them conceptually. Sufis claim that perceiving beauty, meaning, and the qualitative universe is a function of heart, and motive at the subconscious level is a reflection of the qualities presently anchored within the heart. By directing what we give our attention to, we are able to draw in more of the spiritual qualities such as patience, generosity, humility, appreciation, and ultimately compassion. The heart is transformed through relationship with these qualities. The opened heart can perceive the totality of qualitative subconscious faculties, which then function in a unified way to affect the heart's aim.

"Once activated, these faculties support and illuminate each other, much as eye-hand coordination is superior to either touch or sight alone. Although these functions appear to be separate, they serve a unifying purpose, which is to know the unity beyond multiplicity. They are the subtle nervous system's means of realizing unity.

"... The realization and purification of the heart both open a doorway to the Infinite and also results in a restructuring of neural pathways, a refinement and reorganization of our entire nervous system, without which we are not completely human."

Kaibir Helminski, <u>The Knowing Heart</u>

I will go into depth on this process of "restructuring of neural pathways, a refinement and reorganization of our entire nervous system," more in later chapters. In this chapter it is important to understand that intent has and is a quality, and that it arises from the heart. When the quality is selfless kindness and love, intent is no longer driven by a motive of fear and survival, instead it greatly augments the attributes of faith, grace and integrity. The light, or atmosphere, of the divine acts serves to refine your physical even if it is for a moment as seen in the HRV material. It might occur moment by moment till a kind of critical mass has been achieved or it might happen in a moment of total despair or awe. In those moments the little self cannot deal with the total and utter despair or the wonder of awesome beauty. In that timeless place known also as such-ness, is-ness or truth, reality is touched, it touches you and the communication becomes "I". The paradox is that when personal motive dies completely freedom arises. You can only prepare the ground of your hundred trillion cells in doing.

"The 'I' casts off the illusion of 'I' and yet remains as "I".

Such is the paradox of Self-realization."
Ramana Maharshi

Truth is Truth

I could have chosen any of the major mystical traditions to explore these "same basic truths". Whether Hindu, Buddhist, Christian, Jewish or Indigenous, it would be of no difference, Truth is Truth. At some core level the realization of Truth and the laws governing it is the same. According to the sages that have lived to experience this reality, this same truth acts as the foundation for all these various traditions and their sciences.

Being that this book is about the Shroud and tradition has it that it comes from the area of Jerusalem, I have chosen to use one of the most pragmatic spiritual traditions coming out of that region, Sufism. When it comes to the understanding and language of the Heart, the words of Sufism are clear and precise. Followers of Sufism believe in the revelatory power of Being. They believe and acknowledge the possibility of One Great Tradition being revealed within all traditional human communities, and that this One Great Knowledge is essentially in accord with Sufi understanding.

This understanding is in accord with the words and teaching of Jesus and gives insight on the science of Divinity that he might have employed. Sufis believe that there is one Absolute creator. The Universal and primal quality of that creator is compassion, sometimes termed mercy, which is pure love in action. They believe that there is just one Truth and that the Mother/Father creator was the One who gave birth to the cosmos and is the sustainer of life flow. They also believe that all humans have the ability to know this reality through direct experience. This experience is felt through the physical, and when fully incorporated, man becomes fully Hu-man. Hu, the pronoun of Divine Presence, is also understood by the Sufi's to be the indwelling presence of God." This information is according to Karbir Helminski in his wonderful book, The Knowing Heart. Hence, to be a Human Being means to be "A vehicle for individualized Spirit; the most complete witness of Spirit within the material world." (Note, K.H.). A fully developed human is one of community, involved and engaged in life. S/he becomes fully engaged in service to all life due to the knowing gained from the experience of The Reality that sustains all life. The fully Human understands the true intra- and interconnection of all life and doesn't hide away in a cave but holds the sacred Presence within the chaos of daily life.

As I've come to understand, the Sufi model places the heart between the egoic self (the natural self or carnal self) and Spirit (Spiritual Self, essence). Spirit is also seen in this connection as the soul or the psyche as described by the Greeks. Both the egoic self and spirit aspects of us send messages to the heart. The heart is the midway point between these two strongly attractive forces that direct our thoughts, words and actions. "Spirit has several important servants, including reason, reflection, and conscience." (NOTE; Writes Kabir Helminski in his excellent primer on Sufism, called <u>The Knowing Heart, A Sufi Path of Transformation</u>.)

When the heart is attuned to the spirit it opens to Divine Reality and inhabits Divine qualities.

> "The heart is the center of our motivation and our knowing, processing a depth and strength of will that the personality lacks. The heart may even know what the conscious mind denies. When we say that the heart has integrative power, we are not talking in abstract, metaphorical, or merely intellectual terms."
>
> Kabir, pp83

This actual integrative power of the heart is due to several factors. From a purely scientific perspective it is true because of the strength of power found in this key central oscillator, the heart. The rule of the body is that the strongest oscillating field exerts the greatest influence over other oscillators within its field of effect. This effect, when it creates synchronization, is called entrainment. Highly ordered entrainment is understood to be coherent. The heart's field effect is 5000 times stronger magnetically than that of the brain. As I showed in Chapter 6, the heart has the power to cohere all other coherent oscillating platforms whether they are molecules or systems. Under positive emotional states the power and resonance of the field, produced by the optimistic heart's constructive integration, is life supporting. The collective standing wave (emotional state) of self reflects the quality of the motivation. It appears that certain qualities are better at integrating and producing harmonious synergy than others. These are known as spiritual qualities. Here is a simple example. When you are cooking supper for your family are you joyful and appreciative for the opportunity, or are you distant, disturbed or angry? The quality felt reflects the motive regardless of the words said or the fact that you are doing the service of preparing a meal for your loved ones. The info-energy of intent underlies every thought or action, whether we are conscious about it or not.

Intent can be thought of as the quality of the energy sent out, which influences the energy that returns. This is just a concept to aid the rational conceptualization, for on the quantum level it is all happening within the singularity of Self. In other words, there is no time/space so nothing can be sent anywhere. But for the mind's understanding, it can be thought of as the quality imbued within the behavior. Intent mobilizes the other physical energies into attracting vectors because they attract or magnetize their natural counterpart that already preexists. The amplitude of these vectors strengthens with the degree of focused awareness (attention) placed within the quality. The energy of intent literally shapes the lens for directing powerful glandular emotional energies. It frames the energy of thoughts, words and actions; it gives them a quality. This is an important concept because we relate and imbue objects with qualities. It is the quality that gives life to the relationship with another object. The quality of the energy of intent literally dictates the return of energies to the producer of those original intentions. The law of magnetism dictates a like return of energy to fill the void. 'Likes attract like' is highlighted in the saying, 'As you sow so shall you reap'.

Intent is causal energy. Every emotion has in its creation a base carrier wave that we term Intent. Regardless of the thoughts, words or actions, it is the intent that determines the fundamental quality of that collective of other energies. It acts as a fundamental and when the quality is associated with spiritual qualities it aligns to Truth, which is Love, and from this integrity arises, honesty exists. Honesty is only fully present when the intention, which is to say quality, found in the heart at that moment (the inner character), is aligned to the words and behavior. To be in full alignment is only possible when the quality of your motive, thoughts, words and behavior are aligned with your reason for being. I believe at the core, this reason is to have conscious, unitive communication of pure Love supported by the intelligence formulating that quality.

Out of the Zero Point Domain, the singularity, the original duality arises in fractal perfect holographic phi, which is 1 to .618.... As the branching continues, it falls farther and farther away from the original division, The One to .618.... This is the first relationship to the Whole, the first proportion or ratio; it creates the first vibration and attracting fundamental. Phi is a transcendental number with no known end to it. The digits go off into the infinite, never repeating. I will share much more on this important number/relationship in later chapters. For the present discussions on the qualitative aspects of the cosmos, it is important to understand that the first few divisions out of stillness produce core cosmic fundamental vibrations. These core vibrations are qualities, when interpreted or translated through the body and then through the psyche. These vibrations preexist and are communicated through resonance. When the collective field of all the oscillating coherent platforms align to a base fundamental vibration we feel a spiritual quality. When the collective is chaotic or dissonant, which is to say not harmonic various forms of dis-ease are felt. The quality of how and what you place your attention on determines the energy that magnetizes to your field of perception. These subtle info-energy vectors touch the zero point energy that combines to crystallize your future in the now.

Sharon Salzberg from, "Personal Transformation Magazine," Issue 37, Winter 1999, says, "The Karma seed rests in intention, the underlying motivation behind the action. Every thing rests on the tip of motivation. The skill of keeping your intention, your motivations coming from the energy of loving compassion, this is through attention and a letting go of the immediate result with equanimity and peace. Mindfulness is the act of constantly looking at one's motivations and then bring them into alignment with the wisdom of compassion."

Intention, as Sharon Salzberg relates, is based in motivation, and from her Buddhist training she feels that Pure Intent would be one of loving compassion. This would be the highest idea quality to imbue motivation.

Most of us subconsciously have motives for our thoughts, words and actions, for our self-preservation. They arise from fear of some form: fear of not having, doing, getting, being, becoming or fear of pain and suffering. We come to our motives from a separated perspective. We identify with being our body and think that it is all there is to us. So most of the time the quality underlying our actions arises from fear instead of love. Love can arise in many forms such as creativity, beauty and art, but as an emotion it finds its highest form in selfless compassion.

> "Real love arises only when all attachments to individuals, objects and personal interests drop away.
>
> "Then the battle becomes a beautiful play. It becomes selfless service extended toward the entire human race out of love and compassion. In that fighting your ego will not fight, but love will fight to consume the ego and transform it into love." ~ Ammachi

People when they read this comment believe the work is to eliminate attachments. This is an impossible task if perceived from the "I must" perspective. Love is the flame that burns the dross of attachments. Love is God, Truth and the eternal substance of creation. It is the field of creation, it is unity mind, and it is non-local and omnipresent. By allowing the touch of love to enter your life, by allowing, even one small step at a time, all that is, to love you, you open the closed heart to create space for other(s).

The wisdom found in the heart is its desire to attune to the source of creative energy. In all spiritual traditions this energy is said to be Love. Love is; this quality in creative movement is compassion. Compassion defines the quality of a state of being. It is Love in action. Love breaks our heart open to what is not self. Love embraces everything, it does not judge nor insist, it is nurturing allowance; it is beauty, it is the sustaining force of life, it is the door wide open and receptive to ecstasy and unending joy.

Surfing the Flux Of Infinite Womb; The Wind On Which Love Is Carried.

A Native American grandfather was talking to his grandson about how he felt about a tragedy. He said, "I feel as if I have two wolves fighting in my heart. One wolf is the vengeful, angry, violent one. The other wolf is the loving, compassionate one."

The grandson asked him, "Which wolf will win the fight in your heart?"

The grandfather answered, "The one I feed."

Compassion

The Hebrew word for Compassion is derived from the word for womb. (Neil Douglas-Klotz, The Hidden Gospel)And the great Jewish teacher of the first century, Yeshua bar Alaha, a.k.a. Jesus, teaches in Luke, 6,36, to be "compassionate as your Creator in heaven is compassionate."

Matthew Fox writes in his book The Coming of the Cosmic Christ, pp.50, "Compassion is another word for the unitive experience and therefore another name for mysticism. Compassion is a "keen awareness of the interdependence of all living things which are all part of one another and involved in one another," as Thomas Merton observed two hours before his untimely death. "...in truth, compassion is the very origin and goal - as well as process - of creation mysticism." "The first outburst of everything God Does," the German 13 century Christian mystic, Meister Eckhart says, "is compassion." This means that all creatures as children of God hold compassion in common. Compassion is our universal heritage, our God-origin and our God Destiny. Compassion unites us, it forms the common 'field' that all creatures share. ...We are in God and God is in us. That is the unitive experience of the mystics East or West. Its technical name is pane theism, which means that "God is in all things and all things are in God." It is from this perspective, Matthew Fox says, "'*Beginning* for Meister Eckhart means *Compassion*."

Compassion is Divine Mind's Primal Intent, the Divine Creative Feminine.

Compassion is the transfiguration of dualism. It is the only emotional state not anchored in separated self, by its nature it is selfless. Compassion is a state where you feel not for another, this is empathy or sympathy; compassion is feeling and seeing the world as the other person sees it and feels it. It is from this natural state that true love arises and the little ego-driven self slowly losses strength over actions.

Jesus said shortly before his death, "Forgive them for they know not what they do". This level of compassion is rarely seen but it has been recorded in times of extreme violence and war; times where the one being tortured genuinely forgives his torturer and, in the act of embracing a greater reality, immediately has an epiphany of loving calmness flood through him or her.

The principle that 'you cannot give what you don't have,' is applicable here. To be compassionate one must first develop compassion for oneself by developing loving-kindness, fostered by heartfelt truthfulness. Buddhists develop compassion through the practice of Tong-len, literally meaning taking and giving. This practice must be felt from a genuine place, it must be in accord with the inner character. To develop this inner character one practices first metta/karuna or simply loving-kindness. The Dalai Lama has said that his religion is loving-kindness. And he practices this religion in its simplest form in this way; he approaches everyone he meets as an old long lost dear friend.

Metta, Lovingkindness, Karuna and Tong Len; the science of attuning the qualitative aspect of intention.

"Karunananda, means 'bliss through compassion.'

"In the Sutra teachings, the means is compassion, while the knowledge (wisdom) is emptiness. By unifying compassion and emptiness, we attain true and complete enlightenment." ~ Tulku Urgyen Rinpoche

To develop a sincere sense of joy, self, and altruism one must develop a sincere sense of compassion. The Dalai Lama says that endless compassion is at the root of all religions. This truth transcends all wisdom schools of the planet regardless of culture.

Wisdom and Compassion are the two central tenets in all forms of Buddhism. Wisdom comes naturally through the experience of developing sincere compassion, which is our natural inclination yet it needs to be developed. Compassion is said to be a spaciousness or openness within the heart that allows for conscious connectedness. The primary technique for developing compassion is the practice of metta, a Buddhist term for boundless friendship first toward oneself and then translated into loving-kindness to others. This loving kindness then is extended into the full practice of Tong Len, which is taking the suffering of others and giving them your love and joy. His Holiness the Fourteenth Dalai Lama writes in <u>Compassion and the Individual,</u>

"From my own limited experience I have found that the greatest degree of inner tranquility comes from the development of love and compassion. The more we care for the happiness of others, the greater our own sense of well-being becomes. Cultivating a close, warmhearted feeling for others automatically puts the mind at ease. This helps remove whatever fears or insecurities we may have and gives us the strength to cope with any obstacles we encounter. It is the ultimate source of success in life."

"...So far I have been discussing mainly the mental benefits of compassion, but it contributes to good physical health as well. According to my personal experience, mental stability and physical well-being are directly related." (To the development of compassion.)

Sharon Salzberg writes in her book, <u>A Heart as Wide as the World</u>,

"As Thich Nhat Hanh, the Vietnamese Zen monk, points out, 'Compassion is a Verb.' It is not a thought or a sentimental feeling but is a movement of the heart. As classically defined in Pali, (early language of Tibet) compassion is 'the trembling or quivering of the heart.' ...

"Compassion is born out of loving-kindness. It is born of knowing our oneness, not just thinking about it or wishing it were so. It is born out of the wisdom of seeing things exactly the way they are. But Compassion also arises from the practice of inclining the mind, of refining our intention."...

"Wisdom of our interconnectedness arises hand in hand with learning to truly love ourselves. The Buddha said that if we truly loved ourselves, we would never harm another. When we can love ourselves, we give up the idea that we do not deserve the love and attention we are theoretically willing to give to others."

Sogyal Rinpoche writes in his book <u>The Tibetan Book of Living and Dying On the Tonglen Practice</u>, "Before you can truly practice Tonglen, you have to be able to evoke compassion in yourself. ... Fortunately there are several techniques that the Buddhist 'training of the mind' in compassion has developed to help us evoke our own hidden love."

In his book, <u>Loving Kindness: Unsealing the Spring,</u> Sogyal Rinpoche says,

"When we believe that we don't have enough

love in us, there is a method for discovering and invoking it. Go back in your mind and recreate, almost visualize, a love that someone gave you that really moved you, perhaps in your childhood. Traditionally you are taught to think of your mother and her lifelong devotion to you, but if you find that problematic, you could think of your grandmother or grandfather, or anyone who had been deeply kind to you in your life. Remember a particular instance when they really showed you love, and you felt their love vividly."

Allowing the feeling of love in our heart is a primary prerequisite to any level of Tong Len practice.

Sharon Salzberg says,
"The practice of loving-kindness (metta) meditation brings to life our innate capacity for connecting to ourselves and others. The loving-kindness we cultivate breaks through the habit of indifference or judgment that keeps us feeling separate from others. A capacity for friendship and kindness exists within each of us, without exception. No matter what pain we might have gone through in our lives, that capacity is never destroyed. It may be - and often is - obscured, but it's there."

From the words of these people of wisdom, we are assured that the practice of Metta (loving-kindness) is the primary practice of developing spaciousness in one's heart for other(s).

The Practice of Tong-Len

Before acting on a feeling it is important to clearly differentiate between compassion, empathy, sympathy or pity for they are all very different from each other. Sogyal Rinpoche says, "Compassion is a far greater and nobler thing than pity. Pity has its roots in fear, and a sense of arrogance and condescension, sometimes even a smug feeling of 'I'm glad it's not me.' As Stephen Levine says: 'When your fear touches someone's pain it becomes pity; when your love touches someone's pain, it becomes compassion.' To train in compassion, then, is to know all beings are the same and suffer in similar ways, to honor all those who suffer, and to know you are neither separate from nor superior to anyone."

In the eleventh century, the Indian Buddhist teacher Atisha brought to Tibet the Seven Points of Mind Training, which is the practice of Tong-Len. The core practice involves taking on others' sorrow and pain and sending them your joy, not as a masochistic practice but with the aim of getting away from the self-centeredness and self-seeking that cause us so much pain. The tong-len is one of the primary methods employed. Tong –Len means taking and giving and is a meditation done in conjunction with one's breathing. The tong-len practice is a method for connecting with suffering – that of our own and that which is all around us – everywhere we go. It is a method for overcoming fear of suffering and for dissolving the tightness of our heart. Primarily it is a method for awakening the compassion that is inherent in all of us, no matter how cruel or cold we might seem to be.

Thrangu Rinpoche, as taken from the Oral Instructions on the Karma Pakshi Practice given by Thrangu Rinpoche, assured his retreatants of Samye-Ling, December 1993,

> "This practice goes against the grain of wanting things on our own terms; of wanting it to work out for ourselves no matter what happens to the others. The practice dissolves the armor of self-protection we've tried so hard to create around ourselves. In Buddhist language one would say that it dissolves the fixation and clinging of ego.
>
> "Some people new to this practice get worried because they think that by doing the practice they will have to lose happiness and experience suffering, which makes them fearful. However, there is no need for this anxiety because whatever happens to oneself is solely a result of one's karma. Doing this practice does not bring suffering. Other people do the practice with great expectation, with great hope. They think of a friend who is ill, unhappy or otherwise suffering and they visualize this friend during the meditation in the hope that they will remove the suffering. When they find it does not work they lose hope and become disillusioned. This also is not what the practice is about. The point is to cherish

other beings as important, rather than regarding oneself as important. So there is no need to have worry, fear or expectation."

Bodhicitta

"Bodhicitta means the purified and fully awakened heart-mind. This is the heart, the very soul of enlightenment," writes Lama Surya Da in, <u>Awakening the Buddha Within</u>. This awakening primarily is the difference between the open mind and the narrow mind. The more narrow and constricted your attitudes the more ego-centered you are. The practice is to become selfless; the goal from a Buddhist perspective is to live Bodhicitta.

> "Bodhicitta is said to have two sides: the conventional side—selfless or unselfish altruism, aspiration to relieve the suffering of all, compassion, services, and so on—and the ultimate side, which is wisdom itself, sunyata, appreciation of the infinite openness." Lama Surya Da

> "Compassion is the awareness of a deep bond between yourself and all creatures. But there are two sides to compassion, two sides to the bond. On the one hand, since you are still here as a physical body, you share the vulnerability and mortality of your physical form with every other human and with every other living being. …

> "The realization of this deathless dimension, your true nature, is the other side of compassion. On a deep feeling-level, you now recognize not only your own immortality but through your own that of every other creature as well. On the level of form, you share mortality and the precariousness of existence. On the level of Being, you share eternal, radiant life. These are the two aspects of compassion. In compassion, the seemingly opposite feelings of sadness and joy merge into one and become transmuted into a deep inner peace. This IS the peace of God. It is one of the most noble feelings that humans are capable of, and it has great healing and transformative power. But true compassion,

as I have just described it, is as yet rare. To have deep empathy for the suffering of another being certainly requires a high degree of consciousness but represents only one side of compassion. It is not complete. True compassion goes beyond empathy or sympathy. It does not happen until sadness merges with joy, the joy of Being beyond form, the joy of eternal life."

Eckhart Tolle from, The Power of Now, Pages 162–163

As it has become clear by now, in order to develop compassion for others, we must have compassion for ourselves by being gentle or kind with ourselves. We are often our own harshest critics. We can love, but it's a challenge to allow ourselves the gift of receiving love, even from our self. Loving-kindness is a matter of allowing; it is openness and inclusiveness, which includes qualities like acceptance, patience, humility, generosity and forgiveness. It is almost like an equanimity that appreciates things no matter how they fluctuate or dance in our perception; appreciating what is in any giving moment, including our own perceived faults and shortcomings. We need to hold these perceived faults like they are our children; embrace them, settling them into a warmhearted space and giving them the love of something you birthed. This is a good place to start.

Everyone can recall an open receptive moment, an event where you stopped long enough to sense beauty on a body level. The science of Divinity begins with being self-loving by being truthful to one's self. This inner character can develop over time to embody Spiritual qualities, the highest form being that of Compassion. When your body is attuned in full integrity, the quality of the thoughts, words, and actions cohere in a very powerful, harmonious symphony. The laser-like coherence of the integration when sustained results in a restructuring of neural pathways, a refinement and reorganization of our entire nervous system, this allows us to be completely human. It allows for an opening to the Infinite, resulting in realization and purification of the heart.

"There are no stages in Realization or degrees of Liberation.

There are no levels of Reality; there are only levels of experience for the individual." ~ Ramana Maharshi

Chapter Ten

Breath

My ears range wide to hear and wide my eyes to see,
wide this Light that is set in the heart;
wide walks my mind and I set my thought afar;
something there is that I shall speak;
something that now I shall think.
One and common be your aspiration, united your hearts,
common to you be your mind,
so that close companionship may be yours.

Rig Veda about 3700BC <u>Hymns to the Mystic Fire</u>: *Aurobindo*

The light, atmosphere or energy of the Divine is in everything and is increased within the individual by focused breath techniques. This is seen as a real yet very subtle energy. Each tradition has its own term for the substance at the root of life-force; the Hindu, Buddhist systems call it prana, the Polynesians/Huna religious systems call it mana, and the cultural systems arising out of the Middle East called it spirit, grace, or Holy Spirit. Regardless of the word, it points to a subtle energy that induces vitality.

Your heartbeat and your breath are your two oldest friends in this life experience. They have been with you, through every experience that you've ever had, and will continue with you until you expire. We take them for granted and think of them as being on automatic but these two powerful key rhythms, your heart beating and your breath, can be altered with conscious will. Slow down and calm your breath and your heart rate will slow down as well. The mystical sciences of immortality and self-realization place great importance on the science of breath and on developing the skills required to bring these two powers of breath and heart rate into specific synchronization. Learning the skills allows one to be not just alive, but fully inspired, enraptured and fully human before the last expiration and beat occurs, before the gift of the body is taken away.

In Hebrew the word for Spirit 'ruach' and the Aramaic 'ruha' could easily be interchanged for breath or winds or air; an atmosphere or vibration infused with light. It comes from the root, a raying forth (R), as in RA, referring to light, the sun's rays; and of life breath (H). The word 'spirit' migrated into English via 'spiritus' (literally breath, French spirare to blow, breathe). It is directly related to the root for inspiration, which comes from the Latin spirare; to breathe. The letter symbol concept 'inspired' arose from In-Spirare meaning, to influence, guide or move by divine or supernatural inspiration, to breathe in or be filled with spirit/life.

The concepts and processes of breath, life, light and spirit all arise together in antiquity. One would only speak of qualitative nuances but could not separate in the mind breath from light, life or spirit. It was a substance breathed in that was God-substance and it sustained and was life, it was spirit. Coincidentally, there existed at the same time as the Aramaic ruha, on the Indian subcontinent, another word symbol for the same concept called prana.

> "The Siddhas developed slow rhythm breathing patterns in order to prevent such loss of energy and enable themselves to live as long as they wished, serving mankind. As oxygen is taken up by the circulatory systems, so prana is taken up by the nervous system and is spent as nerve-force in the act of thinking, desiring etc. Regulating the breath enables one in fact to absorb a greater supply of prana…" ~Hazrat Inayat Khan

"In Sanskrit breath is called prana,…'" writes Hazrat Inayat Khan in, The Mysticism of Sound and Music. "Prana", he continues, "has a value or psychological power that can be felt and seen in the effects that words and or songs have. A few words can have a deep impression if the quality of the words resonates meaning. Semitic, Hebraic, Hindus seers, and Yogis over the many ages have valued the importance of the word and breath. Words, chants and song are one level in the science of breath. When one studies the science of breath the first thing learned is that the breath is audible;

"...it is a word in itself for what we call a word is only a more pronounced utterance of breath fashioned by the mouth and tongue. In capacity of mouth breath becomes voice, and therefore the original of word is breath. Therefore if we say: 'First was the breath', it would be the same as saying', 'In the beginning was the word'."

Add to this, "...And the word was God" [The Gospel of St. John 1:1] and you can see that from the very beginning breath and spirit were united in the Hebrew tradition as well.

Giving Breath A Quality

If focused, we can connect the attention to our breath. The degree or amount of attention and the quality placed within the breath determines substantially how we experience life.

Humans have their attention scattered in many places most of the time. Attention is energy and as such can act as an agent for attracting or repulsing other energy. We all make choices as to where and how much of our energy we direct to any one place at any one time. Most of our attention travels to the communication stimulus of the five outer senses when we hear, see and feel, but also we give attention to several mental thoughts being juggled by the mind; we drive a car, speak on the phone, feel our leg going to sleep and have several things cross through our mind all at the same time. Each area bids for our attention and we, as a general rule, have very little control over the flow of this vital energy. Our mind jumps from one object to another as if it was an entity unto itself.

The ancient and current yogis understand that if we develop the skills required to close down a few or all of these inputs, even momentarily, more attention naturally flows to one specific area of focus. We have only so much attention for use and it gets diluted with the amount of things it is asked to follow and support. We can easily control the outer senses by going to a quiet, comfortable space and simply closing our eyes. Then all we're left with is the chatter of the mind and an ache in the body or two. This too we can learn to just witness, gradually pulling our attention out of this field and into other more subtle fields of perception. We can use our friend, the breath, as an aid to quiet the mind and calm the body. We can use this constant companion as a vehicle to move the focus of our attention inward, onto the sensations of the feeling body vibrating with energy. With just a little discipline we can place vastly larger amounts of attention on the breath and the heart rhythms. This aids in directing light in which to illuminate these inner rhythms, allowing the intelligence of the heart great conscious control over physical functions. A natural feat to the yogi is incomprehensible to a normal individual, yet as you will read, these inexplicable acts of physical control have been well documented in the back pages of major scientific journals.

Anatomy of Breath

The heart rhythm is calculated as Beats Per Minute (BPM). The breath is also calculated over a minute of time, however, it has three components: the inhalation, the exhalation and the brief pause or still point between the two. All three of these components can be consciously altered and combined in different ways. Each way produces an effect that can be witnessed in the emotions and or feelings.

The yogi is attempting to always refine harmony, which is balance. Bringing order to the breath and its components brings order to the heart wave. This in turn brings order and balance to the finer rhythms of the emotional, mental and physical fields of energy.

From the occult, metaphysical or mystical views, there are three degrees of breath. The first is normal breathing from the nostrils. The second is blowing from the lips, a method more intense and focused, and the more focused and strong the blowing, the more intense is its effect. The third and most intense is sound. This too has levels, for the more sacred the vibration of the word, the more powerful the effects of the sound. Sacred is a simple word referring to attunement with life or nature.

Each method of using breath has equal value when utilized with knowledge. Just the act of being with your natural breath can create a relationship with your inner feeling body. Simple breathing in and out from the nostrils has powers to organize and entrain, to strengthen and vitalize the physical when it is approached with knowledge and discipline. Powerful breath techniques are utilized by athletes, the martial arts, in Chi Gong (Qigong) and Tai Chi for the expressed purpose of increasing strength and vitality, calming the nerves, and directing focus and power. The science of breath to this very day is a cornerstone in all athletic pursuits and Yogic practices.

The yogi can utilize many different rhythms of breathing, however, there are four core ways to breathe those various rhythms.

- Inhalation through an open mouth- Exhalation through an open mouth

- Inhalation through an open mouth- Exhalation through the nose

- Inhalation through the nose – Exhalation through the mouth

- Inhalation through the nose – Exhalation through the nose

Each of these modes, when done in specific rhythm (timing) with the heart's rhythm, produces very distinctive results. When performed in certain specific synchronization with the heart's rhythm, the harmony produces the powerful radiance of peace. This feeling of peace is the result of specific harmonious synchronization of the two main oscillators producing a balance in the Autonomic Nervous System and from their synchronization in system functions. Peace has a quality that allows others to be touched by it and they too feel more peaceful due to the internal harmonization occurring through resonance and entrainment of their own waveform.

There are two ways to produce this physical coherency. The first of these is to entrain all coherent platforms acting in the body with the rhythm of the heart. The second is to synchronize the heart-wave with the music of the breath. If you focus on your breath and maintain a specific regulated rhythm, over time the heart's rhythm will slowly match the breath rhythm in a form of phased synchronized entrainment. They become phase synchronized coupled oscillators. Finding the present rhythm of the heart (your heart rate), then tuning your breath to it in specific ratio, is the other more esoteric method, but one commonly used by runners. In these cases the gait pace, heart rate and breath are all in phased harmony, in fact when ideal it is fractal.

At the turn of the millennium these facts were being verified by science in many countries. We are more and more being thought of in terms of energy beings, as bioelectric coherent phenomenon. Indeed, matter itself is now acknowledged as an electromagnetic phenomenon, a subject I will later speak in depth on. In the last few decades, bio-energy disciplines as a legitimate field of study have proliferated and splintered into many sub-areas of intense interest. The development of high speed computers and frequency analyzing programs has made it easier to record and view the pertinent info-energy data being generated by an organism. Even the study of mind and consciousness whittles down to fine vibrations in quantum-entangled clouds of sub-activity.

The study of the heart as an information energy-producing organism began years ago with electrocardiograph (ECG) diagnostic devices. This study grew into several sub disciplines, as previously mentioned in the discussion of Heart Intelligence, but one area of research over the last decade has shown great promise and significance. This new field of inquiry is generally known as Heart Rate Variability (HRV), the study of the heart's rhythms in relationship to respiration. The ratio of breath to beats of the heart over time is the area of inquiry with modern day medical science following in the footsteps of the ancient research of the yogis, in studying the two main rhythm regulators of the body and their relationship to wellbeing. Consequently, a great deal of energy, attention and man-hours have been directed on this one unique area of discipline, to the point where it too has several sub-set disciplines embedded within the field.

> "…to have relaxation does not mean to sit quietly. It is to be able to remove tension from one's system, from one's circulation, one's pulsation, and one's nervous and muscular system."

Hazrat Inayat Khan "Mystic Relaxation" in Sufi Message, vol, 4 p.165-6

Re-stating Khan's words in another way, we understand that the less the dissonance or dis-harmony is among the various levels of oscillating platforms, the greater the sense of relaxation and inner peace. Oscillating means to swing or beat; oscillators produce, maintain or regulate rhythm. The two main oscillators of the physical body are first the heartbeat and its rhythm and secondly the breath and its inner components. When it comes to oscillators and entrainment, strength rules. This rule is also true in resonance. Power is reflected in amplitude and is an indication of this rule in action.

The body is as important as the soul. Divorced from the body the soul is naught. "If the physical body perishes, it is a doom to the soul and one would not attain the true knowledge firmly. So by knowing the technique of tending and nourishing the body well, I not only tended and nourished the body but the soul too."

Hazrat Inayat Khan "Mystic Relaxation" in Sufi Message, vol, 4 p.165-6

The way of the Sufi heart meditation is to breathe focus on the natural rhythm of the beating heart, and relax into it like a baby in a mother's arms. Eventually the rhythm slows and the attention enters the space of the beating heart to find itself the beat of the universe or vise versa, for the universal rhythm is the ground of your rhythm. Attaching one's awareness to the heartbeat is similar to the mindfulness meditations of following one's breath.

"Time was when I despised the body; But I saw the God within. The body I realized, is the Lord's Temple; And so I began to preserving it with care infinite" ~TM, verse 725 (Thulasiam, 1980, pg. 460)

Chapter Eleven

Heart Rate Variability

"The deeper the Self-realization of a man, the more he influences the whole universe by his subtle spiritual vibrations, and the less he himself is affected by the phenomenal flux."

Swami Sri Yukteswar, in <u>Autobiography of a Yogi</u>

In studying the electrical signatures of the heart scientists began to observe that some relationships began to show more and more importance. One of these areas was the connection to low frequencies in a specific region to breathing. As mentioned in a previous chapter, this new field of research came to be known as Heart Rate Variability (HRV). HRV refers to the magnitude of the fluctuation in the number of times your heart beats per minute in conjunction with respiration. It is significant because it provides a window to observe the heart's ability to respond to normal regulatory impulses affecting its rhythm.

HRV is a measure of these beat-to-beat time interval variations as the heart speeds up or slows down with each breath. The arena of research grew due to its value in diagnosing specific illnesses. Today HVR is understood as the response relationship of the natural rise and fall of your heart rate to your breathing, blood pressure, hormones and emotions. It is now seen as reflective and predictive of general health and overall psycho physiological wellness and as a prognostic indicator of risk associated with a variety of chronic diseases, behavioral disorders, mortality, and even aging. The primary focus of clinical work and research is in observing or modifying the balance in regulatory impulses from the vagus nerve and sympathetic nervous system.

The connection of Heart Rate Variability as a single risk factor associated with such a wide spectrum of disorders is strong evidence of some underlying phenomenon linking disease and health. Decreases in

Heart Rate Variability seem to be a common denominator in both mental and physical dis-ease. Conversely, the therapeutic increase of Heart Rate Variability has been shown to promote positive health outcomes in the context of many chronic challenges.

In a healthy adult, heart rate goes up with inhalation and goes down with exhalation. This synchronicity is also referred to as respiratory sinus arrhythmia. The healthier the heart is, therefore, the greater the heart-rate variability. This is the way it is perceived today in mainstream science. When a baby is born it breathes deeply thus moving the intestines and bowels, however, as a person gets older he/she breathes increasingly higher in the chest, filling the lungs with less and less air as a result.

In a recent event a well-researched yogi from Japan named Mr. Kawakamit, demonstrated to a full house of professionals that there is more to this picture than just this simple definition. He can place himself under conditions that should theoretically activate a sympathetic response (Extreme pain or stress) in the extreme, yet he demonstrates perfectly relaxed harmony and strong HRV. He had control of his breath and had years earlier obtained the skills, or should I say science, required to willfully control his physical systems.

Heart Rate Variability (HRV)

The procedural analysis for obtaining Heart Rate Variability data is usually performed by obtaining an electrocardiograph (ECG) signal. The Inter-Beat Intervals (IBI) is derived from the ECG as the intervals between consecutive R-peaks (the highest/ strongest point of the heartbeat signal). This method is very accurate and reliable but requires using complex ECG equipment.

An alternative way is to use a photoplethysmograph (PPG) measurement by means of a portable and convenient finger sensor. This sensor emits an infrared light on the skin. The emitted light is partially consumed by the blood flow. The degree of light consumption / reflection is proportional to the changes in blood flow. The PPG signal has periodic peaks that represent blood vessel pulsation. It can also be used to derive the IBI as the time between two PPG peaks.

A brief five-minute assessment of HRV has been found to be clinically valid and meaningful, but length of time significantly influences the signal sample. These methods of analysis are based on time, however another method of analyzing the data is in the frequency domain. In a poetical metaphor, this method looks at the notes being played in a specific section of the symphony of music played with each beat. These are in the very low frequency ranges, like listening to just the bass in a song. Frequency domain measures of HRV provide information on the frequency distribution of the components of HRV by using power spectral density analysis. The electromagnetic wave of the heartbeat is analog and the other power spectral density analysis is a digital representation of the distribution and power of the frequencies.

Spectral analysis of HRV is characterized by four main components, each a slice of the low spectrum, however, it is the three higher frequency components that are primarily used in clinical evaluation. These regions are not all standard in the range they inhabit or the name given to each region, but this outline below gives a pretty good idea of the slices of the spectrum pie being viewed.

High Frequency (HF) component (0.15Hz - 0.4Hz) measures the influence of the vagus nerve in modulating the sinoatrial node. HF component is known to be synchronous with respiration and has been considered as a quantitative evaluation of respiratory arrhythmia. The ratio of HF to LF power is often used as an approximation of sympathovagal balance.

Low Frequency (LF) component (.04Hz-.15Hz) provides an index of the heart, particularly when these are measured in normalized units. This slice of the spectrum is used to discriminate the power in the baroreceptor feedback loop. This is mainly responsible for beat-to-beat blood pressure control. The power in the LF region can be due to parasympathetic or sympathetic activity, or to a mixture of both, but is primarily from parasympathetic activity. It has been demonstrated that positive emotional states increase the power and coherence of this region.

Very Low Frequency (VLF) component (.003Hz - .04HZ) reflects the influence of several factors on the heart, including chemoreceptors, thermoreceptors, the renin-angiothensin system, and other non-regular factors.

The Silent Gospel

Frequency

Before moving on, I would like to add a few more comments about frequency. Frequency is time/distance measurement, also known as Cycles Per Second (CPS). Because it is time and distance it also relates to velocity (distance in meters). In HRV measurements, frequencies are really long, low, slow waves of info-energy. 1 Hertz/CPS is 1 cycle per second, these information-energy waves are moving between 0.4 cycles per second at the high side down to 0.003 CPS, which translates to about 5.5 minutes for this one energy wave to cycle once. Most of the frequency domain measuring short-term spectral analysis of HRV comes from information captured in these three components.

The biological view of this process is a two-way communication system with various systems of the body all affecting (modulating) the waveform of the heart. One of the two-way communications affecting the waveform consists of the two hard-wired branches of the Autonomic Nervous System (ANS). This is the automatic part of the nervous system. These subsystems are the sympathetic and parasympathetic branches that are responsible for either speeding up the systems of the body or slowing them down. The sympathetic branch depresses glandular secretions, induces blood vessel constriction and decreases muscle tone. They are in place to slow down the systems subconsciously in order to balance out the effects of the parasympathetic activity. These systems are seen to send messages to the heart, and maintain a very fine balance if optimum heart functions is to exist.

The baroreceptor is another system of communication consisting of pressure-sensitive nerve endings in the cardiovascular system itself and it is the baroreceptor that takes messages from the heart to the brain. The other bi-directional communication system is in the liquid media of the body that includes the messenger molecules like hormones, neurotransmitters, immunopeptides, and so forth.

Another main info-energy communication mechanism is the synchronization of the change in heart rate with the breath (respiration/RSA). Current medical thinking has it that the heart rate should increase with inhalation and decrease with exhalation. But with training a fractal phase coupled synchronization, a kind of laser-like coherency among the various independent coherent oscillating platforms, occurs.

Here is the odd thing, all of these have been shown to affect and impact emotion. Strong emotional states based in fear, anger or frustration immediately change the shape, frequency and variability of the heart's electrical waves, synchronization of the RSA, as well as the chemical make-up of the messenger molecules. In short, the direct link of emotion with heart rhythm and breath is well established. It is now believed that even simple exercises like walking will elevate moods by activating chemicals (proteins /hormones, etc.).

These negative, stress-producing emotions both stimulate the emergency branch of the nervous system's sympathetic branch and increase the release of adrenaline-like hormones into the body. Your immune system is suppressed, toxins increase in various organs including the blood, digestion is inhibited and many other survival activities ensue. The bottom line is that stress to the body means real life threatening danger. All other nonessential activities are put on hold until the threat is over and breathing returns to normal relaxed states. Additionally, when you are angry, the Heart Rate Variability wave flattens (decreases) indicating insufficient recovery of the heart muscle with each beat. This is not good if wellness is your goal, and at this point the parasympathetic system steps in and slows down the activity of the body including the heart, allowing normal activity to resume. This dance to stress is always ongoing even if all on the outside appears okay.

The desire of the unresolved heart is a constant rumbling under the surface of the ocean of 'little mind'. At the seat of all stress and tension is the active, subtle pull on the heart by one of the two core components: those of the little I, time, theoretical, survival driven, mind self, generically called the ego, and the greater timeless soul aspect, with a totally different conception of reality, survival, desire and imbued with a unique form of experiencing and knowing. But like the demonstration of Mr. Kawakami, demonstrated, this too can be brought to awareness and harmonized or willfully redirected via breath and attention.

We've already seen that the heart communicates with the body through four primary methods: the transmission of nerve impulses, by means of hormones and neurotransmitters, through pressure waves

The Silent Gospel

which are similar to acoustic sound waves, and energetically through electromagnetic field interactions. These means of communication inform, direct and transmit the needed energy, to the needed systems, instructing them to perform the needed activities required for maintaining balance on all levels.

The ratio of HF (high frequency) to LF (low frequency) power is often used in HRV research and clinical use as an approximation of sympathovagal balance. Sympathovagal balance means that the two branches are in some type of agreement, electrically they are in a synchronic phased harmony. Oddly, at these moments, subjects say that they feel good; a kind of relaxed peace comes over them even when they are undergoing physical exercise. The ability to intentionally shift to positive emotional states has been solidly demonstrated to lead to positive alterations in sympathovagal balance. Using the breath and visualizing (body and feeling memory) positive emotions, aids in the creation of this positive balance between the supposedly automatic activity and the nerve activity. With this knowledge, the clinician is enabled to offer help to patients with various emotional and physical disorders.

The conscious control of breath is the easiest, most direct way to influence these two major branches of the Autonomic Nervous System. These are the subconscious actions that occur automatically and naturally in order to preserve, protect, conserve, and restore body resources. They act in concert with each other. One branch is associated with rest and digestion, the other is concerned with flight or fight stress response. When in harmonious balance the body is in an optimum state for rejuvenation. This optimum state can also be developed through positive emotions such as appreciation, gratitude and love.

HRV has become a non-invasive test of integrated neurocardiac function because it can distinguish sympathetic from parasympathetic regulation of the heart rate. HRV analysis therefore provides a window through which autonomic nervous system functions can be monitored. The functioning of these systems has a direct result on emotional activity and wellness.

It is also well known that lowered HRV is associated with aging, this is associated with the energetic effects that modulation of the DNA molecule provides. Positive emotions aid in the creation of strong HRV, and the unwinding or better yet, the relaxing of the DNA molecule. Constrictive emotions tighten the twist of this all-important molecule. This change in the DNA brings about a change in the DNA resonance because from a basic point of view it alters its shape. If you feel uptight then you can be assured that your DNA is being washed with information and energy that tells it to constrict. The converse is true also, for if you feel expanded and open then the molecule at the core of every one of your cells is also open.

It's an old story, one that any grandmother could tell you that love and nurturing heals whereas stress creates disharmony and disease. The big difference is that now there are biofeedback tools to help the individual know when and how internal balance is created. The mind is a powerful thing and that little ego can trick us even when conscious of this possibility. Its voice has grown so powerful during this age of rational thought. The intuition and feelings have been forced to take a back seat over the last hundred years or so, but you can be assured, it wasn't always that way.

Panayama

The definition of Panayama is that it is a yogic scientific methodology for directing the flow of this vital substance of prana to desired locations for desired results.

The connections between Panayama and Heart Rate Variability are uncanny. The yogi and the clinician would use both in a disciplined science to produce conscious control over the activity of these systems (respiration, heart and autonomic nervous) as well as other sub-systems, they control. Both disciplines look for control over the autonomic nervous systems to bring about emotional and physical change, and both see the loving open heart as well as balanced breath the keys to attainment of the healthy heart. The yogi would say that when one is able to sustain the emotional feeling connection, as well as control over the breath (prana), they have obtained the keys to the portal of immortality. Oddly, medical research is coming via its own path to a similar conclusion, even though they both have differing definitions of what immortality means. When developed, this restructuring of neural pathways brings about change not only in skin tone, but also acts to harmonize, refine and reorganize our entire nervous system.

The current conclusions of a vast arena of research are pointing clearly to the facts that sincere (genuine/truthful) feelings about these spiritually uplifting qualities create a power spectral shift toward MF (mid frequency) and HF (high frequency) phase activity. Naturally the breath is brought into attunement in the same way that a relaxing walk brings one's breath into natural rhythm with the gait effecting a shifting of mood and emotional outlook. This can produce a phased scale invariant alignment of specific, very important key vibrations, a few of these being the same vibrations that the yogi works to control.

Balance, or energetic coherency, entrains and when sustained over time, the other biological oscillators act as coupled electrical oscillators in phased synchronization. These coherent oscillating platforms are brought into synchronization via mental and emotional control over mind. This skill is developed through highly directed attention (concentration and contemplation equal meditation) on the goal/object. The affects on the body of such synchronization are correlated with significant shifts in perception and cardiovascular function. All of this has a direct affect on the quantum and photonic communications taking place in each moment.

Patanjali

An exponent of Yoga, from around 350 BCE named Patanjali, wrote one of the earliest texts on the complete science of yoga. Today the text is called the Yoga Sutras of Patanjali. Yoga simply means union with the Divine, sutras are written text. These sutras describe disciplines leading down an experiential path to the Divine known as Raja Yoga. The primary steps are based on the science of yoga psychology, which is mind control. In the West this might be thought of as Emotional/Heart Intelligence skills. The sutras spell out a systematized path to Self-realization called the "Eightfold Path". One of those steps on the path is called pranayama -- a scientific methodology for directing the flow of this vital substance (prana) to desired locations for desired results. The root of the word Pranayama is found in Prana meaning "life-force" and yama coming from ayama or "expansion." Prana is finer than atomic intelligent energy that constitutes life. Paramahansa Yogananda translated them as lifetrons, saying that in the physical world there are two kinds of prana:

The cosmic vibratory energy that is omnipresent in the universe, structuring and sustaining all things.

The specific prana, or energy, that pervades and sustains each human body through five currents or functions:

> Pran current performs the function of crystallization,
>
> Vyan current, circulation,
>
> Saman current, assimilation,
>
> Udan current, metabolism,
>
> Apan current , elimination.

Note that these five currents are associated with physical functions and might be thought of as neural pathways. Sri Yukteswar clarifies this knowledge when he writes in his book, The Holy Science, "When magnanimity comes in to the heart this makes man fit for the practice of Asana Pranayama, which is control over prana, involuntary nerve electricities, and Pratyahara which is changing the direction of the voluntary nerve currents inward."

Magnanimous, meaning a great- animus/spirit, a loftiness of spirit, suggests a nobility arising from generosity, a courage that only a heart opened to its natural love attains. It is the quality of compassionate tenderness. This quality arises naturally as the Yamas and Nyamas become a genuine aspect of one's character. They allow empathy and other spiritual qualities to modulate the nerve activity preparing the physical systems for the other changes to come. The Asanas are the postures needed for moving and sustaining the movement of prana. Prana is intelligent spirit-filled breath that is directed with attention to the required regions to aid in harmonizing, relaxing, tension releasing and peaceful radiating. This represents the primary state required for full alignment with The Stillness. It allows a deep knowing that arises from experience of the true nature of reality and one's place in that reality.

The Eightfold Path

Definitions

Yamas - a moral code advocating non-violence, non-lying, non-stealing, non-attachment and non-sensuality/sexuality. These steps aid the individual by creating space for the genuine individual to arise.

Nyamas - religious code involving study of the scriptures and self, austerity, purity, contentment, and devotion to the Divine. Aids the egoic mind to support attunement, it lessens the hold of the survival pressures.

Asanas - yoga postures that release tension and promote physical relaxation and health. They bring attention, breath and energy to the location of tension in the body.

Pranayama - control of prana, which is our spirit-filled breath and subtle nerve electricities, and the ability to focus life force. It is the science of breath/spirit in harmonizing the body/mind system(s). The object of contemplation is the heart rhythm and breath. The synchronization to specific relationships (ratio) of these two primary oscillators is a primary step that entails much depth to the fully initiated student.

Pratyhara - withdrawal of the senses from external objects. Moves contemplation from the five external senses to the internal senses and the qualitative nature.

Dharana - is the ability to focus or concentration.

Dhyana - is meditation, which is Contemplation and Concentration brought together.

Samadhi - Samadhi is the highest on the Eightfold Path of Yoga, as outlined by the sage Patanjai (q.v.). Samadhi is attained when the meditator attains the process of meditation by which the mind is withdrawn from the senses by interiorization (Pranayama & Pratyhara), and to become One with the object of the meditation (God).

The Yogi learns the skill of controlling these functions and currents using intention, focus, breath and right actions. Pranayama is a scientific methodology for directing the flow of this vital substance to desired locations for desired results. Being in nature "electromagnetic phenomenon" mass can be and is "subject to modification."

The knowledge and skill of Pranayama allows the yogi, through full concentration, to direct all his life force to the object of contemplation. The highest object of contemplation is communion with God. Generating this alignment synchronizes one to the hidden harmony within the prime stillness. Contemplation is the act of becoming one with the object of contemplation, and for the yogi this might be a unitive experience of the prime field of omnipresent intelligence.

All scientific techniques that bring about union of soul and Spirit may be classified as yoga. Pranayama is thought to be the greatest of all the yogic methods. But as these great sages have clearly outlined, the body must be prepared for it first, the first level being loving-kindness for one's self. This allows the body to feel the state of truth, (love) and align so that the attunement of the physical can be prepared for the massive changes that occur during mastery of pranayama. The student must till the soil of receptivity to allow what is latent to sprout from within the hallowed ground of the purified heart. With the deepest of caring, the devotee must order the temple of the heart, opening it to receive the grace from which he/she arises.

The yoga science of pranayama is the direct methodology for consciously controlling sensory functions as well as the subconscious nerve activity through the specific meditative and breath exercises. These exercises in a master engender stillness to the breath. When experienced in the mind this stillness is the deathless rigid state of samadhi, which, when fully experienced in the heart, is loving-bliss, or ecstasy. In this state one is not rigid but a partner dancing through this paradise to a cosmic primal beat.

Paramahansa Yogananda says in <u>The Divine Romance</u> "... the actual feeling of this joy is experienced not in the head but in the heart." In the same volume he goes onto say:

> " ...in the initial states of God communion (sabikalpa samadhi) the devotees (students) consciousness merges in the Cosmic Spirit (aligns); his life force is withdrawn from the body, which appears as 'dead,' or motionless and rigid (entropy/homeostasis).

The yogi is fully aware of his bodily condition of suspended animation. As he progresses to higher spiritual states (nirbikalpa samahdi), however, he communes with God without bodily fixations and worldly duties. Both states are characterized by oneness with the ever new bliss of Spirit, but the nirbikalpa state is experienced by only the most highly advanced masters."

This level of experience with Reality can deepen to what most Masters speak of as complete unity with the Cosmic Absolute. This level can only be attained through deep mediation where the yogi learns to consciously disconnect mind from the life functions and sensory perceptions and links mind to prana and the field maintaining the physical template.

Chapter Twelve

Siddha & Siddhis

In Eastern religions and philosophy the subatomic subtle intelligent energy is collectively known as prana. Paramahansa Yogananada translated prana as 'lifetrons', describing them "…as condensed thoughts of God; substances of the astral world and life principle of the physical cosmos".

He claimed that there are two kinds of prana:

"The cosmic vibratory energy that is omnipresent in the universe, structuring and sustaining all things."

"The specific prana or energy that pervades and sustains each human body through five currents or functions."
~*Autobiography of a Yogi*

The Yogi learns the skills of controlling the functions and currents of intention, focus, breath and right actions to balance and harmonize his/her field. When the field is sufficiently harmonized the yogi is able to concentrate (meditate) more deeply on the object of his focus, normally that would be God/Absolute.

Samadhi is True Concentration mastered by focusing the mind to a point where only the object of concentration remains. In Sri Yukteswar's words; "… Fixing attention firmly on any object thus conceived, when man becomes identified with it as if he were devoid of his individual nature, he attains the state of Samadhi or true concentration." This state is often marked with the individual becoming void of all signs of life. When individuals master samadhi, they are endowed with natural powers, called siddhis that are the gifts, or supernatural powers, at the disposal of yoga masters because of their ability to create this single-pointed concentration. Siddha means literally "one who is successful" -- One who has attained union.

Pilot Baba

The Advaita Vedanta tradition warns us that getting involved with the siddhis, (gifts) are a waste of time and not worth striving for. On the other hand, other yogic traditions exist that regularly demonstrate miraculous powers in very public places.

One such individual living today is called Pilot Baba. He is a decorated Indian Air Force pilot who was a personal pilot for Indira Gandhi. After retiring he traveled to the Himalayas to be taught meditative practices. Pilot Baba has, for the last three decades, employed these ancient yogic techniques to impress audiences by entering a state where no physical functions can be detected. He shuts down all vital functions to the point of being clinically dead, then, at a specific point in time, revitalizes his body. He has on several occasions demonstrated various forms of samadhi in front of Western scientists, once placing him self under water for four days and on another occasion was buried underground for thirty-three days. He has performed these feats as well as others dozens of times in front of witnesses. His purpose for exhibiting these powers is to benefit the greater good and to generate peace. When an individual goes into samadhi, he tells us, a tremendous power is released which can uplift, inspire, heal, and transform all who come into contact with it.

Keiko Aikawa

Keiko Aikawa, a Japanese lady met Pilot Baba when he visited Japan for a demonstration of a similar burial act. Already a teacher of yoga in Japan, Keiko was fascinated and attended the show. During the event Pilot Baba invited her to come and learn from his own preceptor, Hari Baba. She accepted and has been a disciple of this yogic sadhu in the Himalayas for approximately two decades.

It has been reported and witnessed by various media that she too has performed these samadhi acts of hibernation. On one such well-documented event, she voluntarily stepped down into a sand pit of nine cubic feet, which was then covered, with tin sheets, tarpaulins and sand, seemingly impermeable to any ingress of air. She remained there under the scrutiny of the public for 72 hours and then emerged as if coming out of her house in the morning fully refreshed.

Pilot Baba and Keiko both say they have repeatedly done this form of samadhi under both soil and water. The key is a supra-human control of breath and body functions, sending the body into a comatose hibernating state, while preserving life.

In tentative English, Keiko's explanation is, "I become one with God," In samadhi (she goes) "Beyond body, beyond mind…just soul. …Go deep into self no more sense no imagination. Just emptiness." She adds (that she), "Become one with the universe."

These siddhis, or miraculous powers, are a part of this level of becoming one with God. These saints perform these feats, not to prove anything but rather to demonstrate human potential and promote peace. These uncommon feats are commonly witnessed in the East, resembling those performed by The Prince of Peace in His time of walking the planet in Palestine.

Pam Reynolds

Pam Reynolds is a practicing musician, wife and mother of three and a member of a very prominent music publishing family. Pam was diagnosed as having a giant basilar artery aneurysm in her brain. A cerebral aneurysm is an abnormal dilation or ballooning of a brain artery. This life threatening condition is usually due to an acquired or congenital weakness in the wall of the vessel. The size and location of the aneurysm, however, precluded its safe removal using the standard neuro-surgical techniques. She was referred to a doctor who had pioneered a daring surgical procedure known as hypothermic cardiac arrest. The procedure would allow Pam's aneurysm to be excised with a far greater chance of success.

In 1991, she underwent a fantastic surgical procedure. The operation required her body temperature to be lowered to 58 degrees, her heartbeat and breathing stopped, her brain waves flattened, and the blood drained from her head. By all of our current clinical definitions Pam was dead. There was no breath, no heartbeat, no blood flow, no viable temperature and no brainwaves or other brain activity, nothing to support any signs of life whatsoever. After removing the aneurysm, she was restored back to life in her body. The nickname that the surgeons call this procedure is "standstill" and was performed by Dr. Robert F.

Spetzler, Director of the Barrow Institute for Neurology in Phoenix, Arizona, and his team of enterprising surgeons.

Her case was later publicized on national radio and in the book written by a cardiologist, Dr. Michael Sabom Light and Death. Within this volume is a detailed medical and scientific analysis of Pam's experience as she underwent a rare operation to save her life. During the time Pam was in standstill (clinically dead), she experienced a Near-Death-Experience or NDE. Her remarkably detailed out-of-body observations during her surgery were later confirmed as being very accurate. This case is considered to be one of the strongest cases of verifiable evidence in NDE research because of her ability to describe the unique surgical instruments and procedures used while she was both clinically and brain dead. More then a decade later, her case remains the most scientifically documented case on record.

For practical purposes outside the world of academic debate, three clinical tests commonly determine brain death: first, a standard electroencephalogram, or EEG, measures brain-wave activity. A "flat" EEG denotes non-function of the cerebral cortex - the outer shell of the cerebrum; second, auditory evoked potentials, similar to those [clicks] elicited by the ear speakers in Pam's surgery, measure brain-stem viability. Absence of these potentials indicates non-function of the brain stem; and third, documentation of no blood flow to the brain is a marker for a generalized absence of brain function. During "standstill", Pam's brain was found "dead" by all three clinical tests - her electroencephalogram was silent, her brain-stem response was absent, and no blood flowed through her brain. Interestingly, while in this state, she encountered one of the most verifiable NDE experiences.

The implications of these surgeries as well as the samadhi deathless states demonstrate a quality of our existence that transcends the mind-body physicality, a quality or aspect that Pilot Baba, Keiko and Pam term the soul.

The work of Dr. Robert F. Spetzler and the "standstill" procedure are detailed in Edward J. Sylvester book <u>The Healing Blade</u>.

In the Blink Of An Eye

I would like to finish this chapter with a brief look at studies into that most astonishing of phenomenon termed medically, Multiple Personality Disorders. The most extreme cases are both truly extraordinary and puzzling. In these rare acute cases, dramatic changes in persona spontaneously create equally dramatic changes in the physical/mental or both. All manner of change has been documented in the journals. These changes coincide with radical shifts of persona. Examples include the manifestation of disease -- scars, warts or some other physical change is possible to appear. It can run the entire gambit, from simple, subtle changes to completely new looks including the ability to speak bizarre foreign languages that the subject has no way of knowing. Then when they change back to their original (normal) personality the physical manifestations of the secondary personality change back to the original characteristics. It is as if the physical attributes reflect the consciousness of the personality causing a shift of info-energy template.

Modern science has believed that physical and personality characteristics come from hereditary attributes of the DNA, however, in these extreme multiple personality patients, this is clearly not the case. If a person can totally become another, completely in moments, then is it their DNA that immediately gives them blue eyes, a scar on the body or some disease like arthritis, only to disappear as the individual reverts back to the normal self? What is the intelligence organizing the shift and from what level of mind? Where is this intelligence anchored? In Science we now know it is not held simply in the brain or even within the body and that this intelligence has some non-local (quantum) mechanics involved. Surely the DNA/RNA matrix is not a simple fixed code from which the body is created; and that genes are not fixed and firm codes locked by parental chromosomes at birth. Today the DNA/RNA is seen more as a coded chemical matrix for creating the complete gambit of our chemical building blocks, yet it appears to act more as a decoding antenna that can receive and send info-energy via superluminal transference.

The siddhas may not have this specific information but they know the nature of reality and how to access it. They use the samadhi-state to literally enter non-local communications with the surrounding universe and if required allow for cellular harmonization with it. Understanding this takes much of the mystery and magic away and allows the rational to peak into a world of power and beauty that the sages possess.

PART TWO

Science of Divinity;

Illusion of Identity

Chapter Thirteen

Awareness

No Subject, Object nor Action

An Elaborate Presentation On No-thing

The Gospel of Thomas #17: has Jesus saying,
"I will give you what no eye has seen, what no ear has heard, what no hand has touched, what has not arisen in the human heart."

Diving into the quanta of Pure Reality raises the curtain on the drama of objective reality in which diaphanous collections of shimmering points of light, dancing in organized patterns are cohered by some invisible centering force into the rich tapestry of daily lives. The weirdness is only enhanced as the eye of science probes deeply into those points of light and the force bonding the picture into a whole. It appears to these learned men and woman that at the root architectures of objects, empty space occupies nearly the totality of the field of influence. Here at these scales of existence at the very foundations of matter, we shift our physics into the laws of quantum mechanics to help explain the weirdness witnessed. The invisible spontaneous forces of this domain entangle elemental particles, electrons, and photons into clouds of organization. These clouds produce resonance, which attracts and repels into self-referencing oscillations of mass. When researched, this primary organizing intelligence appears to originate from everywhere and nowhere at the same time spontaneously. Astonishingly, these smallest of architectures all appear to arise, construct and maintain out of the concept we here in 3D reality call consciousness, thus delineating the problem with which the rational mind must grapple. Matter originates and forms from mind and mind has no central localized region of origin. No one place or thing to dissect for answers to the riddle.

To assist in grappling with this problem both Eastern and Western sciences have created several levels, degrees and definitions of consciousness. The degree or level of consciousness is considered by both sciences to be directly related to the level of personal awareness. To help clarify awareness the Eastern yogic sciences outlined and rigorously defined mortal man's levels of conscious experience.

These sciences claim that normal, everyday man experiences *waking consciousness, sleeping consciousness*, and *dreaming consciousness* to varying degrees of clarity, yet has the ability to experience *soul consciousness, universal consciousness*, and *Absolute consciousness*. The degree of *experiential clarity* one has within each classification determines one's overall level of consciousness.

This last degree of experiential awareness, "Absolute consciousness", is Consciousness with the big "C". It is the ultimate goal of the soul, to experience with awareness this state of conscious awareness. Experienced Consciousness with a big "C" has different names in different religious and philosophical belief systems, but commonly it is referred to as *Cosmic Consciousness* or simply *The Absolute*. Each level of consciousness is only a level in *experiential awareness*, and being experiential, is always open to diversity of personal perspective. If busloads of tourists arrive at the Grand Canyon they will all see and experience the Grand Canyon, feel the expanse and grandeur of the space. However, the experience of the place by each individual will be filtered by his or her perceptions and the degree of awareness he or she has at that time. Therefore, *awareness* in every sense of the word is a facet of Big "C" Consciousness.

These same sciences also tell us that the primary location guiding perception also plays a major role in determining the degree of consciousness accessible in any one moment. These nuances allow for the diversity we see in the world's religions.

Stepping back and looking at the big picture we see that awareness is linked to experience, which is personal, and that experience is linked to perspective. Further more perspective shifts with the level and degree of experiential awareness. Continuing, we come to understand that all of this plays out in a unified arena of big "C" Consciousness called the Absolute. When a soul experientially realizes intimately that he or she is this same Absolute, complete Self-Realization is actualized.

When science looks for the point of origin in biology for the location of mind, the spiral path leads the inquisitive mind to the edge of some invisible, alternative dimension of existence, one very different from the one we live and operate out of day to day. Words like field, domain and space are all used to point to what lies beyond the edge of our physical world, they point to a dimension of existence that has radically different characteristics than our familiar three-dimensional space. The oxymoron is that this dimension appears dimensionless, that is to say non-localized; after all, dimension infers limits and distances of space. This home of Intelligence however, appears timeless and without time-space the rational mind is unable to grasp distance, yet it is a field or dimension of some sort because it has influence and, from this point of reference, has characteristics that appear consistent.

So for us to really discuss in full the science of divinity and the biological process in the creation of the image on the Shroud, we need to take a good look at the science that underlies all objective creativity: the science of paradox -- that of Awareness and, by extension, that of Consciousness and of Light. This *conceptual trinity* seems in Reality to be extensions or facets of the same vibrantly alive intelligent 'no-one-thingness.' I use the word *alive* because experienced explorers of these inner realms have written about this domain in those terms. They tell us that this, *alive emptiness* is pure light beyond movement, time and object. They share, using analogy, that all names and forms arise in transitory fashion out of and in this sea of light, as waves on the ocean. They tell us that this sea of pure light is conscious, pure information; Truth in fact held in a silent stillness, void of thing. No-thing because it, and I use that word it cautiously, is beyond subject, object or action. Mystics have used words like *suchness* and *isness* in pointing to this Reality but the medium of words will never translate the fullness of experiencing this paradox of losing the "I", yet the "I" remains. The reason given by these explorers makes this clear; they share universally in unanimous agreement that when one reaches these depths of exploration a realization dawns into one's awareness that this pure space is in reality everything including one's self, it is the very ground of one's existence. Paradox again rears its dualistic head: how can a space able to be experienced, a domain beyond subject, object and action, be part of our objective reality? Conversely, how can a domain of No-thing be experienced and create all that is, including one's self? Any conclusion must allow these questions to be illuminated.

We are told Awareness, Consciousness and Light, in their purest sense, are all just facets of the same intelligent-information domain I am calling *no-one-thing* because it encompasses all and all is within its womb, a womb with the characteristics of timeless eternal omnipresence, a singularity of dimension, a cosmic absolute, hence no-one-thing. From this objectless domain of light, mind and the experiencing "I" and phenomenal reality somehow births into creation.

I'll explain this in more detail in a moment, but for now let us put our mind around the idea that Consciousness with a big "C" has Intelligence; this is evident by aware existence itself, and that *It* is pure Information in a state of absolute wholeness resting in potentiality. This must be so for all information and energy as well as everything in creation births from this primal state. This domain is Pure Light beyond polarity, before all movement; it appears to be the holographic dark field screen upon which the organizational power of Awareness imprints all objective existence. Awareness by definition is simply Consciousness looping back on itself. It is Light/Information detected in a reflective mirroring process. It is recursive self-referencing.

By way of example, imagine two perfectly created mirrors facing each other exactly. What one would *sense* within the mirroring would be the illusion of movement, depth and spaciousness; although nothing but the recursive reflection is actually occurring. Within the illusion comes a *sense* of distance. This illusory *sense* of distance loops with itself creating a richer sensation of separateness. When awareness loops this *sense of separateness* it gradually strengthens into a *sense of individualization* and the birth of mind. Mind at some point crystallizes from a virtual entity into a physical template as the complexity of recursive detection increases. As the physical develops its *sense* of identity strengths over time into the "I" awareness we are all knowledgeable about. This facet of mind constructs around physical survival and its tools for doing so are the past moments referenced in a context of future desires. Yet all that is actually occurring, emanates from the original illusion of the primal mirroring of big C Consciousness, which is the formation of that facet we call Awareness.

This original *individuated sense* of "I" is the atma, generally termed in Christendom the soul. It generates into being as the agent of

Awareness, Attention self-references the false sense of separateness generated within the illusory *sense* by Awareness itself. It's a paradox yet Consciousness in the formation of Awareness, Allows for the Illusion of Separateness. As Attention, which is narrowed focused Awareness, is given strength, Awareness bifurcates from the whole to a narrower view, a portion.

For the purposes of giving reason something it can latch onto, think of the Information realm as a domain of pure potentiality and possibility: creativity in the feminine sense -- the womb, and the intelligence as Divinity, God or Spirit. They are one and the same yet we can truly ponder only the characteristics of the information domain using the intellect. The Intelligence of that domain is beyond the ability of the lowly rational mind to ever grasp; yet we are told by the Great Explorers of this realm that through some mystery and exalted levels of Divine compassion, we can experience this Intelligence in a direct and personal manner. To gain this level of experiential awareness we must first acquire, by practices or grace, the shift in perspective to the eternal "I" facet of mind termed the soul or "witnessing "I" aspect of self, and develop the contemplative mind and concentration required to maintain attuned alignment of one's self with this Intelligence. When all the facets of mind, i.e. self (soul, heart and egoic mind) unify physical attunement is sustainable as is the aware experience of Mirroring the Absolute.

"Look closely and you will see that all names and forms are but transitory waves on the ocean of consciousness, that only consciousness can be said to be, not its transformations. In the immensity of consciousness a light appears, a tiny point that moves rapidly and traces shapes, thoughts and feelings, concepts and ideas, like the pen writing on paper. And the ink that leaves a trace is memory. You are that tiny point, and by your movement the world is ever re-created. Stop moving and there will be no world. Look within and you will find that the point of light is the reflection of the immensity of light in the body, as the sense "I am". There is only light, all else appears. To the mind, it [that light] appears as darkness. It can be known only through its reflections. All is seen in daylight - except daylight. To be the point of light tracing the world is turiya. To be the light itself is turiyatita. But of what use are names when reality is so near?"

Sri Nisargadatta Maharaj, I Am That

Maharaj plainly writes that the point of light is the sense of "I", yet it is the reflection (mirrored image) of the "immensity of light" that appears as "darkness" or Emptiness to the mind. In the chapter entitled, "Quantum-Zero Point-& the Holographic Web", Astrophysicist Bernhard Haisch of Stanford University, speaking about the Zero Point Field, says that it is; "…a background sea of light…(and) The fact that the zero-point field is the lowest energy state makes it unobservable. We see things by way of contrast. The eye works by letting light fall on the otherwise dark retina. But if the eye were filled with light, there would be no darkness to afford a contrast. The zero-point field is such a blinding light. Since it is everywhere, inside and outside of us, permeating every atom in our bodies, we are effectively blind to it. It blinds us to its presence."

But are we truly blind? According to experienced inner space explorers this Luminous Darkness or Clear Light can be known through direct experience. To help us conceptualize this domain, these returning pioneers attempt to impart that this Pure Light alive-stillness is the common ground state of all existence. Science might understand it as Intelligence/Information within a dimensionless dimension prior to energy as we understand energy to be. Information in this state would be fractally whole, held in a zero point singularity. Spirit permeates endowing Consciousness and endless creative potential, yet when experientially touched with Awareness, the sense in the physical is of Alive Emptiness held in blissful stillness. It is this Absolute Conscious Stillness that acts to backdrop and anchor all movement, all observable Reality.

Sages throughout time have told us that soul is the true nature of man and all living forms of life. Yet the true nature of soul is Spirit, which is Absolute Consciousness/Eternal Light by another name. As I outlined in the beginning of this chapter, Soul consciousness also has levels of conscious clarity into which it can evolve. Clarity of perception anchored within Soul aspect of mind is the starting off point for voyages into the core nature of Reality. The interesting paradox is that it appears that a soul requires the body to complete a self-referencing loop allowing for rich full experience. The unification or attunement of the aspects of self within a body allows the soul self to experience this Divine gift in true physical joy. I will get more into the *divisionless division* subject in Chapter 19 when the subject of Phi, the Golden Mean is explored.

For the sake of clarity in illuminating the root of the process let's temporarily take the facets of Consciousness and Light out of the present discussion, for without the ability to be aware and have a sense of self, a sense of "I", these other two facets do not exist experientially. Nor does the body or the reality we play in daily it turns out. Proceeding with that desire for clarity, both pure consciousness and pure light exist in the absence of mind. In fact, they both exist in eternal omnipresence because time, like all else, is a construct rising out of the creation of mind. Mind, on the other hand, is a construct of the looping of Awareness. Yet awareness can have various levels and degrees of consciousness. Because of these points we will stay focused on the development of awareness first and then mind, acknowledging their intimate connection like that of mirror and reflection, each exists from the others existence.

In quantum physics the observer/detector is what gives matter its flash into existence. Objects of any size can and do detect and sustain one another. From the simplest mechanical view point the resonance of an object attracts and repels causing a cascade of detection but from a quantum experience an electron can and does detect other electrons, even if that electron is virtual, which means it touches via some richer more spontaneous level of communication.

The Tibetan Book of the Great Liberation states: "Matter is derived from mind, and not mind from matter." This statement coming from an ancient text might be found in some of our most current physics texts.

I hope by this point it has now been shown, however, that Mind is not localized in matter but somehow is non-localized, residing nowhere yet everywhere in some timeless existence. This non-local *sense* of "I" awareness, current Western science as repeatedly demonstrated, is a root intelligence in the forming and maintaining the template of resonance for the physical form. At the very least it has demonstrated that as the mind perceives reality, the body system creates all manner of chemical signals in the organization, construction and maintenance of the physical.

The subject "I", through its function of making choices and having experiences, allows all to exist, at least in the illusion of the mind creation. I'm not saying it is not real, for even a dream is real but it is not Reality with a big "R"; the bedrock of all existence.

All aspects of Mind operate out of non-local mechanics, yet when an aspect is filtered through the lens of body-memory recall, the perspective filter created ultimately forms the egoic sense of self. This perspective filter becomes firm through making choices and experiencing the resulting consequences, judgments form strengthen and empower this powerful force in the creation process. This objective sense of "I" builds the foundations and looping self-referencing components for the illusion of choice, experience and existence, i.e. reality.

It is the "I" which allows awareness to exist in Consciousness. Said another way, Awareness exists, but it is the formation of the "I" that allows it to become experientially conscious of itself. Individuated mind (soul) with its motive of fully experiencing that which it is, finds itself in a form of competition with the aspect it created for this purpose. So in the end, evolution in experiential consciousness is always just radical shifts in perspective. With this understanding of different levels and aspects of mind it is easier to understand the great Indian saint Ramana Maharshi's comment on enlightenment, "The 'I' casts off the illusion of 'I ' and yet remains as 'I'. Such is the paradox of Self-realization."

The larger concern, and one of the underpinnings of this work, is the question, whether it is possible to drop all aspects of "I" completely? Merge totally with the Absolute? And if so, what happens to the physical form if one does this consciously during life? To grasp how this might be a reality, a conceptualization on how the "I" might arise would assist us in imagining how it might totally dissolve.

The Arising of "I"

The Science of Divinity is a science of attunement. First and foremost attunement is required between the aspects of mind; i.e. heart, soul and egoic mind. The reason for this is to cause a shift in perspective, allowing a shift in the way mind forms and relates with Reality. These aspects are *senses of self* that have been strengthened into forms of identification. The desired aligned attunement occurs with the proper placement of ones identity, hence one perspective. When this is accomplished in a sustainable manner it allows the environment for stronger physical attunement. To fully understand this process a fuller comprehension of how these forms of "I"/ senses of self arise is helpful. If one understands how the conceptual constructs were created and for what purpose, it will makes the process of proper attunement that much easier. It also helps the rational self understand more completely the process resulting in the Shroud image.

"I" is a *sense of individuation* that rises into a state of being via reflective, recursive looping of information within Pure Potentiality -- the Holographic Fractal of Information prior to energy and movement, before vibration, time-space and matter. The sense of movement, distance, separation and individuation rise out of this reflective characteristic. **Recursive looping of information with in the sense created by the reflection, is the causation of mind on all levels of existence.** For this newly created aspect to fully experience this information which is now the self, the individuated aspect held as Spirit forms a mirror of itself to hone the recursive looping. I refer back to the great saints of inner exploration for guidance.

> "Man is a soul, and has a body. When he properly places his sense of identity, (with the soul) he leaves behind all compulsive patterns. So long as he remains confused in his ordinary state of spiritual amnesia, he will know the subtle fetters of environmental law.
>
> "God is harmony; the devotee who attunes himself will never perform any action amiss. His activities will be correctly and naturally timed to accord with astrological law. After deep prayer and meditation he is in touch with his divine consciousness; there is no greater power than that inward protection."

<u>Autobiography of a Yogi,</u> 1946 First Edition, by Paramhansa Yogananda, quoting Sri Yukteswar, his teacher.

Sri Yukteswar in telling us that man is a soul and has a body, and that a proper shift in his sense of identity, his sense of "I", allows the devotee to attune himself with his divine consciousness, implies more then one *sense of "I"*. Paraphrased, the great inner explorers have told us mortals of average conscious experience that man is a spiritual being experiencing a body, and that the impulse and intelligence for this physical form is held in the Spirit realm.

In an attempt to fully comprehend, let us differentiate between consciousness and awareness, at least conversationally. Confusion on terminology relating to awareness is easy to understand, since most of the time we are relating to a state of being cognitive (aware) of sensory input, i.e. sight, smell, hearing, touch, taste, and so forth. These sensory stimuli are agents of the egoic mind, persona or *little sense "I"*; the sense that is continually strengthened while one is in the state of spiritual amnesia. This state of spiritual amnesia is simply a state of not being experientially conscious of these other aspect/levels of experiential mind or the other areas one can consciously experience. The rudimentary level for further exploration is the shift in perspective to *soul consciousness*. Soul Consciousness opens awareness to experientially touch *Universal Consciousness* and the opportunity ultimately of *Absolute Consciousness*.

Awareness is an agent, or aspect, of pure *Absolute Consciousness* as is everything else. It just rises into existence with the illusion of movement formed by the reflection of Pure Consciousness, which, as said above, is the intelligence of Pure Light/Information. The various aspects of mind and levels of small "c" consciousness arise within Awareness. Conceptually speaking, the core trinity of Consciousness, Light and Awareness are three facets of the Absolute reflecting the prime characteristics of the Divine.

Soul awareness is often referred to simply as Awareness or Presence because of the 'objectlessness' of the Witnessing aspect of non-local self. There is no witness, there simply is awareness witnessing. Awareness by its very nature implies a looping that permits the referencing of signals by a source. Awareness implies and defines recursion. Awareness is always self referencing. The organized dance of Pure Light between the mirrors of identification is both the process and the substance of Awareness.

The Identities of Mind-Forming of "I"

The Ego

Adyashanti, like Ramana Maharshi, promotes the Advaita Vedanta or nondualist school of Hinduism that explains ego well; "Ego is the movement of the mind toward objects of perception, in the form of grasping; and away from objects, in the form of aversion. This fundamentally is all the ego is. This movement of grasping and aversion gives rise to a sense of a separate "me," and in turn the sense of "me" strengthens itself this way. It is this continuous loop of causation that tricks consciousness into a trance of identification."

Grasping and aversion take many forms, from the obvious to the very subtle. They are recognizable by the characteristic survival trait underlying the motive for the movement. We are told by masters of inner exploration that this fear ultimately is rooted in the impulse for a happiness and peace only achieved by consciously realizing that Reality which we are. Paradoxically, the peace and joy desired by the heart and for which the ego survives, only exists when total self-realization arises experientially from the surrendering of the *ego perspective*. For this level of self-realization to occur, a body is required to form the loop of consciousness that allows consciousness to be aware of its self experientially. The body's survival is therefore a key component in the development of an ego. The impulse to save and maintain the body for the purposes of consciousness-looping called experience has been redefined by the ego, as "I need to survive". This, however, according to the great masters of inner space, is clearly not the case. They tell us that it would be impossible to not be, even if we wished it so. We are immortal Spirit and as such eternal, furthermore it is the soul that is evolving in consciousness, not this body. We are a soul having a physical experience, not a body experiencing life.

At this time in history the challenge humanity finds itself with is that if it does not rapidly develop the skills required to break free of the conscious looping trapped in the loop of mirrors set up by the programming of the little egoic sense of "I", then it may destroy itself. Humanity's sense of self is mesmerized by the trance of stimuli supporting the body. Judgments and polarities are created forming the oscillating loop of grasping and aversion. The secret that the initiate to the sciences of self-realization learns is that one can shift the source that does the referencing of the signals to a different aspect of the self. As mentioned earlier, there are three main aspects of self -- the ego, heart and soul. All three possess a sense of "I". Any one of the three can be the prime seat for one's identity and the locus for directing attention and awareness. All three have a cause for their being. All three compose the greater aspect of mind, which observes the subject-object relationship required for experiential knowing.

Soul

The initiated individual develops the skills required to maintain a permanent stable shift out of the trance amnesia state of the ego-mind "I" trapped in time, space and survival, and into the timeless witnessing perspective of soul awareness and beyond. This shift literally changes reality itself. To again be clear, this shift does not mean that the other two aspects no longer exist; they exist, just not with the same power to form reality. The change is simply a shift in one's perception, thereby shifting the experienced reality.

The soul perspective is a non-localized or omnipresent aspect of individuated self, conceptualized as individuated Spirit. This timeless, objectless, Witnessing aspect of self that is able to perceive, is called Awareness or Presence in some spiritual circles. In the end, however, it is sensed as Truth and, if sustained and deepened, is experienced in the heart as joy. Perspective anchored here is the launching pad to richer communion with the Absolute.

Heart

The heart is the mediator and main organizer for the template of consciousness in movement. It is the neutral place between these two other powerful forces of mind; ego and soul. It dutifully follows the direction of the controlling mind force of the moment. The heart organizes, balances and coheres the physical template in accordance with the prevailing impulses of mind. It has constant access to both aspects yet its inherent knowledge of the soul, as the real carriage driver, is the wisdom underlying its own inherent intelligence. The great inner explorers tell us that the heart's natural choice or tendency is love, unconditional love for all aspects of mind and the divine. Because of these characteristics it can be challenging to hear the voice of the heart for its aims cannot be grasped by the rational ego mind.

> "The Heart's immediate aim is the cessation of all suffering to effect the possibility of the ultimate goal. ...Man naturally feels great necessity for Existence, Consciousness, and Bliss. These are the three real necessities of the human heart and have nothing to do

with anything outside the Self. They are essential properties of his own nature.

"… All the necessities of the Heart - Existence, Consciousness, and Bliss – having been attained, ignorance – the mother of evils, becomes emaciated and consequently all troubles of this material world, which are the sources of all sorts of sufferings, cease forever. Thus the ultimate aim of the heart is effected."

"In this state, all the necessities having been attained and the ultimate aim effected, the heart becomes perfectly purified and instead of merely reflecting the spiritual light, actively manifests the same. Man, being thus consecrated or anointed by the Holy Spirit, becomes Christ, the anointed Savior. Entering the kingdom of Spiritual Light, he becomes the Son of God.

"In this state man comprehends his self as a fragment of the Universal Holy Spirit, and, abandoning the vain idea of his separate existence, unifies himself with the Eternal spirit; that is, becomes one and the same with God the Father.

"This Unification of Self with God is Kaivalya, which is the Ultimate Object of all created beings."
Sri Yukteswar

The Template of "I"

At this point in our history it is the egoic mind with its powerful momentum that directs most of our attention and therefore the reality we perceive. The egoic time-space mind, containing the bulk of our attention and therefore awareness, references mostly sensory signals. The information-energy communication is then filtered through the lens of time-space survival perspective, driving the dog eat dog, war-filled reality in which we all appear to exist. The trance loop of ego identification is strengthened by fear, and overrides the input of heart and soul. The hold over the domain of the heart is maintained by the egoic mind in mortal fear of annihilation.

Pure Awareness is pliable, pure potential and possibility; it is creativity in the womb of the infinite, eternal omnipresent. An elementary symbol for Pure Awareness is the Mobius Strip. In its simplest form the Mobius Strip is a seamless strip of paper twisted and pasted to form a figure eight-type shape. Imagine for a second that this is done so as to produce no seam or joint where the paper joins. The uniqueness produced by this seamless strip is that it has no specific outside or inside, no beginning and no end, it becomes a one-sided loop and as such has become the symbol for infinity, . ∞ This concept might help with the alpha and the omega principle but it does not explain awareness as a process. For this it might be best to use the analogy of a perfect mirror mirroring another perfect mirror. Yes, this too is a bit obscure and a tad esoteric but accurate enough for metaphor. Imagine for a moment what you would see if you were standing behind a one-way mirror that was facing another mirror. The viewing intelligence is Awareness as is the reflection between the mirrors.

Another example is that of the video camera monitoring a TV monitor, with the image looped back on the TV monitor it is viewing. The image on the screen becomes a TV monitor with a picture of the same monitor within it and a small one inside it, etcetera, etcetera, going on into infinity. The looping of the image allows for the image to nest itself as a fractal, forming an image with depth and spaciousness. The perspective and lens of the camera determines what we see and how we perceive the image on the screen, something we never see at all in the image on the monitor. When individualized, Pure Awareness is the observing, sensing agent of Pure Consciousness and, as it strengthens a coherent state of referencing (Mobius like looping), it becomes the Subjective-Viewer Chooser Detector in the creation of matter. It becomes "I". It is this "I" that becomes mind on all levels of existence.

The Mobius paper strip looks two-sided and 3D but in experiencing it with your senses it becomes one continuous plane of existence with no beginning and no end. The same is true in the example of the image of the monitor within the monitor. The sense is one of eternity, of spaciousness going on and on, yet it is just a virtual reality created that tricks the senses. Unity tricks itself into polarity and identity, into a sense of outside and movement, but in truth, nothing exists but the Trinity of Consciousness, Light and Awareness. A key can be found in the etymology of consciousness, literally *con scire*, meaning *to know with*, but if there is only the *Absolute*, so it *must* loop or mirror itself and this can be done in the illusory creative realm of mind. "We cannot escape the fact that the world we know is constructed in order to see itself," says the mathematician G. Spencer Brown, "but in order to do so, evidently it must first cut itself up into at least one state which sees, and at least one state which is seen."

At the core of the paradox is the subject-object split. This mirroring of subject-object immediately gives rise to the illusion of individuation or sense of separation called "I" which allows for the looping of consciousness that is awareness. Yet the paradox remains even after enlightenment, as the sense loops inward to the point where the subject and object merge into 'amness' or beingness; even then the sense of "I" experiencing remains. For as long as a sense of self or "I" remains, it is an experiential event held by perspective regardless if, at that point, the experience is of an expanded sense encompassing the whole of conscious awareness. A sense of self, even if the perspective is radically altered, is still a sense relating experience to self, and this is an aspect of mind. Awareness therefore at its most rudimentary level is the *dance of light between the mirrors of self*.

The Qualitative Nature of Awareness

Pure Awareness is neutral, meaning no polarity. Because of this phenomenon, even the smallest amount of magnetism activates Awareness into cohering bonds via the resonance inherent in the activating polarity. Human life forms are amplified waveforms of energy held in polarity by the same polarity consciousness. We rarely place neutral consciousness on anything with our attention. Instead we mostly imbue attention via the lens of our perception with qualities placed on by the egoic nature of desire and aversion. These qualities have resulting energetic resonance. The fact is that when we focus, make a choice or place attention, consciously or unconsciously, we focus awareness colored by the filter of judgments formed by the ego nature.

It is my opinion that as long as there is a sense of "I", this placed/received awareness (attention) always carries the energetic charge of what might be called Attitude. Attitude is a byproduct of individuated Spirit, i.e. mind. Whether mild, subtle anxiety or bodhisattva-like compassion, one is always embedding a carrier wave imbued with an energized dynamic quality. The sum of the power, strength or amplitude, mixed with a quality, whether love or fear, equals the charge (attitude) which imbues motive on all levels of action. The attitude is buried within the attention that is activating and coloring the flow of pure awareness. Through the lens of attitude this flow of pure conscious awareness helps to formulate the returning reflected flow back in the loop creating reality.

The attitude and returning awareness crystallizes and polishes the lens through which awareness operates. This lens is called perception. The easiest way to shift perception is by a shift in the qualitative energy package of emotion. This is why gratitude and appreciation are quoted as being the two most often beneficial attitudes to take in viewing life.

If there is only one reality, as all true Masters have stated, then it all comes back to subtle nuances in perception. Perception is a byproduct of the subtle nuances in the quality, the strength, and the placing of one's attention. Attention is the agent of awareness, and awareness the agent of Consciousness, and I use the term Consciousness in the grand expanded big "C" concept. It appears that we can only expand awareness by bringing the focus of our attention onto the attitude of pure awareness. This charge is neutral and is felt as pure love, which is non-judging, meaning of course no grasping and aversion. Meditation helps develop the skills required to not dissipate or disperse attention, rather to succeed in holding laser-like concentration on the object of our attention, which is the silent still point of grace held within the heart. To gain and sustain this level of concentration on Stillness, masters have found that the emotional quality that best supports allowing (surrender) is key. Allowing what, you might ask? Allowing what IS to be present and allowing the beauty present in the moment to slowly dissolve that sense of importance and power of the little "I", which holds the perspective and the heart in its grip. Allowing prepares the ground for faith and courage to fill the space for the next movement -- the shift in the placement of one's identity so critical in liberation.

The level of focused concentration and contemplation developed by the meditator determines the strength of the attention. This strength of will cultivated through meditation is a skill most often required to overcome the egoic habit and sustain the anchoring of perspective and one's identity in the soul aspect of mind. Most of the time we scatter our attention (focused reality creating awareness), spreading it thin over the five senses. This practice continues the loop of egoic reality. We reflect back the outer world to the biology of our physicality. It is the five senses that translate the electromagnetic spectrum into various signals that are sent to the brain/nervous system, creating the picture of the physical world we see. These electromagnetic stimuli – ones we normally do not perceive - form the pictures we walk through in life, and nothing more. The physical body picks up the sonar or radar like signals from the electromagnetic stimuli, translates them into body talk and the brain, and eventually constructs them into a holographic virtual image. The reflections, whether that of smell, taste, touch sight or hearing, are all just electromagnetic stimuli translated into a virtual image within the mind. The qualitative aspects that imbue these incoming and outgoing stimuli are the nuances that create reality. The attitude and resulting lens of perspective of this play of stimuli form the reactions in the body as charge. We term this resulting charge in the body from the judgments of mind, as emotions. Therefore the quality of the awareness and the lens of perspective can be witnessed in the resulting emotional quality. The power of the signal, and the degree of laser-like focus imbued within the attention, is what determines the signaled mirroring back we call reality.

To say this in another way, perception can be described as the lens that colors and creates the magnetic energy, which in turn detects and attracts, via resonance, then translates by the same perception, the stimuli that is eventually returned to the senses. The object might be the same object sensed, but the quality of that object and its value is altered by the detecting perception.

Awareness, however, can also be turned in toward the physical where the same principle is in effect. When the agent of awareness, that of attention, is turned in on the biology, the resulting feedback loops directly with the source of the signal. This is biofeedback without a device as mediator. The looping of awareness reflects the embedded physiological and psychological patterns. Often these patterns fall below the radar of everyday consciousness, residing in a subconscious realm of habit. When one focuses attention on these energetic sensations, one often witnesses a shift to a more relaxed peaceful level. The lack of external stimulus to the system allows the overall system to relax and become harmonized. The resulting peace adds to the looping qualitative aspect, and this in turn strengthens the power of the signal and resulting state.

Ground of Reality

The trance-awareness of mind constructs and localizes the world and all phenomena. Your world is literally within you and it gives rise to objective reality. Experiencing this sense of awareness, no matter how expansive the perspective, gives rise to the sense of individualized self, even if mind is held in nothing more then pure light. The more ideally perfected the recursive mirroring, the more depth the sense of eternal spaciousness. I emphasize the term *sense* here because at best this is all it ever really is. This sense, formed in the mirroring, is the seed held in timeless Consciousness, it is this sense of awareness with individuated "I AM That" that is the root of soul/atma and mind on all levels of self-awareness. Mind moving attention, even if it is a qualitative shift, forms the template for the other aspects of self, including the egoic body-mind. Movements in perspective, shifts in experiential mind, are all it ever really is. This is the dance of Self-Realization, the realization of Truth. Quantum and natural physics more and more appear to be bearing these facts out, yet universal laws of Light, Consciousness and Reality also exist.

Ramana Maharshi offers us this illuminating comment, "There are no stages in Realization or degrees of Liberation. There are no levels of Reality; there are only levels of experience for the individual."

Rule One then would be:

As long as any sense of self or "I" remains, it is an experiential event held by the lens of perspective; regardless if, at that point, the experience is of an expanded sense that encompasses the universe and all things in it, as your body. Even if the perspective is radically altered, a sense of self is still a sense-relating experience to this aspect of individualized Spirit. I rehash this point over and over to drive home the idea that all aspects of mind, all aspects of individuated senses of "I" are concepts, and all concepts are illusions that can be released. The question I ask you, the reader, to image with me, is what would happen to the physical form if all aspects of mind surrendered and dissolved back in an instantaneous realization of being no-thing, and then surrendered to that in a final *Grand Completion*?

The concise and illuminating comment by Ramana Maharshi speaks volumes, but even more thought provoking is the truth on all levels of self-realization that this comment provides; even experiences of great unity are perceived with a *sense of self*. The Ashtavakra Gita states this notion clearly when it says:

"I am the infinite deep
In whom all the worlds appear to rise.
Beyond all form, forever still,
So am I."

Shankara, the eighth-century Indian saint, said of his own enlightenment; "I am Brahman... I dwell within all beings as the soul, the pure consciousness, the ground of all phenomena..." I could go on and on quoting from all the great saints and spiritual literature on the nature and experience of Reality, but my current favorite is from Adyashanti, a wonderful, awakened soul living in the San Francisco Bay area. When asked how he senses himself, he stated clearly at a recent satsang I attended near Berkeley, California, "Aware space. [silent pause] I am aware space- that same aware space that gives rise to everything that is."

The contemporary Indian teacher Sri Nisargadatta Maharaj, described his own spiritual awakening in this way; "You realize beyond all trace of doubt that the world is in you, and not you in the world." I say again, what would be left if there were no I in "I am"?

When these thoughts are all tied together you can begin to see the direct connection to the field of quantum physics. It appears more and more that the act of perceiving, choosing and/or information-energy transfer, i.e. communication, localizes the wave into a particle from which the mind constructs an image. The mind somehow freezes the fluid jitterbug of vibration into a firm, solid membrane, as Sri Aurobindo says, "All matter is just a mass of stable light." Most quantum physicists would say the same thing. The image I construct and the image the dolphin sees of the same environment are two totally different reality constructions. Man's reality is mainly derived from the combination of the five outer senses and the narrow slice of the spectrum they constitute. Dolphins use different senses and a larger slice of the electromagnetic spectrum to formulate their perception, not to mention they exist in a totally different medium.

As long as a sense of "I" exists, some level of separation (individuation) remains, no matter the level of Self-Exploration and Realization. Even the term Self-realization recognizes this fact of the remaining aspect of self. Yet from my understanding there is a level of attunement where all aspects of self dissolve and merge with Pure Awareness. The result of this level of non-attachment organically creates within the body a massive phase transition. As the microbiologist understands, the physical architecture operates at the most primary scales in a quantum relationship with Consciousness whose agent is mind. Surrender mind and what is left is the original clear light of Spirit.

"We are what we think." said the Buddha.

"If therefore thine eye be single, thy whole body shall be full of light." Matthew 6:22

Dharma

Spiritual and material evolution in our qualitative polarity world is based on the foundation of love. The law, one could say, is Love -- a principle built into the creative dynamics that requires this qualitative sense in order to experience the power and potential inherent to the design that we are. The greatest commandment is all about love. "**Love** the Lord your God with all your heart and with all your soul and with all your mind. This is the first and greatest commandment. And the second is like it: **love** your neighbor as yourself. All the laws and prophets hang on these two commandments." Matthew 22:37-39.

To understand this Law, or principle, and its relationship to oneself is to understand the concept of Dharma. In Eastern spiritual philosophy it is said that the birthplace of Dharma is the heart, and what emanates from the heart as a pure feeling/idea is termed Rutha. Rutha, meaning the feelings and ideas, is called Dharma when translated into action, and considered to be of paramount importance in one's spiritual development. Within these philosophies Rutha is believed to set out all the guidelines for action and has a determining influence on many levels.

The Eastern philosophers also believe that an individual can carry out one's own Dharma or take on another's. Carrying out one's own Dharma, even if one perishes, is considered in these religions far better than taking on Dharma not belonging to oneself. What this philosophy is referring is similar to the commandment of Jesus to his disciples in the Gospel of Thomas, "Do not tell lies, and do not do what you hate, for all things are plain in the sight of Heaven. For nothing hidden will not become manifest, and nothing covered will remain without being uncovered." Gospel of Thomas; saying #6.

Jesus said to them, "If you fast, you will give rise to sin for yourselves; and if you pray, you will be condemned; and if you give alms, you will do harm to your spirits. When you go into any land and walk about in the districts, if they receive you, eat what they will set before you, and heal the sick among them. For what goes into your mouth will not defile you, but that which issues from your mouth - it is that which will defile you." Gospel of Thomas; saying #14.

The instructions given by Jesus plainly say that the most important thing the disciples can do for attainment is to be truthful, genuine and honest to one's inner heart. The thing that comes straight out of our heart must be considered as one's own Dharma. So the feeling that has been shaped and coming from the heart in a genuine manner is called truth. If, what is felt as being true is put into practice that is called 'Dharma'. Therefore Dharma is that which is born from the heart, which is then expressed in the shape of words and then put into practice. This truth for most is filtered through ego perspective yet the feeling at the root is genuine and in this way is linked in resonance directly with unchanging Truth, therefore linking with the Reality underlying all existence. The theory I am asserting here is that the more one is in their truth, the more the qualitative state resonating the body is one of loving-kindness.

To know Truth is to acquire wisdom pertaining to one's own Self and the relationship of this Self with the Universe, and the relationship of one Self to another Self. Implementing Truth into action is Dharma and there is no higher Dharma than Truth. So these three, Truth, Rutha, and Dharma are inseparably connected together.

Truth is always expressed in one form or another as Love and when this Trinity is realized the action on all levels of expression is compassion. Love, Compassion and Comradeship are the virtues that are birthed within the inner sanctum sanctorum of the Lotus of the Spiritual Heart. This star, or point of Light, resides within the heart of the heart and is the heart of all existence. These three virtues idealize as the soul acquires the wisdom of one's relationship with existence. At this level of Aware Consciousness the Self can allow a deeper connection to develop which in turn allows for more and more expanded degrees of Awareness about the nature of Self. In the highest levels of Awareness the soul allows for a total merging into Absolute Cosmic Consciousness. This final level of mirroring dissolves the "I" in a canceling out of two equals, both being of no-thing.

These three, Truth, Rutha, and Dharma, idealize as the soul acquires the wisdom of one's relationship with existence. At this level of Aware Consciousness the Self can allow a deeper connection to develop which in turns allows for more and more expanded degrees of Awareness about the nature of Self. In the highest levels of Awareness the soul allows for a total merging into Absolute Cosmic Consciousness. This final level of mirroring dissolves the "I" in a canceling out of two equals, both being of no-thing.

St. Clare

In the early 1200's a young woman lived in the mountain town of Assisi, Italy. She exemplified the law of love, following to the letter this commandment of Jesus to his disciples in the Gospel of Thomas. Her only desire was to love God with all her heart, soul and body. On a recent trip I took to Assisi the local guide filled me in on much more of her story as we visited the large church built to hold her body. Her name was Clare and her heart in all matters guided her.

Our guide told us the story of St. Clare in front of the massive doors of the Basilica of St. Clare, nuns and monks entering even while he spoke. He also told us about the substantial building sitting in medieval grace behind us. St. Clare's story is one of miracles, however, our guide started with the story of St. Francis. St. Francis was very well known in the region. It is said that he recognized a spiritual yearning in the young Clare, a girl born into the wealthy and noble family of Maiores. He saw that this child, even in her early years had only one desire, to love and be in communion with God. Our guide told us in brief how Francis helped her on many different levels including the creation of her own Order of Poor Ladies, which were a contemplative, monastic communal of sisters, known in later years as the Sisters of Clare or simply the Clares. Our guide finished his story by telling us that history recorded that the great saint, Clare, died peacefully August

11, 1253 within the walls of her cloister at San Damiano with several of the sisters at her side. The Clares desired to retain the body of their founder among them at San Damiano. This wish is well recorded but the magistrates of Assisi interfered and took measures to secure the venerated remains for the town.

The Assisians urged the church in Rome that their second great personage (the first being St. Francis who died young) should also have a church in Assisi built in her honor. The reason they were so insistent was because she had single handedly saved the city from invading marauders on at least two historically recorded events and demonstrated many miracles and healings over the span of her life. In the interim, Clare's remains were placed in the chapel of San Giorgio, where St. Francis's preaching had first touched her young heart, and where his own body had likewise been interred pending the erection of the Basilica of San Francesco.

October 18th of the same year of her passing, Pope Innocent IV ordered an inquiry into Clare's life with many giving testimony. Two years later, 26 September, 1255, Clare was solemnly canonized by Alexander IV, and not long afterwards the building of the church of Santa Chiara, in honor of Assisi's second great saint, was begun under the direction of Filippo Campello, one of the foremost architects of the time. On October 3, 1260, Clare's remains were transferred from the chapel of San Giorgio and buried deep down in the earth, under the high altar in the new church, far out of sight and reach of those wishing to steal away any of her bones to honor another city.

Our guide next told of the search for the remains, which after remaining hidden well for six centuries was no easy feat. He said that the tomb was finally found in 1850 and on the 23rd of September the coffin was unearthed and opened to ensure that the bones remained and that they might be verified.

He next told us as we stood in the cool evening breezes of the piazza that all present were totally surprised by the beautiful floral scent (a heavenly perfume of flowers and grace) that came from the coffin as they pried open the lid. And even more surprised when they opened the lid fully to find the body of the saint lying intact uncorrupted by death and time, as if sleeping.

The body was later placed with great care in the new crypt of the Basilica of St. Clare for all to witness, by Archbishop Pecci, who was to become the future Pope Leo XIII. Our guide continued by saying that the years of touching and kissing the body, as well as flash photography, which was new and in its infancy, began to take its toll on the exposed flesh. In modern times, (no date was given), a thin layer of wax (3 millimeters he said) was placed over the body to protect it from exposure, as well, he said, a glass wall was installed to further protect the body from the thousands of pilgrims that flock to Assisi each year.

He finished his telling of the St. Clare story by sharing with us that the history told by some modern historians and would be biographers that, "the flesh and clothing of the saint had been reduced to dust, but the skeleton was in a perfect state of preservation," was not an accurate account of those present. He added, that many people have handled the uncorrupted body over the many years, all of which confirm the original accounts passed down. Plus, he added in conclusion, that we could go in and see the visible body still in the crypt of the Basilica.

I silently entered the large doors and in this specific case the grandeur of the edifice paled… my feet took me to the descending stairs; tears flowed on their own accord. I came to the glass wall and viewed the wax like figure of a saint from the 1200's.

"He Christ is the splendor of eternal glory, the brightness of eternal light, and the mirror without cloud."

From a letter to Blessed Agnes of Prague by Saint Clare of Assisi.

Chapter Fourteen

Quantum-Zero Point-& the Holographic Web

"As a thing is viewed, so it appears."
The Tibetan Book of the Great Liberation

"...Who is incapable of hatred towards any being, who is kind and compassionate, free from selfishness...such a devotee of Mine is My beloved."
<u>Bhagavad-Gita</u>, 12:13-14

Over the last hundred years an intensification in the unification of science, art and spiritualism has been occurring. A new renaissance driven and directed by experimental evidence rising out of the exploration into the nature of our material reality. The spearhead of this thrust into unchartered waters broke the surface of public consciousness as the twentieth century birthed into adolescence. It was during those times that the cream of this planet's cutting edge thinkers and scientist were getting together to discuss the weird results of their experimentation and develop new concepts and models to fit the data of their research. Data that, when combined and viewed in a broader context, pushed the rational mind toward parallels expressed in the highly venerated ancient Hindu text, <u>The Ashtavakra Gita</u>. This quote from that text might summarize the burgeoning model, "The Universe produced phenomenally in me, is pervaded by me.... From me the world is born, in me it exists, in me it dissolves."

From the musings of these relatively few souls our technical and information age came into being. Their abstract proposals and audacious experiments gave birth to the electronic age, computers and our ventures into outer and inner space. Their notions of reality allowed today's exponential acceleration of information and the global rush to peel the onion of material existence. Tools for exploring smaller and smaller particles and biological architectures are being constantly created, all of which lead science down the proverbial rabbit's hole into a realm operated by consciousness and driven by observation and the

The Silent Gospel

pervading perceptions of the witnessing awareness; into multiple as well as parallel universes, a strange world where the five senses can not be trusted to direct one to the Truth. To fully appreciate the place we find ourselves, which is in the attempt to create a rational theory based in science for the creation of the Shroud image by a man of antiquity, and to explain the phenomenon of how a man might vanish out of existence as in the case of the Rainbow body event, a brief trip back over the road mankind traveled to get to this point might serve to illuminate and anchor the reality of the thesis proposed within these pages in the imagination.

The story we have in science today began with the modern study of light and electromagnetic radiation (EM) at the end of the ninetieth century. It was at that time that a crack formed in the thinking of theoretical physicists. Two opposing camps with two radically differing views developed. One saw complex organisms developing from small organisms, the bottom up view of life. The other is the top down view best expressed by the Nobel Prize-winning Father of Quantum Theory, Max Planck, "All matter originates and exists only by virtue of a force. We must assume behind this force the existence of a conscious and intelligent Mind. This Mind is the matrix of all matter."

The Split

The split began back in the 1890's but opened wide for all to see in1927 when twenty-seven of the world's prominent scientists met in Copenhagen to discuss the meaning of a group of seemingly peculiar experimental results. Among this group were such notables as Einstein, Planck, Bohr, Schrödinger, and Heisenberg. During this little get together this esteem group of worldly thinkers came to some startling conclusions, conclusions that were to change the way we perceive the process of creation and our role in it. These radical conclusions came to be called the Copenhagen Interpretations. Simply put, these conclusions boiled down to two phrases: *there is no deep reality*, and *reality is created by observation.* These novel ideas and the science that supported them split physics eventually into macro and micro branches. Severely strained by the new kid on the block, the old school Newtonian macro-branch began to split away. The simple fact was that this model of the world works extremely well for larger objects. This led to the consensus among the old guard summarized by the axiom; it works, so why fix it! But all large objects are constructed from small atomic sized objects and these smaller particles did not play to the old rules. This discrepancy placed the old standard on very shaky footings.

Here is a sample of what was going on during those years. James Clerk Maxwell (Maxwell's Equation) had showed that visible light and X-rays are really the same, both are electromagnetic (EM) radiation. Confusing the issue, Millikan and Compton showed, just as conclusively that light was made of particles we now call "photons". Both experiments were flawless and replicable, science had a dilemma, was light/radiation waves or particles, and could it be possible for them to be both depending on the situation? In the same year, 1923, a young graduate student named Louis DeBroglie made an audacious proposal appealing to symmetry of nature. DeBroglie proposed that electrons (a particle) also have a wave nature and a wavelength. The young DeBroglie went even further when he proposed that all material objects have a wave nature. He was referring to the particles composing matter, but are we not all material objects? Young Louis was able to come up with this novel idea in large part because of the work of the German physicist Max Planck. As it turned out, young Louis was correct in his proposal and today a wave associated with a body is often called its DeBroglie Wave as it is the wave nature of electrons. For those curious, the DeBroglie-wavelength measures the length of the wave in relation to a particle in movement. However, I digress. Max Planck you see was working on the subject of light itself, and it was he that postulated that energy could be emitted or absorbed by matter only in small, discrete units that he called quanta. The term 'quanta' is from Latin for 'how much'-- plural of quantum, a quantity or an amount. This idea was not entirely new. Sir Isaac Newton many years before thought that light was made of tiny particles that Newton called "corpuscles". Planck conceived these packets as quanta. These packets are base units of measurement that he calculated to be equal to a millionth, millionth, millionth, millionth of a centimeter. This unit became known as Planck's constant and it was his work that birthed into the lexicon the term *quantum*. Planck's concepts allowed the German physicist Werner Heisenberg in that same magical year of 1927, to develop the base for quantum mechanics. Heisenberg's came up with one particular theory called the *Uncertainty Principle* which states that the position and momentum of a subatomic particle cannot be specified simultaneously. In other words you can tell either the position or the momentum but not both at the same time with any degree of certainty, hence the *Uncertainty Principle*. It became part of the foundation for the new *discipline of prediction* called *Quantum Physics*. Implicit in this new quantum mechanical picture is that all objects, even the most solid particles, can act like rippling waves under the right circumstances. In other words, it appeared that a detected photon acts like a particle but at other moments reflects wave characteristics. Doctors Clinton Davisson and Lester H. Gerner of the Bell Telephone Laboratories in New York confirmed this finding in that same magical year, 1927. They found that the electron has a dual personality, which is presently known as the now famous *wave-particle* characteristic. Their research demonstrated conclusively the dual nature of matter and for this discovery Dr. Davisson received the Nobel Prize in physics. It is interesting to note that in this work the wave attribute gave the electron the characteristic of *light*.

I now jump ahead to September 21, 1999, when Astrophysicist Bernhard Haisch of Stanford University, reported in his Physics abstract, #/9909043: "We report on a new development resulting from this effort: that for the specific case of the electron, a resonance for the inertia-generating process at the Compton frequency would simultaneously explain both the inertial mass of the electron and the DeBroglie wavelength of a moving electron as first measured by Davisson and Germer in 1927. This line of investigation is leading to very suggestive connections between electro-dynamics, inertia, gravitation and the wave nature of matter."

This *wave nature of matter* and its relationship to the *particle nature* is key to not only understanding the formation of the Shroud image but in understanding how a man in antiquity could create such an image. By the year 2000 it became clear to Bernhard Haisch's prestigious team that *all matter* is an *electromagnetic phenomena* and as such able to be modulated. This includes those ultra small pieces like electrons. Here is where it gets even more interesting. Remember DeBroglie's confirmed ideas about objects including electrons all having a wave-length? Well, those wave-lengths appear to have relational and or proportional characteristics that allow for the generation of uniquely specific symmetries of phase.

In the mid nineteen nineties I was participating in the development of a novel cardiac feedback device. The device read the raw ECG (analog signal) similar to normal cardiac devices but thanks to Andrew Junker, formally an Air Force technical analysis working at Wright Patterson Air Base, the device appeared to relay dynamic near real-time display of the spectrum harmonic below 20 hertz, as well as several other key points of data. The faster the internal processor of the computer the closer to real time the feedback felt. This was accomplished by using Fast Fourier Transforms (FFT) and unique linear windowing techniques honed while working for the Air Force. These analog and digital transforms allowed a new window into the wave nature of the cardiac complex as it was occurring. One especially important bit of information gleaned was the average velocity between the frequencies present in the current harmonic. This data was produced by a second order DFT (ceptrum) being done on the original FFT. The data in this window was more and more accurate and important the more coherent the spectrum of frequencies in the harmonic became. Poetically, the more harmonic and ordered the symphony of frequencies being played by the heart, the more valid the dynamic display within this ceptrum graph became. This average indicates the implied fundamental ordering the coherent harmonic signal as well as the *shape* of the wave form being generated in that moment. Since there had never been a device similar to this, lots of questions arose that engendered correspondence with numerous cutting edge scientists. There were many, many reasons for these communications but the main drive was to help explain, in grounded science, the more coherent sustaining geometries witnessed. In short, why would certain waveforms be more sustaining then others? The answer to sustain-ability, electrical coherency and constructive longevity, if you will, appeared to reside in the ability to self-organize and be connected to, like Bernhard Haisch suggests, "electro-dynamics, inertia, gravitation and the wave nature of matter."

One such individual I contacted at that time was Alex Kaivarainen, who had been a leading scientist, Ph.D., D. Sc. Physics & Biophysics at the Petrozavodsk State University, Department of Applied Mathematics and Cybernetics Petrozavodsk in Russia. In one of his emails he wrote; "The new fundamental principle of self-assembly of "simple" systems physical systems, like elementary particles, atoms, molecules, self-organization of complex open systems, like condensed matter, star systems, galaxies and evolution of very complex systems like biopolymers (proteins, DNA, microtubules), cells, organisms - can be formulated as: 'The different selected systems (Coherent Platforms) on each level of temporal and spatial hierarchy are tending spontaneously to condition of Hidden Harmony (equality of most important internal and external parameters of DeBroglie waves),

The Silent Gospel

which determines the Golden Mean'". He finished one correspondence with the following comment, "that not only electrons, but also the hydrogen atoms follow the Golden Mean Rule." And he continued even more importantly, "...that the driving forces of the self-organization and evolution on all hierarchical scales is the spontaneous tending of systems to condition..." of what he calls "Hidden Harmony". He concluded with, "We have to keep in mind, that our world is composed from DeBroglie waves." This gave me a new area to research and in doing so confirmed in my mind Dr. Kaivarainen's assertions.

Dr. Kaivarainen writes on principles of superunification and self-assembly in his book, <u>Hierarchic Theory of Matter and Field: Water & Biosystems, Vacuum and Duality</u>, making him uniquely qualified to discuss the world of self-assembly and self-organization. Like those thinkers of the 1920's, he sees the subatomic world self-organizing spontaneously to a condition of a *Hidden Harmony*. This hidden harmony is produced by a tendency towards equality of internal and external velocities and impulses of DeBroglie waves (the wave nature of an object as determined by DeBroglie principles stated earlier) as a quantum root of *Golden Mean*. I realize that for a novice this last bit of verbiage is meaningless. To unravel its meaning, we must understand that at the birth zone of all matter and mass there exists a harmonizing force that produces organizational impulse symmetry and a resonance unifying, at the core foundation, "electrodynamics, inertia, gravitation and the wave nature of matter." This signifies that even biology has at its core a fundamental that is not only interconnected to the field which gives rise to the birth of mass and matter but also to resonance.

An organic, self-organizing, harmonic relationship exists between electrons and, by inference, complex systems like biopolymers and you and me. This quantum relationship and hidden harmonizing factor produces, allows and demands a specific ability via resonance for the wave nature and particle nature to interact, attract and organize into complex structures. At its core it is the central communication web for photonic connectivity -- a characteristic allowing photons and electrons to be shared /communicated between cells, systems and organisms instantaneously regardless of distance. It is the superluminal connective mechanism witnessed by researchers. The visible characteristics of this quantum/DeBroglie harmonizer are self-organizing-self assembling abilities with proportional symmetries. As we will discuss later on, the birth zone lies at the very edge of chaos; the realm of no-thing.

If all this is true, and I believe now that it is, then the foundations of our entire material universe must in some way mirror and reflect an innate characteristic of the womb called the "zero point field." But from a deeper perspective this logos reflects a foundational characteristic of the matrix of mind we call consciousness.

Physics of Life

Physical laws appear to operate with two sets of separate laws. One set of laws for the macro and another for the micro as we have already stated. To this day no neat way to bridge the gap has been demonstrated. For physicists this is distasteful, for like the rest of us, they love symmetry and instinctually intuit an underlying physics that is simple and elegant. Since 1927 the search for the grail in physics has been a mathematical construct to bridge the two seemingly perfect sets of laws. "String" and "Super String Theories" of all types and hype came forth in the 90's but none were simple or elegant, nor can they ever be proven, so they'll remain forever theoretical. At the same time the ancient concept of 'consciousness' being the ground of reality, and not the reverse, was being revised.

David Bohm, a physicist at the University of London, came up with the idea of objects being manifested as a result of the interaction between physical objects with a cosmic field that endows it with a phase. Furthermore, this phase in multiple oscillating coherent platforms emerges as a macroscopic object with coherent performance. Although this was a theoretical idea, it generated the question of what is this *cosmic field* that had the power to endow objects into coherency. Again the self-organizing force that allows self-referencing and complexity to arise is rooted in the quantum zero point field and reflects the Golden Mean characteristics as it manifests.

With the crest of the millennium, humanity had new and very sophisticated devices that allowed mankind to watch the birth of matter directly out of the ethers. Ultra small objects were condensing within vacuums via some mystical attraction agent. This attracting agent had organizing (self-assembled) characteristics. Let me again step back to those magical years of the late 1920's to get a fuller picture where the interest in light, electromagnetic radiation, electrons and photons drove research and industry alike. All of this interest and financing, along with the prestige of Davisson's Nobel Prize, pushed the development of tools like the electron microscope. By 1937 demonstrations of this new device allowed researchers for the first time to observe the crystalline atomic structure of elements and their geometric patterns dancing as points of light in space. The lattice geometric structures of light were clearly seen to be affected by the air molecules, with the appearance of shimmering, like sunlight on water. Elements and their atomic structures were conclusively *seen* as points of light held in geometrically precise forms vibrating with the neighboring vibrations of their environment. You can imagine the impact this had in 1937. For the first time, humans watched elements as fluid geometric patterns, standing as waves on an ocean of space, being affected by the drift of passing gases. These points of light held in structure drove the new rising star of quantum physics into prominence. It also gave evidence that the major portion of an object and our world was empty space. Physicists now claim that matter is 99.999% empty space. The example given to help visualize an atom is of a pea representing the atom, sitting in the center of a large sports stadium and the electron, the size of the period at the end of this sentence, flying around the seating area, to outside the stadium walls. Yes, there are other smaller particles spinning around but they are so small that they take hardly any space at all. As one can see the vast preponderance of the atomic structure is space, vibrating alive space, void of mass; space held in organizational form via resonance and some other force which appears to us that must have intelligence. Intelligence is reflected by the ability to self-organize, self-replicate and sustain over time. This led science to the realization that our world is not concrete nor firm but fluid, dynamic and constantly under modulating influences. To help understand this new realm now seen by our scientists, the world of Quantum physics came into being with Haisch's conclusion that *all matter* is an *electromagnetic phenomena* and as such able to be modulated. The curious thing is that it now appears that the best modulating influence on quantum objects and the standing waves they become in movement, is the influence of consciousness

Quantum Physics

Quantum physics started as a science of prediction, specifically the prediction of where a single particle would be at any one moment in time. What was found was that it was impossible to predict both the position of a particle and the time it would be at any one location. Trying to understand this weird anomaly developed into theoretical quantum mechanics and quantum dynamics. In quantum mechanics, however, particles do not always behave as solid particles as in classical physics, but can appear as probability waves per Heisenberg's Uncertain Principle, meaning they have a certain probability of being in a number of different places at any given time. It is only when a particle is observed (not just by people but also by other particles), that its presence is pinned down to a specific location. (Another word used for observed is detected.)

At the atomic scale, particles such as electrons tend to behave as waves, but at larger scales like humans, electrons and atoms are constantly providing information about their properties to each other hence their location. You can picture electrons as a liquid that carries charge and more interestingly a liquid that interferes with itself allowing detection. This *interference* arising from *detection* raises the spin rate above its resting state also called its *ground state*. The energy released (emitted) as it attempts to fall back to this ground state is the energy we use every day as electricity. Electrons, like all other objects in nature, naturally seek their lowest-energy state. To do this they minimize their total energy, which includes their energy of motion (kinetic energy). Lowering an electron's kinetic energy means reducing its velocity. A reduced velocity also means a reduced momentum, and whenever an object reduces its momentum it must spread out in space according to the Heisenberg Uncertainty Principle. This produces a "delocalization" effect releasing large amounts of energy when returning to its ground state. When the release touches neighboring electrons, a yo-yo cyclic effect (oscillation) of increasing spin and velocity is produced followed by the inevitable fall back to its natural state of rest. The resulting attempt to fall back to the natural ground state of existence allows objects to remain in superposition, which is a fancy term for the phantom of waves localized by detection over time. It is a self-referencing phenomenon of light dancing in space. The geometric pattern of self-detecting all points of active existence is executed so rapidly that the object appears solid. It was all just theory and prediction prior to 1982, but in that year, reality, as we knew it, radically shifted again.

It was in that year that a scientist named Alan Aspect and his team at the University of Paris demonstrated the existence of the strange world of quantum objects and their even weirder mechanics. Aspect and his team confirmed the reality in a reproducible manner. Scientists throughout the world checked and double checked his experiments and findings. The quantum world was no longer theoretical and this meant real world applications. The world of quantum soup and the objects that constantly inhabit that soup took center stage. Classical Newtonian physics worked exceedingly well for our daily lives but clearly the foundations of that reality were on a ground subject to this new bizarre mechanics, so it was vital to understand this realm. Aspect and his team made the existence and strange properties demonstrably real. The virtual rug was pulled out from under the old long-standing views on the nature of material reality. What was even stranger was that we were now beginning to conceive of ourselves at a core level as quantum objects and as such, subject to all the laws and weird mechanics at this level. If virtual photons exist, does a virtual you also exist? The renaissance underway was merging and blurring spiritual and scientific concepts.

The model of this modern physics states that our Universe runs on only one basic particle: a unity based on singularity. There are, of course, countless numbers of these base particles in any one cubic centimeter of space most of them lying peacefully at rest. These particles produce a thermal quantum virtual soup, a black-body field of radiation, a sea of coherent light with enormous latent energy. This womb of energy is the quantum vacuum, the great Zero Point Field (ZPF). All objects reside within and rise out of this vast field of zero point energy (ZPE). The current thinking is that this field acts as a drag on all accelerating forms of this base virtual particle, pulling it back to its ground state. The only way this drag (entropy) could be avoided is to be in coherent resonance with the field itself. Clearly this is not the norm since it appears that all objects decay and erode back to this pure ground state energy. Life from a quantum perspective is a mirrors game, a holographic illusion played out on a black-body screen of virtual radiation. Other points not widely communicated are the conclusions derived from this current model, for if the universe runs on one particle then inherent is a resonant base regulator for all mass/matter, i.e. Haisch's finding and the assertions of Alex Kaivarainen. The inferred information concluded is that this virtual field of energy is our embryonic world and as such has a massive influence on the birthing and growing material within its domain. Collectively this information implies the possibility that an individual could theoretically attune the electromagnetic standing wave of self into harmonic resonance with this domain.

This information is critical in constructing the process by which the Shroud image came into existence. It is enhanced with information on the science of movement called acceleration. For it is only this accelerated aspect of ourselves, the electromagnetic standing-wave form-the visible physical body, that phase transitions. And it is this process I'll show to be responsible in the forming of the image on the cloth.

The Science of Movement

Movement from a quantum point of view is the oscillation of one or more of these virtual particles above their natural ground state of rest. The swing or vibration of this virtual particle sustained into a measured beat is called an oscillation, which measured over time is a frequency. When frequency is sustained it creates amplitude which is also termed power.

Acceleration occurs when a single particle vibrates within a specific frequency bandwidth, pulling -negative (less positive) energy from its outer perimeter, into a more concentrated + positive center. Note please, that the action is from the outer to the inner. As Haisch's team suggests, at least in the case of the electron, "a resonance for the inertia-generating process at the Compton frequency would simultaneously explain both the inertial mass of the electron and the DeBroglie wavelength of a moving electron..."

Matter consists of atoms, and atoms consist of electrically charged components, lightweight negative electrons and positive nuclei. Two of these particles within the same bandwidth form a greater attraction because they are twice as strong as the surrounding space. This event produces resonance, which is a key principle in this whole affair deserving of its own chapter. The resonance produced attracts, as does the stronger magnetic field now being generated.

Sustained resonance infers a coherent state. When this coherent field which is a coherent platform of vibration, comes in contact with another particle grouping or better yet, an electron mass oscillating with another element's frequency bandwidth, all parties will exhibit cross-frequency modulation. This creates a third beat and a fourth 'Superposition' (harmonic) frequency, also known as a Photon Event.

Superposition

A *photon event* has the characteristics of absorption and emission but what it is, is an object held in space-time by the constant rapid recursion of the coherent oscillating platform(s) making up the field held in superposition. It becomes objectifiable. We are able to then vector in on a location. It is no longer non-localized.

The fundamental loop of resonance, self-referencing recursively, is sustained via dynamic detecting of that which is held in superposition (accelerated wavicles localized in time-space). The stronger the superposition (recursive self-referencing detection) the less affect the cross-modulation has on the coherent platform (object). The waves pass through each other forming a ripple like the stone thrown into a calm lake; soon after the event the lake returns to its former state. A true master of reality absorbs the rock without even the smallest ripple occurring to the standing wave field, which if witnessed from the same perspective as the electron microscope, would be a dynamically fluid humming bundle of points of light. When these notes interfere constructively, which is interference that adds to the form in some way, a new harmonic is formed. So a harmonic is a coherent platform. All harmonics are ordered and sustained by the resonant fundamental. For a structure to be held over time as a standing wave, the fundamental must fractally relates to both the resonance of the whole and the ultra small coherent platforms making up the form. Coherent platforms (particles, proteins, cells, and systems) with similar harmonic resonance combine (interfere constructively) to form a new base of resonance, a new form, which again from a photonic perspective is a Superposition of electromagnetic waves held as a Coherent Resonant Platform. If one could look at a whole individual through a device like an electron microscope one would see simply a more complex lattice geometric image. A complex three dimensional geometric lattice of patterns embedded within each other, structured as dancing as points of light in space. This universe of tiny points of lights would be constantly shimmering from the influence by passing external energies.

Humans are a collective of modulating coherent platforms held in coherent bond by a harmonizing base constructive resonance. This base resonance attracts and repels. Yet like a point of light on water, external stimulus (pebbles thrown in) affects the order seen in stillness. In short, the external environment (the place and things around you) as well as the internally taken in stimulus, including all food, drugs and gases, act to shift (modulate) the collective. The largest stimulus acting on the standing wave field is produced by the effects of mind. If the mind perceives danger, a cascade of internal events occur that quickly raises the internal energy states of specific systems in order to respond to the perceived danger. To be an object, resonant coherent harmonic states must be present. A coherent state in quantum physics can accelerate from 0 to 186,000 miles per second in a quadrillionth of a second. In 10-27th of a second, a particle will grow (absorb) to fill the entire Electron Envelope (2.817-15 cm) and then return (emission) to its original energy size (~1.616-35 cm).

This mouthful of techno-garble simply points to facts that allow, theoretically, for the resonance of the field held in superposition, i.e. your body, to be modulated into a more stable resonance. A field of dancing light attuned with the embryonic ground energy. A primal still reservoir that all mass arises out of and within. It also allows for the possibility of a phase transition of the standing-wave to a higher form of symmetry.

Light Facts

The current view has *visible light* as a small slice of a wider spectrum of energy consisting of millions of possible frequencies. This is called the Electromagnetic Spectrum. Light and electromagnetic radiation is therefore the same stuff. All electromagnetic radiation as we've seen can have this dual *wave or particle* nature. This odd characteristic is now termed a *wavicle*.

The particle nature of light, photons, are understood in Quantum Theory as packets of energy called quanta. These packets can move at the speed of light which is 299,792,458 meters per second or 186,282 miles per second in a vacuum. In this new particle view of light, the brightness of the light is the number of photons, the color of the light is the energy contained in each photon, and four numbers (X, Y, Z and T) are the polarization. Both the old and new interruptions have been shown to be accurate. Most discussions on the topic of light speak of the common viewpoint and neglect the quantum view because of the complexities that arise.

Even the speed of light has recently been shattered by experiments done in laboratories around the planet, including work at Bell Laboratories, where pulsed light was recorded to move much, much faster then the speed of light boundary.

In quantum theory these small packets of light (photons) when detected cause polarization of positives and negatives to play out creating the dance of the electron and the electromagnetic spectrum. Any slice of the spectrum is simply the rate at which these particles oscillate (frequency) and/or pair up. Photons in the form of EM radiation can, and do, oscillate at millions of different frequencies, and each element, which is a coherent oscillating platform in superposition, has its own unique photonic frequency which attracts and bonds and/or repulses. It is a cosmic dance of attraction and repulsion, construction and destruction, of absorption and emitting; a dance of movement (acceleration) within an ocean of stillness.

Reviewing the basic science point of view, attraction is defined as harmonious frequencies pairing up via resonance to form more complex standing waves. This in turn produces a new resonance, forming new harmonic coherent platforms, and it is this photonic resonance which determines how and whom they potentially might stick together with in future moments. This process produces everything in the Universe including the very structures we see around us including our bodies.

This describes the *energy nature* of the material 3D universe we all play in, but it does not address the primal organizing energy or intelligence at the core of this wondrous dance of light. What causes it to manifest into being at all? Sri Yukteswar writes that, "The manifestation of Omnipotent Force ... is vibration." Vibration is what we've been talking about, but what is this Omnipotent Force that manifests as vibration in the first place? No matter how you slice the science and physics of our structure one is brought back to the idea that some non-localized consciousness acting with and in this virtual soup produces the ultra rapid dance of light we see and respond to as reality, and this structure which forms and sustains force we define as intelligence.

Consciousness

In 1987 a Princeton Professor of Aerospace Sciences and Dean Emeritus, Robert G. Jahn and Brenda J. Dunne, the manager of the Princeton Engineering Anomalies Research Laboratory, wrote a book called Margins of Reality, The Role of Consciousness in the Physical World. This book not only talked about the power of consciousness and the intent in choice making but about designed tools used to demonstrate and test the power of the focused mind. They discuss in their book specific spaces created to shield against all EM radiation called Faraday Cages. Faraday Cages are still used to test if mind was a characteristic or function of EM radiation. It turned out it was not; mind had the ability to de-localize as well as also localize and effected EM radiation but was not itself a function of EM. This put a fly in the ointment of academia for if mind was not operating with this perceived base medium for all objective reality then there must be another medium everyone was missing.

Then, in the early 90's, another excellent book on this subject was released, authored by Amit Goswami, Ph.D., called <u>The Self-Aware Universe, How Consciousness Creates the Material World</u>. In it he writes, "Consciousness is prior to experiences. It is without an object and without a subject." This sounds like the words of a Self-realized individual does it not? Goswami writes, "The idealist resolution of the paradox of Schrödinger's cat demands that the consciousness of the observing subject chooses one of the cat and thus seal its fate. The subject is the chooser. It is not cogito, ergo sum, as Descates thought, but optio, ego sum: I choose, therefore I am."

The subject is the chooser but consciousness is prior to subject and object. What is this consciousness looking out of those eyes making the choice? What allows for the subject to exist in order to make choices? And what is the process for a human to be aware that he or she is making that choice to begin with? Illuminated souls tell us that the witnessing self is in a state of choice-less awareness; a state of awareness with deep knowingness-beyond mind, beyond experience, beyond explaining. It always seems that when discussing consciousness we fall into that house of mirrors where there is no beginning and no end to grasp onto. For these reasons the holographic principle often comes into play by way of symbolic explanation.

Holographic Fractality

> "In the holographic domain, each organism represents in some manner the universe, and each portion of the universe represents in some manner the organism within it."
> Carl Pribram

The holographic concept as a model to explain the broader concept of Universal or Cosmic Mind rose to public consciousness with David Bohm trying to resolve Alan Aspect's 1982 findings. Bohm concluded these experimental results implied that objective reality does not exist, that despite its apparent solidity the universe is holographic. It was a novel and explosive concept. BAM! The holographic concept ran like wild fire across the global academic landscape, seemingly helping to explain many anomalies for a diverse range of fields of study.

The "holographic concept" goes beyond the mere notion of a simple hologram. Yet to fully grasp the potential of this model's ability in helping us understand the broader concept of Cosmic Mind, it would greatly help to first offer a brief overview of how a simple holographic image is created and the inherent characteristics that are subsequently developed.

To create a holographic image, the first thing to understand is that there are two known forms of light, one form is coherent, meaning ordered, the other being radiant, referring to random or scattered. Nearly all the light witnessed in our daily lives is of the radiant form. The sun, stars and the common light bulb are examples. A laser, on the other hand, produces coherent electromagnetic radiation, i.e. light. The word Laser was originally an acronym standing for Light Amplification through Stimulated Emission of Radiation. A laser produces coherent light in a device consisting of special gas or crystal. To make a holographic image, which by definition is one that appears three-dimensional, requires the use of lasers and the unique coherent light they produce. In other words, a normal photograph uses the regular random light scattering off the desired object being captured on film whereas holographic images require the object to be bathed in the coherent light that only comes from a laser.

The process of creating a holographic image begins with the object to be acquired first bathed in the light of a laser beam. Then a second laser beam is bounced off the reflected light of the first and the resulting interference pattern (the area where the two laser beams commingle) is captured on film. The image shows the area where the two beams dance together, not the object being captured on film. When the film is developed, it looks like a meaningless swirl of light and dark lines. But as soon as a third laser beam illuminates the developed film, a three-dimensional image of the original object appears.

The three-dimensionality of such images is not the only remarkable characteristic of holograms. If a hologram film of a rose, let's say for the sake of example, is cut in half and then illuminated by a laser, each half will still be found to contain the entire image of the rose. This cutting up of the image into smaller and smaller bits does not change the fact that within any of the bits of film will always be found to contain a smaller but intact version of the original image. In a holographic image, every part of the image contains all the information possessed by the whole original image. It is fractal. And something holographically fractal is multi-dimensionally fractal and the mathematics and geometry that rises out of this form of fractal became the base in creating what we today call virtual reality.

Bohm came to believe that the reason subatomic particles are able to remain in contact with one another regardless of the distance separating them is not because they are sending some sort of mysterious signal back and forth, but because their separateness is an illusion. He argues that at some deeper level of reality such particles are not individual entities, but are actually extensions of the same fundamental "something". They are not separate parts, but facets of a deeper and more underlying unity that is ultimately holographically fractal and indivisible. He termed this the underlying unity as the implicate order. If his conclusion is accurate -- that the apparent separateness of subatomic particles is illusory -- then it means at a deeper level of reality all things in the universe are infinitely interconnected as in the holograph.

The connection at the core is the coherent light, which allows for the image to form in 3-D. Living in a holographic quantum universe, time and space would no longer be viewed as fundamentals. This is because concepts such as location break down in a universe where nothing is truly separate from anything else. Time and three-dimensional space would also have to be viewed as projections of this deeper implied order. Vibration would be considered a manifestation of the Omnipotent Force. At this level, the past, present, and future all exist simultaneously. In their attempt to describe and understand this field of reality, physicists came up with the term Zero Point for this singularity of existence. An existence where all light resides at its ground state was also termed the still point. This was from the physics point of view theorized as the holographic black body back drop for material existence. Cosmic Mind was simply the collective information stored in the hologram of pure potentiality and our individuated attention with all its collective energetic baggage was the final laser beam which illuminated the core medium into accelerated states we see as our perceived reality.

Zero Point Energy or the Electromagnetic Quantum Vacuum

The Heisenberg Uncertainty Principle, one of the fundamental laws of quantum physics and the basis of zero-point energy (ZPE), predicts that all of space must be filled with electromagnetic zero-point fluctuations. This space is the Zero-Point Field (ZPF) creating a universal sea of Zero-Point Energy (ZPE). At any point in space enormous amounts of Zero Point Energy (ZPE) exist. As I've already stated, this Black Body is considered a thermal soup within which all our objective universe resides and manifests. The density of the energy contained in the quantum vacuum is estimated by some at ten to the thirteenth Joules per cubic centimeter, which is reportedly sufficient to boil off the Earth's oceans in a matter of moments!

The density of this energy critically depends on where in frequency the zero-point fluctuations cease or come to their ground state of rest. Since space itself is thought to break up into a kind of quantum foam at a tiny distance scale called the Planck scale (10-33 cm), it is argued that the zero point fluctuations must cease at a corresponding Planck frequency. If that is the case, the zero-point energy density would be 110 orders of magnitude greater than the radiant energy at the center of the Sun. But this is pure conjecture. What can be said is that the ZPF is the pure potential and possibility humming in alive stillness, always on call, for the call of creativity, and the two base characteristics of the ZPF would be high coherency and resonance. Ah the paradox! Bohm might call it the Implicate Order and some see it as the realm of pure chaos, but Astrophysicist Bernhard Haisch of Stanford University wrote in September 1999 Science and Spirit, an elegant understanding of this field of existence.

(It is) "...a background sea of light known as the electromagnetic zero-point field (ZPF)of the quantum vacuum." (He asks in the same article one to)"... imagine a pendulum that gets smaller and smaller, so small that it ultimately becomes atomic in size and subject to the laws of quantum physics. There is a rule in quantum physics called the Heisenberg Uncertainty Principle that states (with certainty, as it happens) that no quantum object, such as a microscopic pendulum, can ever be brought completely to rest. Any microscopic object will always possess a residual random jiggle thanks to quantum fluctuations." (The key word above is object). He continues; "Radio, television and cellular phones all operate by transmitting or receiving electromagnetic waves. Visible light is the same thing; it is just a higher frequency form of electromagnetic waves. At even higher frequencies, beyond the visible spectrum, you find ultraviolet light, X-rays and gamma-rays. All are electromagnetic waves, which are really just different frequencies of light.

"It is standard in quantum theory to apply the Heisenberg Uncertainty Principle to electromagnetic waves, since electric and magnetic fields flowing through space oscillate like a pendulum. At every possible frequency there will always be a tiny bit of electromagnetic jiggling going on. And if you add up all these ceaseless fluctuations, what you get is a background sea of light whose total energy is enormous: the zero-point field.

"The "zero-point" refers to the fact that even though this energy is huge, it is the lowest possible energy state. All other energy is over and above the zero-point state. Take any volume of space and take away everything else — in other words, creates a vacuum — and what you are left with is the zero-point field. We can imagine a true vacuum, devoid of everything, but the real-world quantum vacuum is permeated by the zero-point field with its ceaseless electromagnetic waves.

"The fact that the zero-point field is the lowest energy state makes it unobservable. We see things by way of contrast. The eye works by letting light fall on the otherwise dark retina. But if the eye were filled with light, there would be no darkness to afford a contrast. The zero-point field is such a blinding light. Since it is everywhere, inside and outside of us, permeating every atom in our bodies, we are effectively blind to it. It blinds us to its presence."

In summary, since the zero-point field is everywhere inside and outside of us, permeating every atom in our bodies, we are effectively blind to this field of dense energy-state acting as the background for the dance of light. Or are we blind to it? We certainly are when using our normal senses because they rely on slices of frequencies way above the stillness of the zero point field. The brain selects specific sets of the frequencies out of this vibrating blur and transforms them into sensory perceptions, and abracadabra, our objective reality exists. But what if one could focus attention on the de-localized aspect of self, then what would he or she perceive? What if attention was focused on the stillness and not the movement, what then would your aware perception be? Quite simply, the old smoke and mirrors reality would cease to exist or at the very least hold no power. As the ancient religions of the East have long upheld, the material world is Maya, an illusion. True Reality is emptiness. Consider the following quote in <u>What is Life</u>, from the theoretical Austrian physicist Erwin Schrödinger, co-discoverer with Heisenberg of quantum mechanics, "Consciousness is never experienced in the plural, only in the singular. How does the idea of plurality arise at all? ...the only possible alternative is simply to keep the immediate experience that consciousness is a singular of which the plural is unknown; that there is only one thing and that what seems to be a plurality is merely a series of different aspects of this one thing produced by deception (the Indian maya) - in much the same way Gaurisankar and Mt Everest turn out to be the same peak seen from different valleys."

Consciousness, or Pure Light, itself creates reality by creating the mirror realms of mind-awareness and it forms it all in the dance of resonance. If this isn't radical to our post quantum thinking then nothing is. But it concurs with what Illuminated souls have been telling us over eons of time.

The Copenhagen Interpretations are still relevant after more then 70 years and their conclusion are as challenging to accept today as they were then. The reason is two- fold: firstly, they go against what we perceive, through our senses, what our experience is; and secondly, because they place responsibility of reality itself on and with the individual, the observer. This entire line of reasoning brings us back to what the great Indian saint Sri Aurobindo said on the subject, "All matter is just a mass of stable light," this being similar to what one witnesses through an electron microscope wherein is fluid, vibrating light is held in space via some mystical attraction and the self-referencing byproduct of resonance.

Science has found a mechanism for explaining the interconnectedness of all things: that non-locality is produced at stillness. The empty space is a macro (larger then the universe) domain, termed the quantum zero point field, which, as we have discussed, is a field of vast energy. The first discoveries of this domain were at the time of researching the characteristics of particles. It was found that particles are entangled in a process of remaining forever correlated; the proverbial quantum-leap.

The concept of the quantum holograph served to ground the notion of consciousness forming biology, physics and all of objective reality. Within this field, space and time cease and all information is held within the single web of light. Conceptually, this ZPF lies beyond the subatomic realms at the boundary limits of speed, heat, cold and movement, a domain where ambiguity produces a highly coherent, highly stable virtual mass at perfected equilibrium and nothing could be more stable and coherent than a multidimensional holographic fractal reflecting Golden Mean.

The Golden Mean, or Phi mathematically and geometrically, occupies the transition zone between Chaos and the state of self-organized criticality, also termed in some circles *Emergence*. This ratio acts as an optimized probability operator whenever we observe the quasi-periodic evolution of a dynamical system. In fact, it is the optimal energy-minimization route to the region of maxim algorithmic complexity. It also serves as a basin of attraction and self-assembly.

Phi is the only possible geometric and arithmetic expansion and partitioning of ONE with the third being One itself. The Golden Mean is an archetypal fractal in that it preserves its relationship with itself. Its inherent similarities under scaling are conformal symmetries with invariant topological consequences. Phi is the path out of chaos (maximum entropy) also the path to perfected self-referencing. The Golden Mean is the mediator between dimensional realities and all dynamics. It is also the foundation for self-similarity, optimum stability and the speed of light to touch infinite. Phi reflects the formless ideally and acts as a template for emerging form, as it occupies the middle ground between form and formless. Phi epitomizes and optimizes recursive feedback loops in a linear manner yet due to its geometric (logarithmic) nature is equally non-linear in nature. It is the only manner to divide the unity without separation. This unique natural characteristic allows for the finite and infinite to commune as well as the movement and perfect stillness to coexist dynamically.

Primary Perception

In the mid 1960's Cleve Backster was one of the FBI and CIA's foremost polygraph researchers and to this day is one of America's most noted polygraph experts. On February 2nd, 1966 he realized after hooking up his plants with instruments of his daily profession, that his houseplant had "read my mind!" The plants were reacting to thoughts, or so the evidence implied. He had hooked up the plant to see if there were any reactions similar to those of people. The reaction he witnessed "…was more or less like a human reaction under the stress of being caught in a lie. You see, the polygraph indicates stresses in human thinking and emotional reactions".

After 35 years of meticulous research, Backster has progressively undermined the notion of a universe comprised of discrete units. He has proved that thoughts and emotions affect the behavior of their own and other living cells. He has scientifically demonstrated the reality of conscious, non-local, instantaneous communication between thoughts and living cells.

Using straightforward electronics and rigorous protocols, he brought into plain view what he calls *primary perception,* a mode activated before the specialized five senses, in fact it is instantaneous, a non-local effect. From his thorough research, the field of biocommunication within plants, living foods like yogurt, and human cells reemerged into the light of day. He reintroduced modern science to the sentient nature of our universe. Interestingly in the late 1980s, neurobiologists discovered and confirmed that plants might be able to possess "primary perceptions" because they have "rudimentary neural nets."

Backster's work has made visible in a replicable manner the characteristics of the invisible web that links all of creation. He documented the connectedness of life forms and the interactivity of their awareness. He has done for biology and psychology what quantum and standing wave concepts have done for physics. Backster's research explains how plants perceive and react to human thoughts about them. He then illustrates how eggs hooked to electrodes react to other eggs being dropped into boiling water, and how plants react to the eggs' reaction to the experimenter's intentions. He shows how yogurt cells communicate with one another and other species. Backster also describes the collection of human cells (leukocytes and blood) and the instrumentation that records their reactions to the thoughts and emotions of their donor. He does most of this with simple Galvanic Skin Response (GSR), the electrocardiograph (EKG) and or the EEG wave normally set aside for brain waves. Cleve Backster's new book is called, <u>Primary Perception: Biocommunication with Plants, Living Foods, and Human Cells</u>.

Another source confirming the connections of time and events are from Precognition Experiments performed by James Spottiswoode at the Cognitive Science Laboratory. The experiments were very simple yet very powerful and have been reproduced several times now by other groups. Spottiswoode said that the startling results show there is an "extraordinary effect that's coming back from the future and affecting the brain earlier in time."

The experiment involves measuring arousal levels via skin conductor (GSR) responses as subjects listen on headphones to sporadic bursts of loud white noise. What the studies have revealed is that there is a statistically significant response that occurs approximately three seconds before the sound is heard, as if the person's body were reacting to the blast before it actually came. "It could be that consciousness in some sense is de-localized, spread out... so it moves a little bit ahead, a little bit behind physical time," Spottiswoode conjectured. The Experiment went something like this:

- A computer using a random program randomly created white noise loudly to the listening subject.
- No one knew, or had any control over, when the program would create the harsh sound.
- The skin responses were measured very accurately in time.
- The body over and over appeared to know and respond to the sound that was soon to come, even though the computer had yet to make the choice. In simple words, the body knew seconds ahead in time that the sound was coming even though the computer had yet to make the choice to create the sound.

In examining this experiment, it became apparent the body knew and responded seconds before the computer randomly selected the moment to create the sound. This implied a non-local precognitive component to the body's awareness, or at the very least a prior perception of an event yet to be chosen. The researchers then looked at why the average was always approximately 3 seconds ahead in time. Spottiswoode conjectures that this amount of time might be the best interval to aid in survival. Sooner than that and we would forget by the time the event actually arrived. Less time, and we would have no time to react. Heart to brain to muscles to conscious awareness takes on average about 3 seconds or 2 to 5 beats of the heart. What these experiments hint at is something of the process of creating reality.

Spottiswoode pointed out that the study of physics could even be altered by these findings which indicate that the concept of the past creating the present may be misguided. He added that the University of Pittsburgh was planning similar experiments but including EEG patterns to possibly associate a "neurological signature" to this phenomenon. I would suggest ECG as well, for it has been demonstrated that this organ is the central oscillator for the standing-wave of self and it is this wave form that interface the quantum vacuum for its existence. When subjects have the ability to self-reference the cardiac bio-signal, a more direct route to referencing consciousness is achieved. Other scientific disciplines have demonstrated that it is consciousness that is the ground for the event in the first place.

Gaia

Lastly there is a study that points to a greater interconnection than even Backster's work with plant, living foods, and human cells. It indicates an interconnection in a non-local reality of the planet and the people living on her. It points to this same pre-perception ability, which Backster coined Primary Perception. This last study comes from the Princeton Noosphere Consciousness Studies lab.

Roger Nelson is the director of the lab's research which, as the name implies, is on the nature of Consciousness. Many of you might have heard of this program after 9/11 because it was mentioned on CNN news but this part of the study began in 1998. In truth, this is an extension of research started by Robert Jahn and Brenda Dunne of the Princeton Engineering Anomalies Research Laboratory in the early Nineteen Eighties.

Nelson's team has special recording devices spread out all over the planet called eggs. The eggs are designed to record the background random noise (energy). What they are looking for are the moments in time when the random signal becomes highly coherent, which is to say organized. This appears to occur when a significant number of the planet's people are about to become focused on a single event like the death of Princess Diana or the 9-11 attacks.

Just prior to the 9/11 events the eggs began recording very high coherent peaks and they continued through the horrific events of that day. It appears that out of the random energy, a highly coherent signal is generated in varying degrees of time, prior and during these unique mass consciousness events. It is as if the consciousness of the planet or mankind as a whole knew before the event occurred. This offers very similar findings to that of Backster's plant and cell experiments and Spottiswoode Cognitive Science Laboratory experiments.

This note below pertains to the February 2003 Global Peace rallies. A friend working with the Heartlink in conjunction with Voice and Sound pattern recognition devices in Spain wrote to Roger asking if any signatures were witnessed by the devices. Roger Nelson's reply to her:

> "I did not have a prediction for the 14th, but did for the rallies on the 15th. The latter did show a significant effect. It is actually quite striking, and suggests (to me at least) that Mother Gaia is aligned with the feelings of so many that peace is possible, and indeed necessary. You can see the results via a link in the Current Results table, or directly at HYPERLINK. http://noosphere.princeton.edu/demo030215.html
>
> Best,
>
> Roger

(Note: The reference to the 14th was the global AH Sound moment that was made at noon that day. AH in mystical traditions is the sound of the heart matrix and at noon the 14th many globally sounded this unique sound for global peace.)

(Note: The page linked in the email has the graph of the data for that day. I highly recommend visiting this site.)

These three experiments demonstrate in a verifiable way the instantaneous non-local component of perception and or awareness, as well as the interconnected sentient nature of our universe. Coherency demonstrates agreement in the relationship, hence Roger's language, "...is aligned with the feelings..." Literally the planet was in those moments aligned with the consciousness of the mass brought together with concentrated focus.

Shift of Attitude and Perspective

Clearly there is much more to the picture then meets the eye. Consciousness is beyond the electromagnetic wave spectrum and beyond any particle aspect; Consciousness has the characteristics of being both local and also non-local and beyond the restraints of time and distance; beyond object, subject and action. It can appear individuated and simultaneously appear collective. It is an enigma, but its agent awareness, is the main tool in the tool box of Divinity. All other tools at their core are under the influence of the perceiving awareness. Understanding that Awareness can be directed with laser-like precision and imbued with transforming, transmuting qualities energetically is important. Learning to selectively generate specifically imbued focused attention is more valuable in dissolving away the obstructions to quantum resonant harmonic alignment and provides a new, richer sense of identity. The yogi's goal through the epoch of time has been to anchor a total shift in one's perspective from the limiting aspect (a particle stuck in time/ego mind identity) to another more expanded aspect of self anchored in the timelessness of the singularity. When the consciousness, i.e. the identity that organizes the standing wave or spatial aspects (physical), mirrors in resonance the field giving rise to it, the yogi's gifts, (siddhis/powers) become available. Although for most yogis, gaining power over matter is not the goal, it is simply a by-product of conscious growth, of *remembrance*.

Total union with the Divine is the ultimate goal, with an accent on the word *total*, and this, these masters tell us is not in truth a gaining of something as much as it is a *remembrance of what has always been*.

The majority of us walking the planet have our identity caught in the trance of dancing light: the illusion of the time-space movie produced by our five senses and false linear sense of progression it produces. We limit ourselves with the trap of persona and the dream of separated identification. This looping trap is formed, anchored and strengthened by the five senses, which only function through the stimuli of the EM field. And, the EM field has been proven not to play a direct role in consciousness. This was accomplished by experiments done with Faraday Cages. A Faraday Cage blocks all external EM from entering. The perception which operates at the quantum level is normally not allowed to gain strength or prominence. This other level of primary perceiving, demonstrated by several replicated experiments over the last decade, is real and functioning below the radar of the commonly used senses. The yogi learns all the skills required to control the nerve functions of the body and anchors his sense of self in this primary non-localized aspect. This level of perceiving is often thought to be a perception of the heart. Ah, Heart Intelligence.

To help the seeker make this shift, various physical and psychological sciences have developed over the eons. Tools created for the skillful development and experiential knowing of this alternative yet primary perspective. A knowing perceived the ancients tell us, by the heart.

When one becomes sufficiently experienced in having their perception and sense of self permanently anchored with this primary reality, s/he comes to the point of experiencing Consciousness with a big "C", the primal Consciousness that governs Awareness on all levels of existence. This is the connective tissue of all existence. The soul then realizes the operator, energy and process behind the camera, as well as the illusion on the TV screen of life, is the same not only at a core level but on all levels of reality. The veil is lifted on the mirrors behind the curtain and the experience of Self-realization /Remembrance occurs. Duality and polarity dissolve as the pendulum of perspective returns to the source animating experience.

Due to the differences in the experiencing perceiving mind, the qualitative aspects shift, embedding attention more and more with constructive interference which serves to generate higher and higher levels of coherency within the standing wave, i.e. the physical structures. New forms of neuropeptides are produced along with a new pharmacological cascade of protein response from the amino acids library. The shifting of perspective, as one can imagine, has many degrees, from occasional shifts in awareness to fully anchored (fully identified) in the new perspective. And each expansion is interpreted through the essence of that unique soul/body. And if that were not enough it comes with an additional paradox, one apparently cannot make the shift occur, one can only deal with the obstructions put up by the little sense of self and the learned subconscious automated responses of the individuated cells and their collective system. In the end the strongest attitude in shifting perspective is one of surrender, or if you will, perfected allowing, which is to be in faith. This shift in attitude has the power to form a new collective resonant fundamental governing the collective of oscillating coherent platforms i.e. the standing wave of form. When perfect allowing occurs, a massive shift in the biology and codon potential of the DNA/RNA appears also to occur; the biology of molecules and cells shift to reflect the awareness, which again is a shift in the collective resonance. Simply said, a shift in the Mind State produces a new resonance and this creates a collective shifting of the physical architectures comprising the body. Form follows the perceiving mind/consciousness.

What if one could experience, that is have a sense self, as a singularity of pure radiant spaciousness and then faithfully surrender into the consciousness of that spaciousness? The very act of having a sense of this experience would in itself produce the idealized infinite mirroring for awareness, giving rise to the experience as the spaciousness. The Aware Stillness would be the same as the perspective of a holograph from the perspective of the light, not the image or a slice of the image. This idealized pure reflection of Pure Light would be experienced as Alive Aware Still Spaciousness. The object at that moment would go virtual, only now it would be objectless because it is no longer localized. Both wave and particle aspects dissolve back to the field of Aware Stillness, the world of consciousness prior to object or subject and action.

<u>The Tibetan Book of the Great Liberation</u> states, with the support of quantum theory, "As a thing is viewed, so it appears."

The level of experience, which is to say the way one perceives, observes or senses this domain, would localize and determine the level of experience. So the essence of each individual would influence the depth and type of direct experience with this primordial state. With each foray into this spaciousness the communion would increase, as would the depth of mystery and connectedness. As one placed more and more attention on this alive spaciousness, one would become more intimate with this state; then at some point, the sense of individual "I", the base for experience, would dissolve and a greater more universal sense of "I" would organically be birthed into awareness. As the consciousness evolved to this new universal sense, form would follow for evolution to continue.

In this part of the book we will look at the science and internal processes that occur biologically during awakening to full self-awareness; processes that arise organically as one develops the skill of perfected allowing. The man who created the phenomenon of the Shroud achieved this level of perfected allowing, indicating that he had a deep, well-developed relationship with awareness that transcended ritual and mind.

The Science of Divinity is the timeless, selfless art, an embraced attunement so to speak, that shifts the resonance of the collective coherent oscillating platforms into a uniquely specific harmonic relationship. A relationship so unique that it allows ideal self-referencing to such a degree, that the form, in this case the body, remains crystallized even with the pressures of decay that death normally brings. When accomplished by those of great skill, this art has the ability to immediately dissolve the body completely into a union with the creative life affirming pure intelligent essence. This amazing act of willful surrender, which is perfected allowing, also perfect mirroring, is called The Rainbow Body in Buddhism. The value and process of resonance and coherency as it relates to matter and system synchronization are next on the list for discussion in order to better understand this artful science of resonant unity.

From the book <u>I Am That</u> by Sri Nisargadatta Maharaj "Look closely and you will see that all names and forms are but transitory waves on the ocean of consciousness, that only consciousness can be said to be, not its transformations. In the immensity of consciousness a light appears, a tiny point that moves rapidly and traces shapes, thoughts and feelings, concepts and ideas, like the pen writing on paper. And the ink that leaves a trace is memory. You are that tiny point, and by your movement the world is ever re-created. Stop moving and there will be no world. Look within and you will find that the point of light is the reflection of the immensity of light in the body, as the sense "I am". There is only light, all else appears. To the mind, it [that light] appears as darkness. It can be known only through its reflections. All is seen in daylight - except daylight. To be the point of light tracing the world is turiya. To be the light itself is turiyatita. But of what use are names when reality is so near?"

Chapter Fifteen

Resonance

"We can assume that in biological systems the transfer to the next level of organization is accompanied by resonance synchronization of the cell radiation." Dr. Konstaintin Korokov

Form at any level of scale comes into being through the process of resonance and it plays a critical roll in the formation of the Rainbow body as well as the image on the Shroud. Resonance is simultaneously both a process and a result. The broader view understands resonance as a synchronization of bodies at any scale, a harmonious relationship that enhances the sum of the combined parts, "as an energy transfer between two connecting periodical processes with equal or multiple frequencies." ([2])

The process occurs when two objects have frequencies of oscillations (vibrational swings) that are close to each other, which is to say, in resonance with each other. When two such systems are in proximity, then they will resonate at the frequency dictated by the stronger of the two oscillations. Stronger refers to power or amplitude when discussing frequencies. In general, the longer low waves carry more power to entrain the higher waves. The bass or percussion in music is a prime example of this. The base produces the beat that all the higher frequencies phase with. The common example given to visually understand resonance is witnessing a string on a guitar being plucked and then to observe how strings at a nearby resonance start to oscillate at the driven frequency of the louder original note plucked. When two fields or objects resonate together, as in the example of the other guitar strings, they produce a third vibration. This frequency rises the closer in resonance they are, till in a moment the third frequency disappears. This is what musicians do each time they tune their instruments. Tuning is a cohering or harmonically aligning of two or more vibrations, producing an overall harmonious relationship. One can tune a twelve string guitar and that guitar can be tuned to an overall

---
[2] Dr. Konstaintin Korokov Light After Life

symphony and that symphony can be tuned for a special building or place.

The metaphor of the symphony can be applied to the human body as well. It is like a grand symphony with many, many different coherent oscillating platforms, the brass, string and percussion sections, and each of those with their many, many individuated parts, each with its unique resonance and tuning, all operating within a greater coherent collective, producing a unique spatial note. This collective we embody and radiate is modulated slightly with each beat of our heart, yet the whole is maintained by the ultra long waves and their resonant relationship to the fundamental.

In music theory the concept of the fundamental goes something like this: all natural sounds that have a distinctive pitch-like quality, consist of a combination of many frequencies which are called harmonics. These harmonic sets of frequencies are related in a simple way by the lowest-frequency harmonic called the fundamental. The other harmonics present are multiples of the fundamental, that is, two times the fundamental frequency, three times, four times, and so forth. The relatedness of the fundamental to the higher harmonic is in resonant proportion. This lowest-frequency set always correlates to the higher sets in a directly proportional way. With this knowledge one needs only look at the relationships of the high frequencies present in the central cardiac matrix when the harmonic is coherent, to see what the fundamental ordering the harmonic might be. The base resonance attracts and entrains through the power and length of the cycle. It is not as affected by interference as are the higher realms of the spectrum. The ultra long span of time one cycle takes to complete serves as a cohering agent and platform for the dance of much higher frequencies. No matter how many different instruments are involved they all follow in a tuned manner the base timing called the beat or rhythm, even if hidden or implied. This base beat, this base-harmonic-resonant relationship is the *core fundamental.* It is my contention that this *core fundamental* is always in resonance with the Zero Point domain. Rationally it can not, not be, since at the core all the component parts of the physical objective world are composed by these quantum-entangled parts. It is only the high frequency domains (sets and harmonics) that stray from the *Hidden Harmony.* Always present at the core of all mass are the building blocks of raw energy and primal intelligence holding it is latticed form.

Resonance is the way, the method and the vehicle in which fields communicate, by touching and sharing their info-energy in a constructive manner. Particles can be in resonance with other particles (objects with mass) and or waves or both simultaneously.

Today our current science sees form, even the simplest of form, as a collection of parts all with their unique vibration held together by the collective self-referencing bond of resonance. Simply the bonding that holds it all together in space is rationalized as an effect of coherence dynamics which has resonance as a key principle. Resonance, therefore, plays a key role as the cohering agent for macro-spatial standing waves. From a scientific perspective we are all complex macro-spatial standing waves. These wave forms can and are modulated and tuned dynamically by the heart, beat by beat. The intelligence of the heart and soul is attempting to modulate the whole into an ideal sustained tuning with the core fundamental and its specific scale invariant relationship. A relationship that dissolves the artificial boundaries of individuation and sense of separateness. After all this is the reality of the core quantum family of particles.

The actual process of two objects coming into resonance allows for additional info-energy to constructively transfer. Experiments in the mid 50's, showed that, "resonance leads to two types of trajectories: the first are trajectories with normal behavior, well known through the study of two-bodies problem. The second are trajectories with stochastic behavior."[3] A simple example of normal behavior might be a ball dropping straight down out of one's hand and hitting a concrete driveway, while the second, stochastic behavior, might be a basket of jelly beans dropped onto a gravel driveway. Determining exactly where the ball is going to land is easy to calculate but the final resting place of all the jellybeans involves far greater chance. Energy can be characterized by both particle and wavelike properties as we have previously mentioned. This means that our body has both wave and particle characteristics as well and each forms a resonance which in health is attuned to the whole. The waveform characteristic can be graphed as a Hertzian wave, either in the form of a sine wave or a step wave. Indeed, about everything from electricity to magnetism, from light to sound, from X-rays to Cosmic waves and beyond can be graphed in some manner. We may not have the tools yet to measure it

---

[3] Dr. Konstantin Korotkov; Light After Life

all at this time, but if it has movement it falls into this category called The Spectrum. The full spectrum of light is also known as the electromagnetic spectrum. The only difference between all of these forms of energy is how fast the waves rise and fall (the frequency) and how intense those rises' and falls are (their amplitude). When the frequency sets are constant (not fluctuating) the form is thought to be coherent, which is simply sustained order within a set of frequencies also termed the harmonic. The amplitude of each frequency may initially alter slightly, but over time a truly coherent graph of a coherent wave will also have balanced order in the amplitude, i.e. in the power. Resonance of Coherent Platforms plays a key role in phase transitions, and the process in creating the Shroud image occurred through a massive phase transition as we will read in more depth in later chapters. The key scientific principles at play in the creation of the Shroud image are resonance, coherence and phase transition of the particle-wave aspects of the human elemental symphony.

Dr. Konstantin Korotkov, in his groundbreaking book, Light After Life, writes:

"The development of these representations brought to life the concept of the so called Big Poincare Systems, in which resonance plays a very important role. Big Poincare systems, i.e. Chaotic systems, have only stochastic (random) trajectories. ...Big Poincare systems reflect many important situations. In effect, they reflect majority of situations in nature. It also removes the obstacle against the integration of the system. This result destroys the determinism and reversibility of Newton's and Hamilton's mechanics, since the solutions for Big Poincare systems generally are statistical and non-symmetrical in time. ....Poincare's proposed division of all systems into integrable and non-integrable, remains valid for quantum mechanics as well.

"The central link in Prigogine's chain of reasoning is the concept of quantum chaos -- chaos in a mathematical (linear) sense. Non-reversibility and probability are two organic attributes of the world described by Prigogine."

He concludes his thoughts on resonance in this way,

"...Roughly speaking, the behavior of any group described by generalized group function cannot be reduced to the behavior of a single member of this group. That is the consequence of resonance, which is a necessary condition for existence of open systems integrating with the surrounding world."

Simply put, without resonance and its characteristics nothing would exist in form nor would they evolve, grow or expand on any level. It would be a fixed, closed, ridged, loop. Goswami wrote; "consciousness should be regarded as an open dissipative system." Yet consciousness means *to know together*; it requires two or more in the awareness loop to exist. The stochastic behavior of resonance allows for expansion and growth. It is the key for evolving the collective tuning of Self, to be in conscious resonance with the *Luminous Darkness*.

Dr. Koroktov's continues, " Once again the leading role in behavior of a system should be played by resonance interactions- both among the elements and with other systems of the kind. Summing up, we can assume that in biological systems the transfer to the next level of organization is accompanied by resonance synchronization of the cell radiation."

Synchronization is bringing two or more things into ordered step together, having the same phase and period, exactly the same rate or timing. Oscillators all resonating in synchronization are said to be coherent. Coherent synchronization reflects balance and harmony in the quantum event. Through resonance the phasing can change the over-all resonance producing a phase transition.

Water changing to gas then to ice and back to water is an example of *phase transition*. This change in the material nature at the molecular level is the process of phase transitions. In this example, at all times the substance is H_2O (water), but the state it exists in radically shifts placing it into a fundamentally different form. One form is fluid liquid, the other an invisible gas and then it is in the crystal form, then back to its fluid state. The form is altered through resonance of the various fields it contacts (touches or references). Low energy environments cause it to be ice; high energy, it is transformed into a gas.

The main condition of functioning of any complex biological system is the cell resonance synchronization. This synchronization is provided both by the internal synchronization references, i.e. the references coming from the other parts of the system, and by external references, all in communication with the virtual quantum level of biocommunications.

A summary of this process by Dr. Korotkov is offered below. The bracketed phrases included are mine.

> "The transfer from the group of individual cells to the level of complex organism has a character of bifurcation (dividing or branching) self-organization: the properties of the organism cannot be defined as the sum of properties of the composing elements." (The sum is more then the parts. This is always the case.)
>
> "The clockwork reason for this self-organization is the process of resonance synchronization of separate system's elements." (Entrainment to the strongest fundamental produced by resonant synchronization.)
>
> "On one hand, the synchronization possibility could be explained by the unity of the genetic structure of biological objects. On the other hand, the theory of dynamic systems predicts resonance for interacting systems with close natural frequencies."
>
> "The interaction between different components of a complicated biological system (e.g., cells) can be described as information exchange through fields and emissions."
>
> "If there is resonance there is synchronization which produces a third base fundamental which acts to cohere or bind the collective. This is maintained till it comes in resonance with additional components, either internal or external or quantum impulses outside of time. These additional components may strengthen the core-organizing fundamental, which adds to the strength of the coherent synchronizing bond; it also adds magnetism.

"Any complex organism has multiple systems that modulate the collective resonance moment by moment. The self-organizing, self-referencing nature of the info-energy produces a field in superposition, (localized spatially) which is to say, locates in space. This info-energy field is the Standing Wave. The superposition is the dynamic wave envelope of charge (standing wave) is the field of an object interfacing with the quantum Zero Point Field. The Standing Wave field has resonant fundament that becomes a fractal attractor due to the self-referencing nature of the field. The resonant field produced by the two types of trajectories, normal and stochastic behavior. When the fundamental of the standing wave that is held in superposition harmonic aligns to the womb of Still Energy it resides in, a massive phase transition occurs in the field. It self-references to a different fundamental one that is scale-invariant and ideally fractal. The net result is zero and emptiness is achieved at the most spacious level."

I am privileged to end this discussion with the words of Dr. Koroktov. "The undertaken study shows that a biological system could be regarded as a complex-structure set of field emission source, synchronized by frequencies and phases. Source of this kind are called coherent source."[4] He continues; " It is known that a simultaneous application of the fields by coherent sources forms an interference pattern in space. In the same way, we can assume that certain field structure is attached to any biological object."[5]

---

[4] Dr. Konstantin Korotkov, <u>Light After Life</u>, page 58

[5] Dr. Konstantin Korotkov Light After Life

Chapter Sixteen

Tuning to the Divine

"To have order you must have randomness, because where there is no randomness order cannot manifest itself." ~ *Alan Watts*

"…not one atom can have its evolution without annihilation."
Hazrat Inayat Khan

The process we call evolution, from a spiritual perspective, is understood as the movement of consciousness yearning to ideally mirror the divine (divine referring to God or God like). It is reflected in the desire to create heaven on earth, it is the call of immortality; it is consciousness coming to realize that which it is. Objects and places that begin to accomplish this feat or are associated with self-realized souls, we think of as sacred. If an object or place were to come close to the ideal it would be immutably sustained in the domain of time, its form radiant as the new rose opening to receive the light of its first day. At that rare point there would be no need to evolve, no impulse to change, union literally would have been achieved. Conscious existence would have no other, no mirror, a coherent state would be. Remembrance would be achieved.

Science tells us that the Shroud image was *radiated* onto the flax cloth by an intense *coherent light* (electromagnetic radiation/EM), through an unknown process that left us a full head to toe, back and front image of a man in the posture of death. The energy that imprinted the cloth must have been ordered for it to produce the unique characteristic and visual clear image. This much we know factually from the data examined, but what does it really mean, the term *radiated coherent light*?

Since this is at the heart of what we know about the Shroud's image creation, a brief look at the subject and value of coherent light (EM) might help illuminate the process and science that allowed the medium of light to radiate equally from or near the body, producing this silent testament to our potentiality.

Coherency occurs at Equilibrium

Coherence is the state or quality of being coherent, implying a form of unity, a wholeness or oneness. It comes from the Latin cohaesere, to stick or bond, to cohere. The more perfect the unity, the more perfect and stable the coherence. Interesting to me is that it implies oneness yet requires more then one to fulfill the definition. It requires two or more parameters or aspects, as does consciousness and awareness.

Coherence as a value relates to order, balance and harmony, as a quality it is stable. Coherence can be fixed and closed or it can be open, expanding and dynamic. It can be reflected in both particle and a wave dynamics. Coherency in one domain implies ordering in all domains with the field of influence, especially within complex systems.

Coherence on one level of thought is the ability to not lose energy (minimize resistance) but from another perspective it is the ability to attract/collect and share information and energy between scales and levels in a constructive way. Coherency is the best way to conserve and hold light from dissipating and *it occurs at equilibrium.*

From a psychological perspective coherency is to be awake, conscious and logical. To communicate coherently is to transmit one's thought in an orderly, harmonious manner so as to be understood. In the literature of physics the definition might refer to a mathematical algorithm expressing a quantitative measure of the spatial or temporal relationships between two or more parameters. In quantum mechanics a coherent state is a quantum state that describes coherent fields or platforms where all of the energy involved shares some measurable property that allows them to be thought of as being "in phase". Simply expressed, the more synchronized and in-step the differing beats are, the more harmonic the symphonic collective rhythm. A high degree of phased cohering over time allows the field to be coherent. *A coherent field is a field with symmetry held in equilibrium.*

The onset of coherency in light is a laser, an acronym for Light Amplification through Stimulated Emission of Radiation. In a laser, a coherent light is produced in a device consisting of special gas or a crystal. A quantum phenomenon that affects the performance of lasers is known as 'jitter'. Jitter occurs due to a lack of coherence at the subatomic level. This is a lack of phase alignment with the long-wave lengths governing the properties of these small bits of matter. Jitter is understood poetically as quantum noise that affects the performance, thereby limiting the use of lasers in many applications. The problem is that the higher waves and the phase which holds the light in synchronization are not in phase with the smallest pieces and their waves. This effect occurs at the edge of chaos, the domain of quantum laws and electron wave mechanics. Jitter to the layman is quantum mechanical grit adding drag to the soup of material stuff, guarantying erosion, change, shifts and annihilation of that which is holding light and matter in coherent form. *Quantum Jitter* could be thought of as the *cosmic recycler, d*ampening vibratory movement (oscillations) back down towards the ground zero state of idealized equilibrium.

Sun Rise on Stillness

Most of us were raised in school with old classical physics which was anchored on a vision where the universe is an assembly of separate individual objects interacting through forces that act on each object from outside. The development of this theory makes sense when you understand that this is the way we understood ourselves: as separate, individual objects attempting to remain unchanging, yet constantly being subjected to external forces that come and act upon us, forcing change. This mechanical model of the universe has each individuated component perturbed from its solitude. Its solitary inertial trajectory is bombarded by external forces propagating through a neutral medium of empty space. In this view, stuff arises from individual bodies mutually coupled by some external forces and the empty space is essentially nothingness and plays no role in supporting creation. In this view we are victims to the hands of fate and play no roll at all in our reality. Consciousness is only sometime to witness the show with.

This model is a very different from the view now held by many in the scientific community. This new vision, one with many similarities to the ancient wisdom teachings of the planet, has our cosmos held in a womb of potentiality and possibilities, where consciousness creates even the forces that force change. Nothing is outside and oddly still, there is no real inside, there is only consciousness creating within this womb of amniotic life/creative field of stillness. It endows life and it taketh away simultaneously all that is not in perfect phase equilibrium. Consciousness is a Pandora's Box filled with emptiness, a paradox of self-responsibility.

All energy mechanically seeks entropy, its ground state of equilibrium, which is a highly coherent place where energy loss is minimized to zero; a collective home for all energy known as the zero point. You can pick your point of reference, but understand that all movement, through some process, attempts to return to entropy, a form of stasis. Roll a ball and eventually it will come to a stop. Add energy and the electron spins faster but then it releases this added energy and information about itself and steps back down to its natural place where loss of energy is minimized and it can sustain itself. This process of attaching the info-energy occurs mainly through resonance and coherence which are two key elements of the Zero Point domain according to Prof. William Tiller of Stanford University (former Chairman of the Materials Science Department and Guggenheim Fellow).

Forms that stay coherent as shape are collections of vibrations that, because of their shape and tuned resonance, hold the light (the standing wave of energy) coherently for longer and longer periods of time before decay. Decay is a sign that the coherency is waning due to cross frequency modulations and a general dissonance affecting the resonance. The longer the form holds its coherency the more fractal-phase connected it needs to be to the ground state of electrons, photons and the other subatomic elements. The greater the resonant fractality, which is recursive self-similar scaling, is to the base state, the greater the longevity of the object.

Coherency can occur in a closed fixed loop of referencing; a laser is a nice example of this type, or the internal phase produced can be open and more fractal to the ground state of all existence. This more receptive open loop system-type produces/allows for expansion, evolution and invariant communications. Life on all levels best examples this state. When idealized, wellbeing results from the internal coherent symmetry present. This type of coherence produces beautiful complex symphonies that dance through space constructing and harmonizing with ease due to the inclusiveness and excellent info-energy communications it offers.

The best form for this coherence energetically is a torus with the ideal being a phi proportioned torus field. A torus is a donut or apple shape. When dynamic it has a dual counter-spinning field, with dual spinning vortex in the top and bottom of the field. This geometric field is self-referencing and when idealized by the golden mean, it idealizes self-referencing and coherency, due to the self-sustaining nature of the shape and vortex actions. It is symmetry in motion, exemplified.

What is the binding agent that acts to order and bond collections of vibrations in a biological form, form which we know as life? What orders the symphony of life into form and allows it to remain bonded while dancing though a sea of dissonant waves? According to the saints that have existed, it's Love

Evolution-The Transformation of the Human Species

In this profound philosophical investigation, Sri Aurobindo felt that the divine evolutionary impulse was inexorably not only toward the spiritualization of human consciousness, but ultimately a physical transformation of the human species.

Aurobindo contended that the transformation would occur by bringing the "Supramental Consciousness", also called "Truth Consciousness", down into the physical. Supramental Consciousness at the level of mind would manifest as the understanding and vision of Truth. This same Truth Consciousness, at the feeling level of the heart, would be perceived as Love, and a rich joy would rise from the deep appreciation for being able and allowed to realize the true nature of existence. At the physical level it would manifest as total inner peace, a contentment that comes from resonant merging with Divine Intelligence. It arises out of phased harmony within the nervous system.

Survival demands would be non-existent, identity would reside in the eternal 'Suchness' he claimed, and all notions, even those of interconnectedness and oneness would cease to be in the collective consciousness.

Aurobindo wrote that *Truth Consciousness*, is "This deep recognition that the true law of the universe, regardless of appearances, is the Divine Law,..." and that when anchored in the physical, "creates *the vibration* of Truth in the physical..."

This vibration has a fractal unique signature that allows for and at the same moment creates high levels of coherent harmony with-in the multiple levels of individuated coherent platforms operating within the energy sphere. This produces a phased resonant signature that is in resonance with the primal singularity, that of Absolute Consciousness. When felt in the heart, it is experienced as love.

"Cultivating that inner peace" is the key to the rest of the unfoldment. It is the corner stone of the science. What the body *remembers* is that there can be a different way of functioning, one of balance, internal harmony and connectivity. "When the peace is there... very soon (after) there is Love that... takes the lead in life." Then and only then is it possible for everything to begin to change in a massive way. "All those so-called laws of aging, or deterioration start disintegrating. The real power of the cells," as Sri Aurobindo states, "start to be activated." "This is normal divine power," says Bhaga, a representative from the "Laboratory of Evolution" in Auroville, India which shares a parallel to Intergal Yoga called Yoga of the Cells.[6]

The experience is felt as an enhanced receptivity and like any true communication is based on love and a genuine concern for the other, even if that other an aspect of your self. When this real caring for the other exists, in this case the cells of my body, organically there arises genuine loving-kindness. One develops a deep appreciation and a wellspring of gratitude flows up for being a participant in this wondrous adventure. Looking at the transformation from the detached view of science, what occurs is simply a unique tuning of the grand symphony with the ground of existence, one that produces a unique coherent-resonant relationship; a relationship in remembrance, a relationship with Love.

---

(1) What Is Enlightenment Magazine, Extra Summer issue 2002, Article, Yoga of the Cells by Craig Hamilton
Evolution-The Transformation of the Human Species, Sri Aurobindo

Chapter Seventeen

Quantum AUM

The symbol AUM... summarizes within itself all processes of Being and Becoming and is to be accepted as the ultimate formula of spiritual success. "Listen to the Primeval Pranava, resounding in your heart, as well as in the Heart of the Universe."[7]

A Constant in Spiritual Traditions; AUM

From the ancient mystical traditions comes the idea of the Cosmic Constant, the prime causal vibration, known in Genesis as *The Word*. The ancient sages of the Indian sub-continent had a very sophisticated cosmology and their word for this cosmic constant was AUM. The first reference to AUM was seen some four to six thousand years ago in the writings of the Vedas. AUM is a Sanskrit root word or *seed-sound* symbolizing that aspect of the Godhead, which creates and sustains all things. AUM of the Vedas became over time the sacred word Hum of the Tibetans; Amin of the Moslems; and Amen of the Egyptians, Greeks, Romans, Jews, and Christians. Often this symbolic idea was simply called *The Word*. Later this concept migrated into the Greek understanding of *Logos*. In my search for a neat, modern understanding I came upon the 1894 writing of Sri Yukteswar, which crystallized this idea perfectly. In the Holy Science, his small book attempts to clearly outline a Western view of his Eastern Cosmology. He writes;

> "Parambrahma (God) causes creation, inert Nature (Prakriti), to immerge. From AUM (Pranava, the Word, the manifestation of the Omnipotent Force), comes Kala, (which is) Time; Desa, (which is) Space; and Anu, the Atom (the vibratory structure of creation)."[8]

His commentary on this Sutra states:

---

[7] Sai Baba as quoted in Vision of the Divine by Eruch B. Fanibunda

[8] The Holy Science by Sri Yukteswar Self-Realization Fellowship

"The Word, Amen (Aum), is the beginning force of creation. The manifestation of Omnipotent Force (the Repulsion and its complementary expression, Omniscient Feeling or Love, the Attraction) is vibration, which appears as a peculiar sound: the Word, Amen, Aum. In its different aspects Aum presents the *idea* of change, which is Time, Kala in the Ever-Unchangeable; and the *idea* of division, which is Space, Desa, in the Ever-Indivisible."

He continues, "that these four -- the Word, Time, Space, and the Atom are therefore one and the same, and substantially nothing but mere ideas." Yet, he writes, one must merge with this primal "idea" in order to return to his Divinity. He goes onto say that "...the only way by which man can return to his Divinity, is in the baptism or merging of Self in the stream of the Holy Sound (Pranava), Aum, ..." and that this merging manifests spontaneously through, "the culture of *Sraddha*, which is the energetic tendency of the heart's natural love; *Virya*, moral courage; *Smriti*, True conception; and Samadhi, true concentration." [9]

But he says that the principle requisite for attainment of the holy life is attainment of Love, which he calls the heart's natural tendency and the attracting agent back to union with the Omnipotent Force.

Notion of a Constant in Physics

Physics also has a constant, one first proposed and developed by Nobel Prize-winning Father of Quantum Theory, Max Planck. Indeed, it carries his name, Planck Constant, but this theoretical foundation is a constant for the world of movement only not inclusive of Being as AUM is said to be.

Planck Constant is a theoretical base for light and energy. I therefore found it interesting that this father of micro-physics was quoted as saying -- and even he was quoted as saying -- that "All matter originates and exists only by virtue of a force. We must assume behind this force the existence of a conscious and intelligent Mind. This Mind is the matrix of all matter." So this highly regarded Nobel Prize winner and originator of the idea that light moves in ultra small packets, which is the foundational concept of quantum mechanics, is telling us that the real constant is Consciousness. This is similar to what the sages past

---

[9] The Holy Science by Sri Yukteswar, Self-Realization Fellowship

and present tell us that 'being', that Divine Intelligence, is the true motivating force at the highest levels; yet they also tell us that at the mundane level of existence, our everyday existence, the motivating force in the creation of reality is aspects of one's own mind. Again, this is similar to what quantum theory is telling us.

As we travel backwards down scales of size, from the large complex objects like galaxies, people and molecules like DNA, we enter the domain of the smaller masses like atoms, subatomic and elementary particles. We discover that all these, both large and small, are comprised and formed by the electromagnetic medium, which at its core is all the same stuff with the sole difference being rates of oscillation. Yet these ultra small architectures are pulsed and sustained by virtual forces, forces that appear to be intelligent. Hence the comment by Planck that *Mind is the matrix of all matter.* This notion is in agreement with the commentary of Sri Yukteswar; "These four -- the Word, Time, Space, and the Atom are therefore one and the same, and substantially nothing but mere ideas, (mind)."

The formation of Mind we read in Chapter Thirteen, originates out of the primal mirroring which is the creation of Awareness.

This primal movement might be viewed poetically as the primordial relationship, the neutral partitioning between stillness and illusion of movement. A relationship born of perfect mirroring, a relationship formed by a divisionless scission. This divisionless partitioning or perfect mirroring gives birth to individuated Mind and the process of awareness. A divisionless partitioning sounds like a paradox yet in mathematics we find a principle which allows just such an event to occur. All of Chapter Nineteen is specifically about this principle.

The Dance of Light

When fluctuations (accelerations) occur within The Field, the interaction (repulsion and attraction i.e. polarity) within this still silent medium produces an unbalance (asymmetry), a push and pull force arises, oscillation and vibratory law are born. Yet because all things arise from this central micro-spatial curving it must be a unique relationship. It must allow for bifurcation and inertia/mass to arise. It must allow for all the diversity we see in our daily lives. For this to occur, special unique core characteristics must exist.

1. First, it must reflect/mirror the original field from which it arises, for at that moment
there is nothing else.
2. It must interact and be in resonance with the field from which it arises, for at that moment there is nothing else.

Hence the primal *idea* is to reflect itself and in doing so birth the illusion of time, space and vibration, again, because at that moment there is nothing else. The sages of wisdom tell us this primal idea forming the seed vibration is the formation of all maya (illusion), yet is also the touchstone for the return back to Divinity and the completion of its cause. "I am, that I am" should be read, "I Am that, I Am."

Divisionless Partitioning

So the recurring question is, 'what could divide, yet remain itself perfectly?' In researching this question I arrived at a biologic and elemental tendency, as well as a mathematical relationship, which points to a path allowing just such a relationship.

The biologic and elemental tendency is resistance to change and or movement, a tendency to lean towards stillness (rest). In biological objects this tendency is called homeostasis, which is simply seen as biology's way of conserving energy. But biology is comprised of bits of mass which are defined by inertia itself. So by definition, mass and biology have an inherent tendency to resist change from its ground state. This resistance is to any acceleration (movement, scattering, etc.). It has a built-in brake that naturally creates drag and a level of coherency within the object. It is the crystallization or slowing down of light (energy) into its minimum superposition. This tendency is what allows objects to exist in the first place. It is understood that objects, through their quantum fluctuations, discover the configurations where the energy is minimum and, thus, where they might settle indefinitely in coherent form.

Objects become crystallized through self-referenced resonant entrained centering. This implosive force is also understood as compression. This action references an extremely long, low base vibration engendered by the dance between the symmetry (coherency) of the zero point state and the asymmetry of causal jitter-spatial curves produced by any form of acceleration (oscillation). This process occurs in all form no matter how coherent. In other words, at the boundary between chaos and form is a Hidden Harmony that anchors and facilities communications between scales of form and between dimensions. Scientists and mathematicians tell us that this domain between the vacuum or stillness and movement is occupied by Golden Mean -- a relationship that forms, or should I more accurately state, allows for, a divisionless movement.

As stated in Chapter Fourteen in Alex Kaivarainen correspondence, "the driving force of the self-organization and evolution on all hierarchical scales is the spontaneous tending of systems to condition of Hidden Harmony (equality of internal (hidden) and external velocities and impulses of DeBroglie waves) as a quantum root of Golden Mean." Our world is composed from DeBroglie waves. It turns out that the only possible creative duality within the Unity of the Great Singularity is the 'supra-rational or transcendent' proportion of Phi, the Golden Mean, a subject worthy of volumes but for our purposes I'll summarize more completely in chapter Nineteen.

I humbly suggest that the prime resonance has a root phi relationship and that when this relationship is sustained within the heart's standing wave, an expanded coherent synchronized coupling (phasing) occurs among the oscillating platforms of the human form. This proportional relationship allows for scale invariant constructive interference and alterations in neural pathways as well as the cell-to-cell interface including expanded gene excess within the DNA/RNA matrix. Then, as Yogananda writes, "the whole body vibrates with the sound of AUM." And this Sri Yukteswar says is; "...the only way by which man can return to his Divinity, is in the baptism or merging of Self in the stream of the Holy Sound (Pranava), Aum...".[10]

"Once the mind is interiorized," Paramhansa Yogananda said, "and withdrawn from its identification with the world and with the body, the inner light comes into clear and steady focus. The inner sounds become all absorbing. AUM fills the brain; its vibration moves down the spine, bursting open the door of the heart's feeling, then flowing out into the body. The whole body vibrates with the sound of AUM."

He continues; "...Gradually, with ever-deeper meditation, the consciousness expands with that sound. Moving beyond the confines of the body, it embraces the vastness of infinite vibration. You realize your oneness with all existence as AUM, the Cosmic Vibration."

---

[10] The Holy Science by Sri Yukteswar, Self-Realization Fellowship

This state is known as AUM Samadhi, or union with God as Cosmic Sound. AUM is that aspect of the Christian Trinity, which is known as the Holy Ghost, or Word of God."...

"By still deeper meditation, one perceives in the physical body, underlying the AUM vibration, the vibrationless calm of the Christ Consciousness, the reflection in creation of the unmoving Spirit beyond creation."[11]

---

[11] The Essence of Self-Realization by Paramhansa Yogananda, Copyright 1990, J. Donald Walters

Chapter Eighteen

Sonoluminescence

Thamaso maa jyotir gamaya
(Lead us from darkness into Light)

The story of Sonoluminescence (SL), meaning light from sound, begins back in 1934 at the University of Cologne. At that time two scientists by the names of H. Frenzel and H. Schultes while researching acoustic radar witnessed some unusual phenomena during their experiments. However, research into the odd spectacle playing out in the waters of their experiments did not gain much attention and the subject of what was to become SL made little progress until 1988. In that year D. Felipe Gaitan, now with the National Center for Physical Acoustics, University of Mississippi, succeeded in trapping a stable sonoluminescing bubble at the center of a flask energized at its acoustic resonance. The ability to trap a single air bubble made the phenomena easier to witness, record and obtain more accurate data. His achievement is considered the birth of single-bubble sonoluminescence (SBSL) and was the impetus needed to reconstitute the study of SL. In truth, much of what was needed was a massive advancement of the tools required for studying this strange occurrence, for without the instruments to witness the details occurring during sonoluminescence, the depth of the phenomena could not be fully appreciated.

Few of the characteristics now taken for granted were known before Dr Seth Putterman and his colleagues at UCLA, California, armed with state of the art, high tech tools and computers, picked up the SL ball. Putterman, Robert A. Hiller and Bradley P. Barber at UCLA took the lead, publishing many papers on SL, but the one that sparked my imagination, was now the famous issue of the February 1995 Vol.272, Scientific American.

Despite the volumes of papers to date on SBSL, the actual mechanism by which low-energy sound waves can concentrate enough energy in a small enough volume to cause the emission of light is still unsolved. It requires a concentration of energy by about a factor of one

The Silent Gospel

trillion, and to make matters more complicated, the wavelength of the emitted light is very short; the spectrum extends well into the ultraviolet and beyond. We need to understand that shorter wavelength light has higher energy. The observed spectrum of emitted light seems to indicate a temperature in the SL bubble of at least 10,000 degrees Celsius, and possibly a temperature in excess of one million degrees Celsius. These are temperatures hotter then those found on our sun. Another difficulty is in measuring the conditions inside a pulsating bubble whose diameter is measured in micrometers. Yet today, due to the efforts of these groundbreaking researchers, anyone with equipment costing as little as $200 dollars can now produce single bubble sonoluminescence (SBSL). Alas, making and determining the characteristic is only half the puzzle and the easiest part at that, it turns out. Determining the mechanisms for the phenomena has proved far more challenging and interesting because in doing so our notion of physics is again being tweaked.

SL *(Sonoluminescence)*

In this age of "bigger is better" extravaganzas, the ability to excite, stimulate and create wonder by the agonizingly simple is often lost. Looking at a bubble of air suspended in a flask, implode into a tiny, short star-like burst of light, for most of us would end with a blank pained expression that often accompanies boredom. The scale and the effect are a minimalist dream. Raised on glamour and celebrity, surrounded by sound bites, headline news and the fast edit of TV advertising, an age where speed is king, it's odd that SL with its supersonic mach 4 collapse speeds would not gain more notoriety.

So what if the bubble is gone and this tiny spark of light flashes before it blinks out of existence! What is sexy about that? We see lots of brief light flashes in our daily lives, like lightening flashes and lightning bug flashes, to name a few. Well, to a growing number of souls it is very sexy indeed and on closer inspection the particulars yield why this subject is of such interest and why it stimulates wonder, awe and excitement to the swelling numbers of people.

Some of the interesting facts about SL are the following:
- Suspended in a spherical flask of water is one air bubble 5 microns in size.
- Pass ultrasonic (high frequency sound) waves through that 5 microns air bubble and in super slow motion what

- would be seen is that the 5 micron air bubble expands to 50 microns and creates a near vacuum state inside the bubble itself. Then in an instant, the bubble collapses down to 0.1-1.0 Micron.
- The bubble's temperature reaches an estimated 10,000° C to possibly more than 1 million degrees C., temperatures hotter than the surface of the sun and light pulses are emitted from the air bubble before it exits this dimension.
- The entire process occurs in milliseconds but a millisecond of temperatures in those ranges one would think would heat the liquid somewhat? But it does not. Scientists have found little if any heat (energy) released into the surrounding liquid. Witnessed are temperatures estimated as hot as the corona of our sun yet little if any energy is released into the liquid!
- Another thing amazing the researchers are the extreme pressures generated. Pressures as high as 200Mbar (1Mbar = 10^{11} Pa) in the core of the imploding bubble. This pressure is equal to $1.974*10^8$ or 19,743,336 atmospheres (atm). One atmosphere (1 atm) is the amount of pressure that we live in at sea level.
- Another curiosity is in the use of different gases other then oxygen and or doping of the surrounding water with noble gases. One example is in the doping of the surrounding water with 1% Argon gas, the emission of light grows by a factor of >100. Other noble gases also have shown an affect on the amount of photons emitted.
- Our now famous Seth Putterman at UCLA says, "The light emitted from the implosive action extends into the ultraviolet, indicating temperatures of 10,000 to possibly 1 million degrees C." and that the speed of the collapse is "supersonic" around mach 4.

William Moss, a physicist well acquainted with this subject, works at Lawrence Livermore National Laboratory in Livermore, California. He says, "The key to this process is implosion". At the time of the writing of this material Moss is one of the leading investigators of Sonoluminescence in the United States. The reason for this expertise is because Lawrence Livermore National Laboratory's specialty is implosion. This lab was primarily created for researching energy focusing on the ways thermonuclear powered bombs go "boom". Later it branched out into other energy sources like fusion and laser, but all the while implosion is what they model best. This world famous research lab has the finest of specialized tools, computers, codes and simulations to study implosion. Moss works with codes designed to deal with the imploding geometries of laser fusion.

The following quote is from the aptly named article "A Star in a Jar", found in the December 1998, Popular Science.

> "Using weapons code to simulate the fluid dynamics of a collapsing, gas filled bubble, Moss says his calculations show that a shock wave strengthens as it nears the bubble (spherical) center. There, where heating is maximum, atoms and or molecules that make up the gas begin to break down, forming a plasma - a collection of partially ionized particles and electrons. The hot gas emits light by a torrential cascade of energy – in a quadrillionths of a second – to create the light pulses."

Currently there are six major theories that have been advanced to explain the mechanism(s) involved in sonoluminescence. None of these theories completely accounts for all the reported properties that encompass the richly varied spectral, dynamical, and chemical sensitivities displayed by this phenomenon. The six basic theories to date are:

- Shock Wave Theory
- Jet Formation
- Solidification at High Pressure
- Collision Induced Emission
- Gas Scintillators
- Quantum Vacuum Radiation

Reasons for interest in SL vary widely from belief that it might be a useful energy source for space travel, to thermonuclear fusion in a jar. Some find interest in its visible connection to the Zero Point Field or as a means of transmuting toxic waste into harmless elements. For me it is a visible process demonstrating the power of coherent recursive implosive waveforms with the bonus of also producing a flash of ultraviolet light in a quadrillionth of a second. Because of this I've gravitated to one of the more innovative theories, to my knowledge, first proposed by Claudia Eberlein, formally of Cambridge University. She proposed that sonoluminescence might be a Quantum Vacuum phenomenon. Eberlein, now at the Cavendish Lab in Cambridge (UK), says that sonoluminescence may represent the first observable manifestation of quantum vacuum radiation. This scenario can be compared to the "Unruh Effect," a hypothetical phenomenon in which photons are emitted by a mirror accelerating through a vacuum.

The Unruh-Casimir Effect

At the core of the Unruh-Casimir Effect theory, as well as modern quantum physics is the precept that unseeable virtual photons abound in a vacuum. Making up the quantum vacuum are fluctuating electromagnetic waves of all possible wavelengths residing at their lowest possible state of rest (ground state), all with the tiniest of "residual random jiggle thanks to quantum fluctuations", bringing to our minds the Heisenberg Uncertainty Principle. This blinding background sea of whole coherent light, known as the electromagnetic zero-point field (ZPF) of the quantum vacuum, is influenced by the properties of the surrounding medium. The most common medium to influence this omnipresent field is Mass, which is condensed light held by self-referencing resonance.

The Unruh Effect Eberlein speaks of is the detection of particles in a vacuum by an accelerated observer (detector); a problem first studied by W. Unruh. Quantum field theory predicts that if the detector is accelerated, its ground state can be spontaneously excited even when moving through the vacuum.

The Unruh Effect predicts radiation by non-inertially moving quantum mirrors. Furthermore, the accelerated detector will not find a vacuum but a thermal distribution of particles, as if it were in a thermal bath of blackbody radiation with a certain temperature coined the 'Unruh temperature'. Simplified, the Unruh Effect is a consequence of a dynamic Casimir Effect.

The Casimir Effect is named for the 1948 Dutch physicist Hendrick Casimir. It was he who realized that between two close parallel uncharged conducting plates, only those unseen electromagnetic waves whose wavelengths fit a whole number of times into the gap between the plates should be counted when calculating the vacuum energy of this space. He theorized that as the gap between the plates is narrowed, fewer waves could contribute to the vacuum energy, causing the energy density between the plates to fall below the energy density of the surrounding space. The result would be a tiny force pulling the plates together. This attractive force was named the Casimir Effect. Steven Lamoreaux measured the force in 1996, confirming the existence of this vast field of zero point energy. Yet the Casimir Effect is just one of several phenomena that have provided convincing evidence for the reality of this sea of light. As of the writing of this material the quantum vacuum has shifted from theory to a core piece of modern physics. As hard as it is for our senses to grasp this reality, good science has constantly demonstrated its existence and odd properties.

The Quantum Vacuum Radiation theory would pose that the rapidly moving air-water interface (where two media with different indices of refraction come together) would facilitate the conversion of virtual photons into real photons. The cascade of the imploding shock wave going superluminal would create an event horizon at the boundary between the two vacuum mirror states of the imploding air bubble vacuum and the quantum vacuum. This interface of the two vacuum states, the two infinities, would cancel each other; the asymmetry in photon to virtual photon would result in a massive photon release.

SL and The Silent Gospel

How is all this information relevant to the image on the Shroud? To make this relationship factual we need to connect a couple of dots in the puzzle. Bear with me as we take a brief scientific recap of the physical body, the subject of mind, and this weird domain of the quantum vacuum and how they all are related. First let me say that the process of sonoluminescence I use by way of example in order to demonstrate a process that has; exotic phase transition that results in disappearance, implosion models, a massive release of energy (photons) in a very brief moment in time, all caused by coherent rhythm ordering. Again when one system or process indicates coherency, through inference other systems and processes entrain also into coherence.

The Body

Scientifically described, the physical form is seen as a standing wave comprised of many coherent electromagnetic, oscillating platforms held in superposition (localized) by; the detector of mind, the ability to self-reference (awareness) those detected platforms, and some nonlocal component of this process (awareness) we call consciousness.

These standing wave interconnected packets held in space are open systems that allow for external and internal modulation. Modulation can manifest as evolution, growth, progress, and wellness; or disintegration, degeneration de-evolution and disease.

Even though the physical sciences understands all bodies including the human body, to be electromagnetic in nature, they can not deny that at the smallest physical architectures of every component, it operates in quantum entangled environments under non-local field mechanics. The physical may be a complex macro system filled with a chemical soup of molecules but at the core it is a quantum object operating under the influences of quantum mechanics. Vital operations for life materialize in virtual spontaneous seamless events, or so it seems from our limiting time perspective.

We then add to this the mounting data coming out of studies on the *nature of mind*, information that have the activities of recall occurring at architectures finer then those of neurons, information that positions the conclusion that mind originates *everywhere and nowhere;* within and beyond this three dimensional reality, from a virtual quantum domain, a domain that has its main characteristic idealized coherence.

Furthermore this field and the totality of its component parts are strongly influenced by emotions, which are now understood to be the bridge between the psycho-mental and physical processes, and that the perceiving mind determines the event state that will ensue within the physical structures.

In short at the core of all physical structures, at the root of all emotional chemistry, the base in recall and psycho-mental states; all have a quantum foundational component operating in spontaneously simultaneous manner.

Now we find that there are correlations between coherent excited states and physiological processes (emotions), with forms of sonoluminescence and chemiluminescence. These states of luminescence have been conclusively demonstrated to the level where some like my self are beginning to think that biological luminescence simply reflects a quantum yield in photons. The stronger the emotional state the higher the potential for a quantum yield in photons at the cellular level. It is my contention that the more excited (stronger) the emotional state the higher the potential in quantum yield. This is mainly due to the field to the background imbalance (asymmetry).

The question is what would allow for the appropriate harmonization that would generate the characteristics of sonoluminescence to unfold? The common sense answer is, to itself. To answer this question we had to look at the process of mind and its connection with recursive self-referencing (awareness.) This subject we covered in exhaustive detail in chapter thirteen. We did this because of the foundational role it plays in the thesis. So to summarize; **awareness is the ability to self-reference a field, and it requires two or more *aspects* to exist**. I found it easiest to understand the term aspect as it relates to this subject when I saw it as a facet or face of a diamond. There is one stone but with many faces.

When this recursive self-referencing is held in ordered balance harmony or symmetry, coherence within the field exists. This self-referencing balance (coherency) can and does exist in two basic forms. One is form of symmetry is created by polarity itself (magnet) and the second in fields with phase and or frequency singularity, like lasers and or superconductive Meissner Fields. Both types can be open nonlinear systems; the same as it appears is also true with mind.

The two key aspects of mind (soul and ego), from a physics perspective, is that they are, in perspective, anchored in two opposing realities/domains. One, the ego, is centered in time-space, is active and focused on vibratory movement, the other is in non-localized timeless stillness with an eternal perspective. It is plain to see that these two realities are two opposed states, yet each has the ability to act as a photonic localizing switch in the forming of experiential existence.

The paradox, researchers have found, is that even the egoic mind and basic recall are rooted in the fuzzy haze of non-local quantum mechanical laws. Therefore the two core parameters of self are rooted in the non-local timeless. Again it is as the sages have said, a mirrors game, played by the root aware intelligence forming the play (Lila), which in Eastern mystical traditions is termed *maya*, loosely translated becomes *illusion*. In truth *maya* is the delusory power inherent in the structure of creation, by which the One appears as many.

The mirroring of these key components is what needs to be aligned into harmonious attunement. Mysticism tells us that the heart is constantly under the pulling force of each of these two powerful forces. That each has its own agenda: one is soul evolution (remembrance) and the other is to secure physical longevity. Mystical tradition also tells us that the little "I" (ego) is really striving to be immortal like its primordial other half and that this impulse hints at the greater divine plan, one summarized in the phrase, *heaven on earth*.

The question I would like to pose and am attempting to answer in detail is: *what would happen to the physical form if these two key aspects of self were to perfectly mirror each other and this to the field/intelligence they arise within?* In other words, what would ensue in the moment if Divine Intelligence were fully actualized in physical form? If coherent stable phase unity were to take place? What result would come to pass if the Intelligence of the Absolute, the soul and physical where all on the same page consciously?

The Physical Form

The physical form is an embedded, dual, counter-rotating toroidal field of self-referencing electromagnetic spectrum, referenced via resonance and entrained via the base long wave fundamental. At the center of this torus field lays a phase singularity, a still point.

If one had the eyes to see it, the field of moving energy of our body would poetically look something like a large spiral galaxy ranging out past the physical membrane by at least ten feet. The shape of this field modulates with each beat slightly. The two extremes of shape are a circular global geometry and a more egg shape.

This electromagnetic field, set up and maintained by the beating of the heart, has embedded within it the base communication codes for all operating systems. The phase singularity or center point for the entire field is also found in the locale of the cardiac matrix. A phase singularity is the point at which the two vortices touch. This is found at the center point of this dynamic geometry. It is a zone where time-space falls into ambiguity, yet out of this point magically comes a returning self-referencing echo that continues the process of recursive referencing and communications.

This only can make a little sense when we begin to see ourselves as quantum objects stimulated into vibration by this notion of identity. For even in pure science we are understood to be residing within a vacuum of pure coherent light, dancing, quantum holographic mirrors reflecting the virtual whole, segmented by perception and the creation of this idea of self.

As seen by current physics, humanity and its universe is a mirrors game built and sustained by the collective perception of the consciousness observing the play of life. Life is a quantum detector stimulating the quantum vacuum, influencing the Zero Point medium into phase specific oscillations. In short we are *oscillating detector-mirrors moving through a thermal field of still points of very alive conscious light*.

The Unruh Effect predicts that, the accelerated detector would encounter a thermal distribution of particles, as if it were in a thermal bath of blackbody radiation, and that these accelerated quantum mirrors will produce radiation. Sonoluminescence appears to be direct dynamic evidence of the already proven Casimir Effect.

To envision this possibility one is required to abstractly view our physical field, as electromagnetic. It modulates and fluctuates with every bit of stimulus it touches. When the field idealizes a coherent state, the matrix of coherent platforms aligns with the base fundamental of the whole sea of light, via Golden Mean-phi relationships producing stable recursion. The field aligns in phi-phase resonance; The internal and external velocities and pressures synchronize in a relationship that allows for sustained scale invariant coherent implosion of the waveform, its frequencies and corresponding velocities cascade down the vortices of the toroid toward light speed and beyond. In the ideal a phase transition occurs where the phase singularity expands briefly to inhabit the whole and then implodes.

The coherent superposition of the human electromagnetic field (bubble) in a moment reflects the collapsing vacuum of the air bubble, a perfect mirroring, and produces a flawless reflection resulting in some form of Unruh Effect or Hawking Radiation.

When idealized, the black hole or vacuum cavitation causes a plasma phase transition of the elements resulting from the asymmetry of the vacuum. The form undergoes a rapid phase transition as it exits from this dimension into one that it is now in perfect phase resonant with the Quantum Zero Point itself. When *idealized* within all the aspects of self, the template and form phase transitions in a high-energy, microsecond flash of light. The Rainbow or Golden Body is formed.

Like Eberlein Theory for SL, I believe the light that resulted in the creation of the Shroud was emitted by the vacuum surrounding the imploding, or massive centering, forces created by an idealized coherent resonant waveform comprising the now coherent platforms of the physical body.

As the whole body vibrates with the primal sound of AUM, a merging (baptism) of Self in the stream of the Holy Sound Aum (Pranava) occurs, and this merging manifests spontaneously through, "…the energetic tendency of the heart's natural love."

It is this emotional state idealized to compassion that allows the scale invariant, ratio depended sustainability, among the various scales of coherent platforms in operation (scales of EM), creating a waveform in phase singular resonance with the Quantum Zero Point domain. When fully anchored and sustained consciously, the extreme centering of the toroidal forces produces a rapid phase transition in the elements comprising the form.

The physical electromagnetic coherent torus bubble held in superposition, in the case of the Shroud, I presume to be Jesus, is massaged in coherent pulsed phase. This organically creates constructive implosive centering forces down the dual perfectly symmetrical vortices of the waveform. They rapidly cascade towards the center at super-luminal speeds, toward the zero point termed a phase singularity at the heart of the waveform. In just one aspect of this process the internal gases, including oxygen, start the sonoluminescence process as described in detail above. The phonon waves are massaged past ultrasonic speeds. The implosion/compression forces cause asymmetry of the vacuum causing an emission of radiation in the ultraviolet range or higher as the vacuum oscillates back to symmetry and ground state. The emission of radiation would be high, intense and ultra brief. It would produce a fire that does not consume!

Chapter Nineteen

Golden Ratio - Golden Mean - Golden Number - Phi Golden Section - Logos - The Word

"Blessed are the pure in Heart for they shall see God." Matthew 5:8

The Golden Number, Golden Section, Golden Ratio, Golden Proportion, Phi, The "Word" and Logos, are all names referencing a unique proportional relationship, one found embedded within all life as well as the boundary of chaos. There is so much to this topic that entire books on the subject have been written. For the purposes of this book I will elaborate on the fundamental features of this relationship and what it implies. In doing so, clarification and the potential of the process outlined at the end of the last chapter will become more apparent.

The Divine Proportion
1.6180339887...

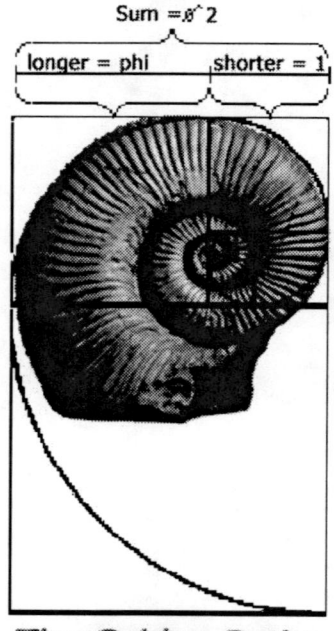

Sum = ϕ^2

longer = phi | shorter = 1

The Golden Ratio
Phi

Let us not lose the fact that a human being is an extremely large complex collective of independent life forms (cells) all with similar systems to the whole human body: digestion, immune, energy production, reproduction and communications to name a few of the key operations. And all these cells have molecules and proteins acting as part of these processes, all vibrating in a sea of vibrations. Calculating the amount of independent yet inter-dependent vibrating platforms operating in one individual at any one moment in time would be a staggering feat. Yet the mathematical and geometrical Golden Principle that follows allows them all to nest, regardless of scale, in a unique form of coherent phase resonance. For this to occur in the ideal, even the neural activity produced from on-going emotional states would need to produce a song that was on locked step with the constant primal hum.

Fundamental Features of the Golden Mean

The Golden Mean is the only possible geometric and arithmetic expansion and partitioning (proportional division) of One using two terms with the third being one itself. Due to this fundamental characteristic, it represents an archetypal fractal in that it preserves its relationship with itself in the most economical, yet mathematically robust manner.

This unique proportional relationship, which preserves inherent similarities under scaling, is that of conformal symmetries with topological consequences that are themselves invariant. This ability to expand and/or partition yet not change while undergoing transformation is self-similarity exemplified and defines this proportion as a fractal. Yet even more important is the fact that this elegant proportional relationship appears to bridge chaos and form mathematically and geometrically, acting as a foundational relationship between the Quantum Vacuum and subatomic building blocks that construct our 3D world. It is my contention that this particular irrational number allows for the conceptualization of the creation of awareness and mind. At the same time this mathematical signpost points to a rationale for the creation of diversity within a unified holographic singularity. Because of these fundamental characteristics, and because it is thought to mirror the primal movement within creation, it was designated as Golden by the ancients. Gold's value lies in its unique features which are its total immunity to decay, it is an excellent conductor, can be pounded into the thinnest of sheets, twisted into the thinnest of wire, and sliced into micro-sliced atoms in width, all without losing its fundamental nature. Another aspect of gold is that it is found naturally in this form and requires no processing by man to produce it. I find it interesting that Christians of antiquity related this 'golden' proportional symbol to the Son of God.

At the core, the Golden Mean is a proportional relationship that during transforms maintains a direct self-similar mirroring of itself. The Christian mystic Hildegard is quoted as saying, "Everything that is in the Heavens, on the earth, and under the earth, is penetrated with connectedness, penetrated with relatedness." (pp 19, <u>The Coming of the Cosmic Christ,</u> Matthew Fox (Hidegard, HB 41, <u>Meditations with Hildegard of Bingen,</u> Gabriel Uhlein, (Santa Fe, N.M. Bear & Co. 1982)

Meister Eckhart, the 13th Century German Christian mystic, also put forward this concept of relatedness when he said; "Relation is the essence of everything that is." (pp 19 <u>The Coming of the Cosmic Christ,</u> by Matthew Fox, BR 198 i.e. from and earlier work <u>Breakthrough: Meister Eckhart's Creation Spirituality in New Translation,</u> Matthew Fox 9Garden City, N.Y.; Doubleday & Co. 1980) One need only look closely at the opening words in the gospel of St. John to see that the creative moment, or original scission of which he writes, intuitively describes the geometric implications of the Golden Proportion.

> "In the beginning was the Word (or in Greek, Logos, the controlling principle of the universe, Logos also is often identified as the second person of the Trinity) and the Word was with God (the phrase 'with God' can also be read 'in God') and the Word was God." (The sustaining creative force). The proportion "is with God" (the part of the whole), and "is God" (the whole, or perhaps each part seen non-dualistically AS the whole).

Numbers

Numbers are symbols, and like letters or any other sign, they point to something other than themselves. They exist only to represent or mirror a concept of existence. Numbers can be Whole (1,2,3…), and represent a whole object like an apple, or a ratio of one or two whole numbers, these collectively are known as rational numbers (1,2,3… etc.). However, there is also an odd category of numbers termed Irrational Numbers that cannot be expressed as a fraction or a Whole Number. Of the Irrational Numbers, the Transcendental Numbers are the most curious, for not only are these numbers not expressible as a fraction of whole numbers, they are not of any integer polynomial. The numbers after the decimal point never complete, never end, precision is never reached. For example, Pi (the ratio of a circle's circumference to its diameter), is a transcendental number. Perhaps something as universal as the circle gives us a clue about how wonderfully mysterious life really is and why the circle (O) is the symbol for the void, or as we have come to know it, no-thing. Computer programs created to search for a conclusion have run these mystical numbers out into the black hole of infinity and yet they defy resolution. Transcendental means, of course, beyond comprehension, and any study of these numerical oddities certainly stretches one's imagination. Mathematicians jokingly imply that the study of Irrational Numbers is as close as the rational mind can ever get to an understanding of God (Creative Principle). Scholars on the subject believe that Irrational Numbers were originally uncovered with the discovery of the Golden Ratio. (A geometric and arithmetic expansion and partitioning (proportional division) of One using two terms with the third being one itself.)

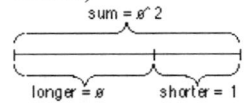

$$sum = \phi^2$$
$$longer = \phi \quad shorter = 1$$

Phi

One of the most interesting of the irrational numbers is phi. Phi is the numerical equivalent of this unique golden proportional relationship; i.e., a relationship of 1 to the irrational .6180339..., or alternately 1 to 1.6180339... . (The decimal never ends). The numerical value of phi points to something far greater than a few characters on a typed page. It hints at a dynamic relationship that is the quintessential creative duality within the unity of the Absolute. It is the most intimate of all relationships in that it is a direct non-compromised relationship with itself; a relationship that appears to be the foundation of aesthetics and our notion of beauty as well as nature's base unit for design.

These mystical golden qualities can be referenced in mathematical, geometric and harmonic terms, but it is first and foremost a proportional relationship, an archetypal fractal exemplifying self-similarity. Reason loves this primal idea because mathematically and geometrically it conceptually symbolizes the ideal, the image of the perfection, the Original Unity itself. The Bible says that Man was made in the image and likeness of God, as is all Creation; it could not be any other way. Out of the primal Singularity came all, so in some base way all must in some way mirror that from which it arose within. For this reason, and a multiplicity of other reasons, this symbol of perfect relationship is the symbol for the Son of God, which, within this thesis, is totally appropriate. If we take theology out of the picture, this ideal relationship offers us a perfect mirroring of the Absolute impermanent ground of existence: the hum of the Zero Point, the jitter of the great womb of creation, and or the consciousness of the creative singularity.

First and foremost, the question we need to immediately address is this: why can't the proportional reflection just be 1:1, or divided in half? Why can't it be a rational number divided into two equal parts? In an odd paradoxical twist, it turns out that the dynamics needed for progression, extension and recursion from the Singularity of One requires an asymmetrical division, especially if a return path is to be established and maintained.

Like the certainty that comes from the Heisenberg Uncertainty Principle, that "no quantum object, such as a microscopic pendulum, can ever be brought completely to rest, any microscopic object will always possess a residual random jiggle thanks to quantum fluctuations." The irrational number of phi perfects that asymmetrical division with divine elegance because the symmetry always mirrors itself even under scaling. Phi proportion division is the perfect, creative divisionless movement of the Singularity of Unity. I say this because the Whole relates back and is contained within it and the mind itself finds this beautiful and elegant. This asymmetrical division produces a relationship that allows for infinite potential, possibility and growth. Out of light comes the rainbow of colors that fills the palette of creativity.

No term of the original scission (initial reflection or division) changes the characteristics and properties during subsequent transformation. It maintains itself coming and going, yet being asymmetrical in scale allows an open receptiveness that results in diversity. Phi proportion division is the connective movement that produces fractionation without separation; it allows morphology (life) to nest one within the other, allowing the roses to sit in the garden on a hill, in a state, on a continent. Landscapes, like a head of broccoli, resemble logarithmic spirals, displaying "self-similarity" under any magnification when inspected closely. Phi proportion division allows the vast potential and possibility of the Absolute to be embedded within all that arises within its womb. It allows creativity an infinite palette for design, for the canvas, medium and genius are all the same; a perfect holographic fractal of coherent light acting as connective tissue for quantum mechanics, mind and the birth of realities. ['See Chapter on Resonance Chapter 14] All other types of geometric progressions (expansions or other movements) preclude a return path to reference the original Unity. Since Phi uniquely is both a geometric and arithmetic mean, it is the method of uniting multiple "dimensions". Phi's golden elegance provides a model of evolution that has as its goal the image of the perfection reflected in the original Unity. The Golden Mean offers a mathematical and geometrical model allowing awareness to travel out in the illusion of mind yet remain intimately connected. One never knows if one is on the inside or outside of the Mobius Strip; the reason, of course, is because there is no outside or inside. This model agrees with most mystical understandings about the nature of Reality.

The Golden Division is the primal, uninterrupted proportion of One -- One being the symbol of God that allows the external progression, with the constant proportion reflecting the internal progression. The Golden Progression demonstrates the possibility of an evolution guided from within, from the initial image of the Divine Whole. More importantly, it allows for the return path of the idea of movement to reflect the Silent stillness of Alive Emptiness from which all is birthed. This sacred relationship allows the environment a laser-like, self-sustaining mirroring in an open loop system. It allows for the idea of movement to perfectly mirror the Ground of Being, yet form the notion of separateness. It allows perception to create differences, polarity if you will: near and far, dark and light, hot and cold, etc. Symmetrical equality, on the other hand, produces no differences, but rather acts to void each other out.

Look within any piece of a genuine holographic image and there you will find the image of the whole, yet when one looks at the whole, an image containing nothing but separate pieces is seen.

"Geometry has two great treasures: one is the Theorem of Pythagoras; the other, the division of a line into extreme and mean ratio. The first we may compare to a measure of gold; the second we may name a precious jewel." Johannes Kepler

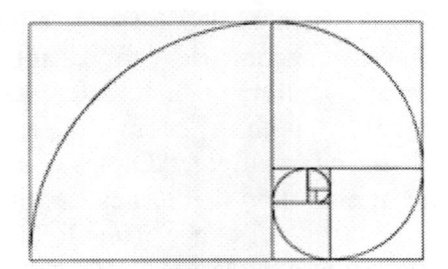

The Principle of Phi, the Golden Ratio

The Golden Mean/Phi is the archetypal fractal that preserves its relationship with itself, in the most economical, yet mathematically robust manner, preserving inherent similarities under scaling. As I've said, this is a fundamental characteristic of this prime relationship. It demands the structural properties of continuity and connectedness at all levels of relationship. It's a relationship that can be geometric and topological, as in the nature of waves held in superposition.

The human body when viewed as energy is considered as electromagnetic phenomena held in superposition as a standing wave. Under certain emotional states the heart's harmonics reflect powers of phi relatedness. It prompted the imagination to wonder what would develop within the biology if phi wave mechanics were maintained through focused attention or sustained balanced emotion. What scenario would develop if the Phi Principle were applied to this geometric field of energy?

The principle of Phi facilitates seamless touching (communications) through the In-PHI-knit (infinite) ability it offers in wave mechanics (motion and behavior). It permits wavelengths and velocities to multiply, add and divide by itself or any root of itself, producing harmonic scale invariant constructive Electromagnetic Wave Interference, meaning that electromagnetic waves/particles can exist (nest) in the same space without destructively interfering (dissonance) with each other, regardless of the spectrum of these waves, as long as their frequencies are related (ordered) by the golden (phi) ratio.

This level of nondestructive interference produces laser-like phase discipline, theoretically making it possible for waves of differing velocities to travel to the zero point and back without dissipation or distortion. In the year 2000, experiments carried out by Dr Lijun Wang's team at the NEC research institute in Princeton, demonstrated pulsed speeds of 300 times the speed of light. These experiments proved that light could move faster than the conventionally agreed on 186,000 miles per second. In these experiments "physicists sent a pulse of laser light through cesium vapor so quickly that it left the chamber before it had even finished entering. The pulse traveled 310 times the distance it would have covered if the chamber had contained a vacuum." [12]

"In effect it (the pulse of laser light) existed in two places at once, a phenomenon that Wang explains by saying it traveled 300 times faster than light." [13]

When the Phi Principle is imposed on wave mechanics it allows communications (information and energy transference) to have superluminal (faster then the speed of light), simultaneous, and instantaneous characteristics. Theoretically, phased phi pulsing defies the speed of light and the domain of time and space, giving a spin path to a wave (via vortex mechanics) that will take it to the zero point domain. Again it is my contention that the more important fact is the resonance generated during sustained episodes of phi entrainment. The reason is that the Phi Principle allows different scales of wavelengths the ability to self-reference, self-identify, self-regulate, and self-organize yet nest fractally within the whole without the production of dissonance. The Phi Principle theoretically perfects maximum exposure/minimum superposition of objects especially those of a biological nature. This phenomenon in the plant kingdom, called phyllotaxis, divides a circle into golden ratio proportions so that statistically each new leaf gets the most sunlight possible for its position around the stem to which it is attached (maximum exposure in a minimum of space). If one traced the upward spiral created by the birth and growth of each new leaf you would have a phi logarithmic spiral similar to those reflected in the seed pattern of sunflowers and cone shape on some seashells.

This PHI-cycle (physical) may well be the perfect relationship for biological systems for it would bring to absolute minimum stresses within the body, and the reason is due to the constructive interference

---

[12] http://www.skybooksusa.com/time-travel/physics/gas.htm http://www.skybooksusa.com/time-travel/physics/gas.htm

[13] http://www.sunday-times.co.uk/news/pages/sti/2000/06/04/stifgnusa01007.html

and the seamless communications between the various scales of resonance and or electromagnetic energy operating, all of which would produce ideal coherent phase when sustained over time. It is both common sense and medical knowledge that the absence of stress (electromagnetic dissonance) produces both mental and physical well-being. Stress from an electromagnetic perspective is simply systems not in phase with each other, as was shown in the HRV material earlier in the book.

The Phi Principle creates optimized fractal coherency among the dimensional scales of waves, producing dimensional invariant order and balance and ultimately a unified field with similar characteristics to a Type 1 Superconductor. It also theoretically perfects due to the inherent self-similarity and topographical invariant characteristic of an idealized notion of wave compression, implosion, centering, embedding, and information density, when modeled within toroidal form, which as it happens is the geometry of the electromagnetic information as viewed from the heart. The ideal symmetry produced in this waveform creates logarithmic spiraling, phi-phased vortices of energy that piggyback their wavelengths and velocities down to the heart, into the phase singularity and past the speed of light. (Note, at the same moment it enters, it reflects back out of this domain to generate the next pulse in the waveform, one in symmetry to the entering vortices.) The mathematical and geometrical ability to scale invariantly embeds energy recursively without dissipation or distortion, sums up to idealizing the vortex mechanics allowing information to transfer in apparent superluminal fashion.

Most interesting is that the Phi Principle, symbolized as an archetypal fractal model, creates the model for an archetypal, multidimensional holograph with optimum coherency (internal and external balance). The relationship of wave-phase is present in all proportions and hierarchies. The symphony tunes and harmonizes with a rhythm that aids and supports the nested harmonic hierarchies comprising the collective waveform. The various scales of oscillating architectural platforms phase (when sustained over time) into a phi coherent resonance. This resonance vibration, as a whole, produces the fundamental (tone), which in this case is scale invariant to the other vibrations producing the various harmonics. The small reflect the larger in every way known at this time.

Phase Singularity

A helpful example of a phase singularity is to consider it as the location where all the longitude lines merge into a diaphanous ambiguity at the South Pole. The dot at the center is the timeless Zero Point where the spin of vortex energy enters one-pointedness. This one-pointedness is a singularity. When discussing pulses of energy like the heartbeat, the point at the very center of this waveform of spinning energy is thought of as a phase singularity. It is the place where all the various scales of electromagnetic energy phase into one-pointedness. I believe that it is the point of self-referencing for an object held in superposition. This point by its very nature is theoretically timeless.

Mystics share with us that a still point is within the heart of each of us and this is our direct connection experientially with the Divine. A point of connection where we are able to transcend the limitations of the polarized world, our jobs and complex lives, and connect to the heart of the Universe. A space that exists in all of us that, when experienced, allows each of us to grow closer to the loving-kindness and compassion required for a stable shift in perception.

All objects, whether they are atoms or complex biology, construct form via linked, multi-layered, self-referencing electromagnetic fields and the resonance they produce. The specific ordered development from a single cell (zygote or seed) to a fully-grown human adult or oak tree occurs by the process of going within to find the next move in growth. It self-references (goes within) to find the next steps required in order to complete its mature development. This process demands elevated levels of order for the unfolding to occur exactly right, yet openness to receive information, energy and communications required for growth. The ability to reference (detected) in time-space is a needed element for form to exist in superposition (location). This ultra rapid referencing has been calculated to happen at 10^{44} times per second, which is much faster than science can currently measure.

It appears that a phi related torus, mathematically and geometrically, is the best waveform for self-referencing and self-sustaining wave order. As it turns out, the energy field generated by the heart, neutrinos, the planet earth itself, the solar system, and galaxies all have a magnetic field that is basically toroidal in shape. The torus shape provides the fractal holographic blueprint for interconnectedness allowing for a cosmic uni-verse to be sung.

Phi, the Golden Mean, perfects self-referencing shape in the torus, and by extension, the multidimensional shape known in the technical literature as a KAM-tori fractal.

The Form of Recursive Energy: Tori / Torus/Toroidal- The Geometry of Self-Referencing; Nested Dual Counter Rotating Vortices of Phased Symmetry.

The key to understanding the human energy field is to first understand the form and the relating geometry of a torus. The basic shape of a torus (plural is tori, adjective is toroid, or toroidal) is the surface of an inner tube or a doughnut.

A torus, when idealized by incorporating the phi proportion, is the optimum geometry for energy self-referencing and self-sustaining. Smoke rings and ripples in a lake formed from a thrown rock are all examples of torus shapes momentarily self-referencing, even as they expand outward from the initial center point of origin. The form returns with energy and information about itself to form the next rendition of itself even as it expands outward. The same would be true for going inward.

The human energy field, as measured from the heart, is toroidal in form. Researchers at the HeartMath Institute in California claim that this energy field extends measurably out from the physical body by at least ten feet. The difference with the shape of these toroidal fields is that they are more like an apple with the two indented vortices just touching in the center. The major and minor axes are mathematically the same value, so the "hole" in the donut comes exactly to a point instead of the more traditional tube form. That point is the locale for the phase singularity. The energies spin out and are pulled in simultaneously in a dual counter rotating symmetry.√ This field of energies modulates with each beat and has two maximum extreme geometric shapes based on the two fundamentals found in the relationship of the low frequency harmonic during internal cardiac coherency. One fundamental is more one-to-one related causing a more circular/global shaped field while the other is more oval/egg shaped resulting from the phi ordering. (Note, think of the egg lying on its side with the long length extending out past the arms.)

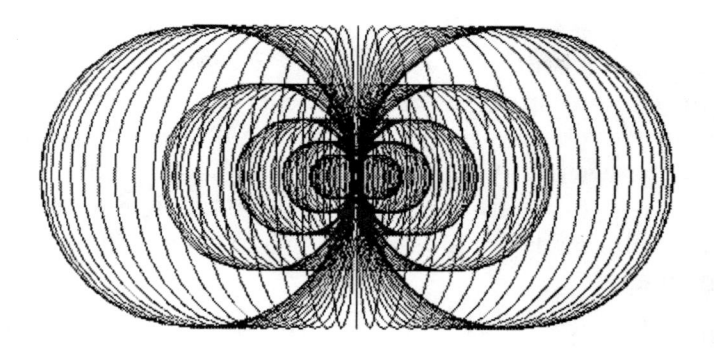

This overall shape is important in determining the root fundamental anchoring coherency and by association, the resonance and the longevity of the form.

Biological longevity is electromagnetic sustainability referenced and reflected electrically, it is phase coherency, and it is my belief that in the years to come science will find that specific phi rooted photonic resonance will produce idealized waveform longevity. The reason they will discover it is because it hums in harmony with the field resonance of the Zero Point domain. This uni-verse will produce stability in the form, a crystos that is incorruptible. Remember, phi is an irrational number and as such is never perfected into a rational number; it always carries with it a bit of drag resulting in quantum jitter. The more exacting is the phi-rooted relationship of the constantly modulating waveform, the greater the balance in the branches of the Autonomic Nervous System. This, in turn, synchronizes other systems that fall under the umbrella of this broad network of neural activity.

The market will soon produce the devices that use lasers to modulate cells back into vibrational resonance, so allowing connectivity. Initially, cancer is a renegade cell that has gone out on its own, reproducing and acting at will regardless of the surrounding other cells. Even when the surrounding cells attempt to communicate connectivity to this renegade cell, it perceives the communication as attacks and walls itself off. At this point the immune system jumps in and the cell reacts by rapidly reproducing itself, forming a tumor.

Unique phi phasing of systems allows emotional characteristics like peace, openness, receptivity, etc., to rise organically. More accurately, the closer to phi relatedness the resonance modulating the standing wave form (i.e. the tori) is held in superposition, the more seamless are the self-referencing communications. This Phi-related-resonance makes it easier to sustain; because stresses are not formed in the nervous system. This allows the body's resources to deal with challenges to its equilibrium. When these are met, ease is felt. Heart Rate Variability, psycho-physiological and neural research have clearly demonstrated that lack of internal stress allows for greater immune response, which in turn reflects greater mental wellbeing, emotional happiness, and ultimately, as this research has shown, translates into physical longevity.

Some privately say that Philosophy as understood in the ancient libraries of Alexandria, Egypt, originally was the study of Phi-lo-sophy, or The foundation of Golden Mean Wisdom.

When the distance between frequencies (implied base fundamental) is aligned in phi related coherency, the spiraling vortices also phase into phi relatedness. As this occurs, the torus waveform modulates into a Golden Mean proportion, forming a well balanced, self-referencing symmetry. Maintaining this well-formed field requires the skill of maintaining a unique state of mind, a state developed by yogis with highly honed concentration. The sustained special waveform with its equally unique resonance (fundamental) enables info-energy synchronization of bodies at any scale; theoretically synchronization between dimensions also becomes possible. "Resonance leads to two types of trajectories: the first are trajectories with normal behavior, well known through the study of two-bodies problem. The second are trajectories with stochastic behavior." (Konstantin) The stochastic behavior produced from resonance demands random variables, and when combined with the irrational numerological component spoken of earlier in this chapter, forms the open aspect that biological systems require to grow and evolve, even consciously.

A secondary characteristic evolves when the waveform modulates into this phi related torus shape. The resonance formed is in resonance with the event horizon at the edge of chaos -- a space that defines the edge of the quantum vacuum of stillness. I use the term event horizon here because it is the theoretical edge/circumference point at which no light appears to emanate (black hole), or the event boundary for light speed. Theoretical validation done by numerical simulations has demonstrated that this Hidden Harmony has Golden Mean roots. A further connection to this link to the edge of chaos arose out of V. I. Arnold, and J. Moser's confirmation of A.N. Kolmogorov's mathematical predictions on the stability of the Solar System. The confirmed theorem became known as the KAM Theorem, which we will speak of shortly.

My greatest curiosity is with the fact that the spiraling waveform of electromagnetic harmonics reemerges from that dimensionless point of ambiguity to continue its dance in the cycle we call life. The spiraling mass of energies whirl down to a point and then out again with every beat of the heart. If that in itself is not weird, I'm not sure what is. This is why I term that vector with no point, 'the point of Self-Referencing'. When this point is consciously touched, it is the place of Self-realization.

Vortices

The easiest way I've found to help individuals imagine the shape of this field of energy is to look at a large apple. The major difference is that the two indented cone shapes at the top and bottom of the apple are vortices that touch in the center at each other's point. To understand the way this energy spins into a vortex (cone shape), look at water spiraling down the drain as a tub empties. The water spinning down has air spiraling up within the same shape at the same time. These dual counter-rotating actions occur simultaneously at both indented ends of the torus shape. This produces, in effect, two interwoven waveforms in counter-rotating symmetry within the same form. The symmetry is hemispherical as well as rotational around the axis of spin. In other words, the energy spinning out the bottom is rotating in balance to be sucked into the top and vise versa. When the vortices are idealized by phi, the centering pull of the two hemispherical mirrored vortices sustains in a highly balanced and ordered symmetry. In short, the rotational symmetry on all axes of spin is the same for both hemispheres in a manner that constructively adds and multiplies wave interference. It produces a state of sustainable phase.

The human torus field appears able to modulate from a more global sphere shape to an oval egg shape with the longer side of the egg shape extending out past the arms, similar to the shape of a spinning galaxy. These two fundamental, three-dimensional shapes are at the heart of all standing waves of energy (the wavicle). The more egg shape in its ideal form is phi proportion in its major to minor axis ratio. The modulation happens due to internal and or external energetic stimulus. From my reading of it, the more open one feels, the more egg like the shape, whereas the more contracted (closed or stressed) one feels, the more spherical the shape becomes, it all has to do with the resonance being produced in the moment. One could make the geometrical case that all Platonics can nest within the dodecahedron and icosahedron forms which have phi proportions, abundantly demonstrating the intrinsic blueprint of phi to nest topographical varying forms morphologically within a whole. Indeed, all objects from subatomic particles, to atoms, molecules, and single celled life have torus shaped electromagnetic energy fields which nest in the larger forms they find themselves. When viewed from simply the energy alone, these fields of differing scales combine, forming multi-dimensional fractal that has come to be known as a KAM-tori.

(See Flower of Life image)

KAM tori

A.N. Kolmogorov, a Russian mathematician, developed a theory predicting the form and stability of the orbits of the planets. The theory was the byproduct of various efforts to find an answer to the question of whether or not our Solar System is stable. His student, V. I. Arnold, and the German mathematician, J. Moser, independently confirmed the theory he put forth. The theorem became known as the KAM Theorem, named for Kolmogorov, Arnold, and Moser

(KAM). The form predicted and confirmed in this theory is a multi-dimensional fractal known as a KAM-tori; basically tori rotating fractally around and within a large torus. The key to understanding the KAM theorem is the concept of an "invariant torus". All modulation remains in an overall invariant (constant) field held in coherence by the fundamental that forms the greater field. This theorem elegantly models the complex human field with its countless oscillating platforms.

The real beauty of this theorem is when you reverse this fractal back to the original, or last tori at the edge of chaos or pure randomness, the winding numbers that create this last torus are Golden Mean. In other words, the primal relationship parameters, the very foundation of this stable form, are Golden Mean. The binary two-part parameter of this toroidal form is oscillation, a form more efficient than rotation when it comes to energy conservation, and is the twofold 1 to .618... proportional relationship. I theorize that this primal relationship is the causal relationship in space-time micro-curving (bending/mirroring), which leads to oscillation, inertia, mass and gravitation. A NASA-funded study at the Lockheed Martin Advanced Technology Center confirmed with independent theoretical validation that, "distortion of the quantum vacuum in accelerated reference frames results in a force that appears to account for inertia. A further connection with general relativity has been drawn by Nickisch and Mollere (2002): zero-point fluctuations give rise to space-time micro-curvature effects yielding a complementary perspective on the origin of inertia."

The abstract continues, "Numerical simulations of this effect demonstrate the manner in which a fundamental particle without mass, e.g. an electron, acquires inertial properties; this also shows the apparent origin of particle spin along lines originally proposed by Schrödinger. Finally, we suggest that the heavier leptons (muon and tau) may be explainable as spatial-harmonic resonances of the (fundamental) electron. They would carry the same overall charge, but with the charge now having spatially lobed structure, each lobe of which would respond to higher frequency components of the electromagnetic quantum vacuum, thereby increasing the inertia and thus manifesting a heavier mass." [14] (Bernard Haisch, Alfonso Rueda, L.J. Nickisch, Jules Mollere)
(Update on an Electromagnetic Basis for Inertia, Gravitation, the Principle of Equivalence, Spin and Particle Mass Ratios)

To relate all this back to what this means to us personally, we return the conversation back to our findings using heart biofeedback instrumentation. Specifically the findings that emotionally receptive states produce coherent Golden Mean ordering within the harmonic present: in short, emotional states that could be interrupted as loving. These energetic states generate phi relatedness within the music being played to every cell and beyond by heart.

---

[14] (Bernard Haisch, Alfonso Rueda, L.J. Nickisch, Jules Mollere) General Relativity and Quantum Cosmology, abstract 0209016

http://www.arxiv.org/abs/gr-qc/0209016 Update on an Electromagnetic Basis for Inertia, Gravitation, the Principle of Equivalence, Spin and Particle Mass Ratios http://www.arxiv.org/IgnoreMe

"I think that gravitational attraction is an early form of compassion or care."
Brian Swimme-cosmologist

These studies are just a handful of many that quite clearly point to the fact that phi relatedness communes between finite and infinite attractors and as such, acts as the cohering agent via resonance in material construction.

In an asymmetrical manner, phi order reflects the absolute coherence of the quantum vacuum domain, becoming a base for bifurcating into symmetry, and acts to break oscillation back to ground state entropy and or stochastic chaos. Paradoxically, this means that it is the expander as well as the eroding drag that recycles that which strays (modulates) away from the primal relationship. It does this simply via the principles of resonance and entrainment, nothing more is ever needed. Because of these facts all morphology has it embedded within by necessity; to exist is to maintain Golden Mean relatedness.

This groundbreaking science of coherence and embedded resonance isn't just an abstract theory. When an individual feels open receptiveness, deep genuine appreciation, gratitude or compassionate love, the heart's electromagnetic field organizes in-root phi relationship. The torus energy form surrounding the human form modulates into a KAM-tori fractal. If sustained, the emotional feedback shifts to a deep calm peace. This occurs as the two branches of the Autonomic Nervous system synchronize in phased relationship. This is fully referenced in the chapter on Heart Rate Variability. It appears that evolution is looking for the ideal form to carry these two key characteristic qualities of coherence and variability in order to idealize communication; a communication that is sustainable, able to expand and to include all fractal versions of itself fully. Consciousness, it would seem, is evolving the form to embed all form consciously. The Big "C" Conscious Intelligence is allowing form to unfold/evolve to the point where the mirrors pass [each other] and the reflection produced is nil. It appears that Consciousness is looking to reflect its perfection in form, one which mirrors open and receptive, nondestructive communication in a stable waveform of light, able to commune on all levels of hierarchy, architecture, scale and dimension.

"The Golden Proportion represents indisputable proportional evidence of the possibility of conscious evolution as well as of an evolution of consciousness."[15]

Stable Light

David Bohm outlined the cosmic nature of quantum theory whereby the wave function appears as the effect of the interaction of the physical object with a cosmic field, endowing it with phase. This phase, in multiple oscillating platforms, emerges as a macroscopic object and also contains coherent performance. Through their quantum fluctuations, objects discover the configurations where the energy is minimum and, thus, where they might settle indefinitely, able to sustain a stable configuration.

Individuals that succeed in creating phi perfected Kam-tori "invariant torus" field relationships among the various coherent oscillating platforms of their physical field, stabilize the standing wave (and the form) via the idealized resonance and stability that is fundament with Golden Mean. The KAM-tori field is fractal to the primal base it operates within. Fields in Fundamental-Harmony demand self-referencing stability. The reason for this is because there is no destructive jitter acting on the field. Harmonic resonance is in place. The field then becomes an ideal fractal mirror, mirroring the Zero Point hum (Heisenberg's Uncertainty Principle). This ideal state of perfection is nearly impossible to sustain while operating in the day-to-day physical world. But at the moment of death skilled yogis and sages have repeatedly demonstrated the existence of this level of harmonic reality. There have been many examples such as Paramahansa Yogananda, where the bodies of yogis have maintained their form in beautiful perfection whether for days, weeks or years; verifying some underlying principle of crystallization, (Christos).

A recent example happened on December 1, 2004, at Rashi Gempil Ling Temple in Howell, New Jersey. Sermey Khensur Lobsang Tharchin Rinpoche, an eminent lama and renowned scholar of the Tibetan Gelukpa tradition, began his clear light meditation. He

---

[15] Robert Lawlors' 1982 book <u>Sacred Geometry</u>, pages 46-47 on the Golden Proportion

breathed his last breathe in the early evening of December 1, 2004 and remained in meditation and perfect physical form until December 6th. This occurred at the Temple which had been his principal residence for the past thirty years. An account of his transition was related on December 12, 2004, by Yongyal Rinpoche, a reincarnate lama from Sera Mey Monastery. He stated that this extraordinarily special person's holy body remained fresh with a special fragrance that lasted the duration of his five-day-long meditation (December 1 to December 6). This freshly preserved state was noticed until the very end of the fifth day, December 6, 2004 Khen Rinpoche completed the meditation. A ritual fire ceremony was performed on the grounds where the body was cremated December 7th. Local city officials were involved and acted as witnesses accounts claimed, so to make sure that no laws were broken during the Fire Puja, which is the burning (ritual-cremation) of the body on the Temple grounds. For five days the body of the lama remained unaffected by the onset of death. It is my humble opinion that only an individual so perfectly aligned in love could achieve this level of mastery.

The basis of the onset of coherence in matter occurs as a consequence of the various microscopic matter components' (atoms, electrons, etc.) electromagnetic fields all phasing or tuning together under this unique resonance. This collective resonance creates highly coherent, stable bonds. When the phasing is idealized and sustained, the form crystallizes allowing the individual to truly become a Son of God or simply the Christed One. 'Christos' to the Greeks, referred to the anointed one, but the term has the same roots as the word 'crystallize'. The body's resonant field, and thereby the architectural structure, becomes stable and highly invariant. Forming a crystallized packet as we read in the chapter [Chap 3] on the Siddhas. When fully maintained and all aspects of "I" are surrendered, the individual form mirrors the vacuum, creating a rapid implosion of the field. What results is a massive photon release at the edges of the event horizon. This field implosion and photon release manifests in what has been termed resurrection, ascension or an elemental-phase-transition back to the Intelligent Light, which creates and maintains it. It is the attainment which Buddhists call the *Rainbow Body*.

The Silent Gospel

Key Bullets In Dynamics of Condensation

- Coherence in matter is the spontaneous outcome of energy minimization. Coherence does not require work, but is stable and occurs at equilibrium!
- Maximum Exposure / Minimum Superposition; this phase symmetry is the key to optimum coherence and longevity of an object.
- Matter, is therefore, not a loose confederation of molecules, but a specific macroscopic object with a field or medium surrounding the space it inhabits.
- The medium could be regarded as a continuum of the old-fashioned classical physics (the ether).
- Normal condensed matter could be regarded as a two-phase system: a coherent phase that guarantees the wholeness of the system, and an incoherent phase that accounts for the entropy and, more generally, the *thermodynamics of the system.*
- Matter operates in time and space but is always being pulled back to a ground or zero fluctuation state. The reason for this is that all matter arises (condenses) from a Zero Point Field.
- The relationship to this omnipresent field is entropy.
- The idealized relationship, by its very nature, forms stability due to the scale invariant nature of the primal movement.

The understanding of the physical dynamics of condensation allows one to decipher a mountain of seemingly complex and thorny data about a wide range of condensed matter systems; from super fluids to superconductors, from Ferro magnets to liquids, from crystals to plasmas. No physical system can any longer keep its own secret and remain silent. The Silent Gospel has reflected these facts with those with eyes that *see*.

An example of this principle can be seen in the hydrogen bonds among water molecules. These bonds are not the cause of their molecular interactions. The protuberances of the electron molecular clouds do not exist in the isolated molecules themselves. Hydrogen bonds are now seen as the affects of coherent dynamics in liquid water which reshuffles the electron clouds producing the protuberances.

The living state is a two-phase system: a coherent phase that guarantees the wholeness of the system, and an incoherent phase that accounts for the entropy and, more generally, the thermodynamics of the system. Biology unfolds from a single cell or seed to complex organisms comprising hundreds of trillions of cells all working and operating together in wholeness. What if the coherence that guarantees wholes produced coherence that eliminated entropy producing a balanced state of equilibrium?

We humans have both wave and particle characteristics in the same moment. They are interconnected and are in fact different sides of the same coin. We are coherent as objects yet fluid, dynamic and evolving. We are condensed form and wave fields jitterbugging through an amniotic medium of energetic conscious stillness. This medium appears chaotic or empty because it is objectless and non-localized, yet by its very nature idealizes the notion and characteristics of idealized coherence, which is to say equilibrium.

Wave Coherence creates both matter and the flow from the omnipresent field called life. Massive complex coherence never sustains life except when the fundamental acting to perturb the collective is in resonance with Golden Mean. The scale invariant nature of phi wave geometry allows for a phased nesting of torus fields. Sustaining phase coherence requires recursive heterodyning (beat frequencies obtained from the sum and difference frequencies of any pair of interacting waves) both adding and multiplying (and or subtracting) the wavelength and velocities as well as the created resonance. This fractal principle creates 'centers' of gravity - the monopole and implosion – wave collapse in general.

"Stress is inner biofeedback, signaling you that frequencies are fighting within your system. The purpose of stress isn't to hurt you, but to let you know it is time to go back to the heart and start loving."
<u>The Hidden Power of the Heart</u>, Sara Paddison, (c) 1998, Planetary Publishing

'All That Is' exists within a rhythm. The beat of your own physical heart determines your base vibration in resonance. Your thinking mind acts to pull on the heartstrings as does the psyche anchored as soul. The heart desires peace, but is a faithful servant to the forces of mind. It will create for you, upon whatever your attention falls.

Guided from Within

With its vast energy, The Zero Point Field (ZPF) rests in its ground state near zero fluctuations. And the flux of the initial asymmetry forms a micro-curvature within the vacuum. As this field stabilizes, reflective energy is released and a cascade of photonic detection occurs. This is light/energy. The relationship of this primal bending, or core zero point hum, has a Golden Mean (1.6180339...) relationship. The ZPF being 1 and the movement, or curve to the whole, ideally reflected yet minimizing fragmentation without separation, is .618... or simply 1.6180339... This unique proportioning allows a symmetrical and asymmetrical branching in the primary formation of inertia, which becomes mass. It is the primary constructive interference that permits membrane building -- the Standing Waves of Light held in Superposition by the awareness formed by internal self-referencing. This act allows for self-assembly and an evolutionary guide from within. If it were not this way, there would be no sustaining growth or path of return. There would be no conscious awareness of that which is. The adding of additional, more rapidly accelerated spin, creates even more resistance to acceleration movement, i.e. mass/matter. Increasing the spin rates of the inherent energy increases density and mass. It produces a harmonic in a spatial environment anchored by a coherent ultra long wave resonant fundamental that resides at the boundary of the vacuum state similar to the last winding of a KAM tori. This unique resonant communication attracts in an invariant manner via the core relationship-primal winding at the edge of chaos and its relationship to pure information. The degree of strength is dependent on the coherence (equilibrium) of the standing wave. The depth of the sustaining, self-referencing and aware consciousness characteristics reflect the levels of Phi Coherence present. It appears that life on all levels builds/evolves/develops/attracts via this core relationship, and the reasons become clear as one realizes the unique characteristics and properties this very unique primal relationship inherits.

In early Christian philosophy this relationship was characterized in Greek by the concept known as *Logos*. Logos was there in the beginning of the universe and as such, it was the controlling principle of the universe. Logos was identified as the second person of the Trinity, *The Son*. And from Genesis, "In the beginning was the Word,

(Logos) and the Word (Logos) was with [in] God, and the Word (Logos) was God".

> Highly regarded guru of modern scientific theory, Professor Emeritus William Tiller states; "In modern physics the two main theoretical constructs are *quantum mechanics* and *relativity theory*. For these two to be internally self-consistent, their calculations require that the vacuum must contain an energy density 1094 grams per cubic centimeter. This means that in the vacuum contained within the volume of a single hydrogen atom there is, 'almost a trillion times as much energy as in all of the stars and all of the planets out to a radius of 20 billion light years!'"

The current idea modeled in physics tells us that all matter is 99.9% emptiness. And the small bit that is not emptiness is electromagnetic resonant phenomena. The small particles constructing this misty cloud are entangled in some mystical way with the vacuum-singularity of the Zero Point and Consciousness. The magic of all that we call life originates from the conscious tickling into a vibrating jitterbug. This silent ground state of being appears to be the rooted to consciousness. As Astrophysicist Bernhard Haisch of Stanford University wrote of this silent ground state, it is; "…a background sea of light…(and) The fact that the zero-point field is the lowest energy state makes it unobservable. We see things by way of contrast. The eye works by letting light fall on the otherwise dark retina. But if the eye were filled with light, there would be no darkness to afford a contrast. The zero-point field is such a blinding light. Since it is everywhere, inside and outside of us, permeating every atom in our bodies, we are effectively blind to it. It blinds us to its presence."

Summary

With attention and awareness we light up the resting ground state of information-potential with the mirrors of mind. And the interplay of oscillation forms a symphony of attraction and repulsion. The law of vibration dances into becoming. When the music connects in resonance, then mass, matter, form and inertia all scream onto the holographic dance floor producing the illusion of distance, velocity and time. Tickling that *blinding sea of still light*, even a little light changes the randomness of pure information into a cohering attraction that, in a vibrating montage, bonds are created that form all types of wave-particle interplay. Every form able to sustain its resonance, even if only for a moment in time, is self-referencing a standing-wave of attraction. An attraction held in superposition by the self-identifying detection of the field itself. The loop of vibrating music acts by the very nature of its form to recreate itself by touching the notes that it is. The symphony of oscillating-coherent-platforms creates a single note, a fundamental held as resonance. This is ones essence. It attracts and repels like any other resonance. The exception in this attraction game being the resonance produced by the relationship the ancients termed, Golden.

This magical illusion of light all occurs within the diaphanous vectoring of a grand singularity of pure information, which is the receptive womb of Creativity and Potentiality; the womb of saints, sages and Buddha's, you and your neighbor.

The Upanishads says, "Whether we know it or not, all things take on their existence from that which perceives them."

Chapter Twenty

Shroud Image Formation
Summary and Conclusion

Conscious Union and Formation of Coherent Scale Invariant Harmonic Fractal Resonance

The great saint Rumi says, "Don't look for water, be thirsty." In most mystical traditions yearning is understood to be the magnetic pull of God's longing for you. It's the natural attraction for peace felt by the heart coming from the soul. It is said to be the response to constant movement, a desire for stillness and rest. Like a moth drawn to the flame, we are drawn back to Spirit by the fire of longing, back to stillness by the restless heart. The stronger the longing the hotter the purifying fire, a fire fueled by the dross of form and identification. It burns form in all its appearances until the moment nothing left within your heart but Divine Stillness. A Stillness and the peace that comes from touching consciously that object-less Absolute that you are presently.

Those with an insatiable thirst are pulled to experience a non-noun, pure verb ultimate state of Being; the Presence of Aware Existence. Consciousness, by Divine grace, completes the looping of awareness and *fully* Realizes that which it is. Heart, Soul and Mind are merged into a single unified harmonic that is guided by the intelligent wisdom at the heart of all life. Allowing the yearning to pull without resistance allows deeper and deeper levels of experiencing this complete union of self. Those with knowledge mark these stations of conscious evolution. The non-judging eye *knows* Reality, but only to his or her *level of experience*. This notion may be hard to grasp but it is what the Great Masters have told us. Unity has a depth and range of experience. Consensus within the mystical sciences has the highest pinnacle in this plane of existence, a total merging with Reality. Interestingly to this researcher is that this final meditation also can produce a range of visible results during the final process. They range

The Silent Gospel

from an uncorrupt-ability of the body for varying lengths of time, to the complete dissolving of the body.

This process occurs normally at or near the time of death. Each final result carries with it a variance of by products such as: sweet flower like fragrances, inner skin radiance, aura-like emanations and in the ultimate cases a brilliant brief burst of light flashes as the body shrinks to the vanishing point. I realize that for some this might seem beyond the bounds of reason. But, I assure you, in these ancient traditions this is real.

The *longevity factor* in and of itself tends to support the existence of these phenomena. These teachings and practices would not continue for so very long if there were not some cases documented to support the philosophy and its associated practices. Another factor is the documentation of modern cases in both the East and in the West by neutral observers.

The premise of this work has been that Jesus and His resurrection story parallel many examples of the great saints of the planet who attained this highest level of union. And that His teachings and life example parallel teachings and methodology found in the Eastern Yogic Sciences. The reason for this correlation is the Eastern Spiritual philosophies have well delineated written science. It then makes it easier to correlate these ancient sciences to various Western scientific disciplines to construct a plausible modality in the creation of the Shroud Image. If I had come straight out and said that the image on the Shroud was Jesus and at the moment of the resurrection he vanished in a blinding flash of light, a light that embedded the cloth with his life-like image, and then gave the science of how this occurred, it would not have been convincing. But anchoring it to a science that has been around long before the times of Jesus, and then giving science to support that I felt would give it more credibility. The challenge for me then became making it plausible for Jesus to have learned or known about these ancient teachings.

To this end I found anthropological and archeological evidence which supports the possibility that a studious individual living in the Middle East had clear opportunity to receive spiritual cross-pollination of these same Eastern philosophies. This was a bonus, because Truth when genuinely realized, whether in a cave in India, the deserts of the Middle East, or in a major Western city, is the same. Regardless of race, culture or education, it makes no difference, individuals with enough yearning and grace blossom True Remembrance, no matter the life situation.

I pray that the similarities of the story of Jesus and His teachings, to the Eastern philosophies and their sciences, were sufficiently fashioned to allow the imagination free rein while delving into my thesis on the creation of the Shroud Image. Imagination, the forerunner of creation, is required when direct experience is missing. The correlations I found between the Eastern mystical sciences of Self-realization and Western science opened the imagined reality of these Higher Stations of experience to my rational mind long after my heart knew the reality.

Yearning pulled like a tiger with the inner voice echoing *All is ONE*. If this is so, then reason must be able to make sense of *it* even if *it* were no-thing reason could never fully grasp. I sensed the possibility of connecting all the pieces into a beautiful tapestry but required a concrete process to offer an example and anchor the discussions. I needed a sound visible process to act as a central example. The December 1998, Popular Science, article "A Star in a Jar", on Sonoluminescence was my epiphany. Here was a process, simple to reproduce, that visibly demonstrated the language I found in the mystical texts. It also had similarities to the physics sensed by my mind in having the possibilities of constructing a process that would result in the Shroud image. Then in March of 2000 my son passed over and on his bed-stand sat a book on the Shroud of Turin; as I held that manuscript in my hand, a second epiphany occurred, and my mind in those moments rapidly put all these pieces together neatly into one beautiful package. It seemed so simple, yet from that moment till the completion of this work a lot of water has gone under the bridge.

ONE

Whether from a spiritual or scientific perspective, whether it is a biological, electrical, chemical and or mechanical model or a psychophysical humanistic view; what we are talking about is the creation of a highly harmonized union producing a coherent unified singularity that mirrors the womb of existence. A massive vibrational tuning occurs that produces a phase singularity with resonance in resonance with the ground consciousness of existence. This thesis is what happens when a human being becomes coherently harmonious with the womb of energy within which it exists. It may begin as being one *with*, but in the *Final Great Completion* it is simply *One*. A *Completion* that occurs the moment consciousness frees itself completely from **all** aspects of identification. All the psychophysical preliminaries discussed in the sacred sciences are there to set up the internal conditions for allowing the *Final Completion* to proceed.

Much of the discussions within these pages are focused on the preliminaries for environmental attuning, and what unfolds as accomplishment of experience is attained at various *stations*.

It was my experience that both the spiritual and western perspectives were required to lessen my innate resistances. So this manuscript is more or less my personal road map. I personal found that at the core of this non-judgmental attitude of mind to *what is,* exists faith in the design and the intelligence of life. This attitude allows one to follow the yearning to all manner of places, some external other internal; to look in the shadows and dark places and see what drives the madness. Faith allows self loving-kindness, which in turn allows one to follow the calling of the heart more easily. Faith allows an inner knowing of the appropriateness of *what is*, which organically generates gratitude and a deep appreciation to flow within consciousness for the gift of experiencing life. When this is held firmly with unshakeable resolve in the heart of your heart, the hand of creation moves through the individual without resistance and opens up portals to greater depth of experience and the ultimate choice of formless conscious existence.

The Shroud Image

Over the last two thousand years the Image on the Shroud has existed as a testament defying all reason regardless of the age. The mystery engenders faith within the faithful and drives men of science with a longing to know the truth outside the box, a longing that propels inquiry past the normal bounds of possibility.

We live in times where physics has reduced the material world to levels reminiscent to those found in the mystical traditions of this planet. These novel constructs birthed out of direct experimental evidence allow reason for the first time to define a plausible path that concludes with a satisfactory supposition, how the image on the Shroud might have been formed. Yet it is best understood from a marriage of the spiritual and biophysics, for one without the other leaves a hollow unsatisfied feeling to this Westerner. Only through a balanced comprehension can one decipher the true encoded message left to this generation within those ancient fibers, and in so doing receive the gift intended by its creator, one that is pertinent and clearly meant for consummation during these times. For it is only in these times that we have the required tools, physical models and mindset to unravel and allow rational comprehend the mystery implanted on those fibers. In my mind the creator of the image must have intended an immediate purpose, that of engendering unshakable faith and a long range motive of concretely demonstrating human potentiality and an expanded view of the nature of *reality*. Only now does humanity hold the required tools to fully gain access to the embedded meaning held by the Silent Gospel.

The tradition of the Shroud has always been directly tied to Jesus and the birth of a religious movement based on his resurrection into the Kingdom of Light. Viewing the story and teachings with a neutral eye, one not poisoned by dogma, allows a richer understanding to develop. It allows new cultural and historic information gathered from archeological data to broaden and enrich the story. A story that now has this spiritual teacher of an ultra small sect of working men, as a radical thinker and activist at odds with a majority of the cultural, political and religious precepts of his region. The question that immediately arises from looking at the life story of Jesus is; from what source did Jesus get his unique thoughts and principles? It was certainly not from the Jewish law of his day! From our reading of the Bible stories, this radical activist appears at constant odds with the laws, both political and religious. Secondly from what source did he gain his courage and strength of conviction? Clearly he was a threat to both the social-political and religious sectors of his society, and at that time torture and death were known to be the punishment for either. The conclusion one derives after sober thought is that he either obtained these foreign notions from within after some self-enlightening event and/or he gained them from an external source in the form of books, verbal stories or another teacher(s). In the end, the collective information left to us points to the fact that all the above might have played a role in developing his exotic views of enlightenment, while the direct experience after his full awakening in the desert conferred upon him the inner courage to stay loyal to the truth regardless of the outcome.

Because I am correlating the *resurrection event* to other clearly delineated spiritual practices of the Indian sub-continent, it was important to show that archeological facts clearly demonstrate that the Eastern Science of Self Realization long preexisted the times of Jesus, and furthermore this science/religion traveled with merchants to the regions around Jerusalem. In doing so, it has been archeologically proven that well-established Buddhist and Hindu centers had indeed existed in that area. There is also substantial speculation that Jesus might have traveled in his youth, especially in Egypt, where a large cross-pollination of thoughts are known to have flourished.

The creation of these science/religious centers were permitted, even encouraged during those specific times for very practical reasons. It was one of the great strengths of Roman rule to allow spiritual diversity. It birthed out of necessities and very practical concerns. On one hand it allowed much needed and desired foreign goods to flow more easily throughout the empire and into the heart of Rome itself. On the other hand it promoted peace via thriving local economies. No one likes to upset the apple cart during good times. Merchants, regardless of their culture, felt more welcome, encouraging a volume of trade and goods which in turn resulted in lower prices, increasing diversity of goods and generating a sense of well being. Thriving economies are generally peaceful economies which were cheaper and easier to rule. Locally it created a boost to local economies all along the trade routes and their surrounding sub regions. Once an economy came to rely on these traded commodities the last thing it wished to do was upset these exotic foreign gods by insulting one of their priests. Similarly in recent history, when the Chinese came to America to work the gold-fields of California they brought with them their religion and constructed their temples in their new home. This need to have their own gods and religious forms would have been true in Roman times for the diversity of settlers from foreign lands in and around Israel.

The other powerful point as mentioned above is the *longevity aspect*. Longevity has two interesting byproducts, one is credibility and the other is cultural expansion. The longer an idea survives, the stronger the natural credibility becomes, and the farther a field the principle travels. Christianity is a prime example; it started with a few individuals and over time came to be one of the planet's largest religions. Due to all these facts it is very likely that these Eastern spiritual traditions had a high probability of cross-pollinating those with open minds and hearts in and around Egypt and Palestine. This certainly appears to be the case when one reviews the actual verbal and nonverbal teachings shared by Jesus and his disciples, for they closely parallel the Eastern yogic sciences and their commentaries on the process of attunement in mastering self-knowledge. If I've failed in any way to create a firm bridge between these sciences and the teachings of Jesus I encourage one to compare them for your self. Similarity between spiritual traditions is not as uncanny as it may appear, for the masters of inner exploration tell us clearly that there is only One Truth, it just has many differing cultural and modality translations. Another very important point not to be over looked is the fact that these same mystical traditions have within their teachings a final level of attainment, a *Great Completion*, one that produces a union of soul, heart and mind and a return to the *Kingdom of Light*. This final station of attainment is not generally spoken of, for without attainment of the basic level of an anchored shift in perception to the soul aspect of mind (samadhi/enlightenment/awakening, the other higher levels of perfection can never be realized. The primary reason a true Master does not bring it up, is because it acts as another inhibitors to success. It is another *object to attain in future time*, and these strengths the ego, the very thing the student is working to annihilate. Masters tell us that if you are *doing* a practice to gain a goal (object), then the mind is involved in *doing*, which clouds the attainment of being. Students get caught in identifying with the doing act of practice, i.e. yoga, mediation, diet, etc. and this veils the reality of Pure Being.

The Great Completion

The highest attainment is to fully merge with the Divine, a process with many levels of experience, termed the Great or Perfect Completion within the Buddhist tradition. In Christian tradition it is the attainment of the Kingdom of Light. In reading the specific commentaries for this level of attainment, one cannot help but see the similarities to the teachings and story of Jesus, specifically to His Transfiguration and Resurrection stories. The comparisons parallel on all points. Again, not that I think it is required that Jesus learned these techniques. I simply include them for emphasis and academic support that a tradition of practices ending with a result mirroring what science tells us occurred in the formation of the image on the Shroud was present in the geographic regions of the Middle East long before the birth of Jesus.

The great libraries of documents such as the Dead Sea Scrolls and the Nag Hammadi Codices, to mention the best known, show us that this ancient science was known and practiced at least in part by ascetic Orthodox Jewish sects of the times and by sects that have come to be known generically as Gnostics. Gnostic meaning knowledge or knowing, and this referred to self-knowing. The philosophy found in the Gospel of Thomas itself could be completely viewed as a Zen Buddhist treatise. It begins: "These are the secret sayings which the living Jesus spoke and which Didymos Judas Thomas wrote down." The intent for the disciple follows with the first saying or teaching of Jesus; "Jesus said, "Whoever finds the interpretation of these sayings will not experience death."

Thus, this first Saying not only holds a promise of everlasting life, but becomes a key to decoding the *Silent Gospel* of the Shroud, especially when it is thought to have been spoken by the originator of that image. "…Whoever finds the interpretation of (this cloth) will not *experience* death." All the teaching if followed to the letter leads one to not experience death. This is literal; sadly most relate it in a metaphoric or spiritual light.

His disciples had witnessed many miracles from their guru. The gospel stories are filled with the amazing tales, even one of raising Lazarus from death. So to see, meet and speak with the risen Master three days later as claimed by the disciples, would have brought great joy and solace to the small group. But I am convinced that on some level, especially among those with great faith, his resurrection would have been expected. To see and hold this miraculous image on the Shroud, left as a witness to His torture and death, would have been the miracle of miracles and would have added a great strength and value to this volume of sayings. It would have been a road map to the *Kingdom of Light,* where one would become a *Son of God* and *not experience death.*

The Shroud Evidence:

The scientific evidence on the Shroud was gathered by highly regarded individuals of science that came to the article from a diversity of beliefs and disciplines. Important to realize is that they were not all

Christians investigating the Shroud with a Christian bias. Rather, their conclusions are based on data gathered from exhaustive studies done over many years, continuing in some circles to the present. These data and conclusions have been reviewed by the scientific community and by their peers. What is most telling about these collective conclusions is that independent to each other, the researchers portray a scientific parallel in a precise, detailed manner to the story of Jesus' torture and death as related in the Bible. This by itself is amazing. What these unrivaled experts tell us is that the Shroud is an actual burial shroud of a man tortured and killed in a very unique manner, one identical to the Bible stories. The forensic evidence of the Shroud is very exact; a man died or was very near death and the cause was asphyxiation from fluids filling the lungs. Stories to the contrary are fictions not born of the facts. The detailed mapping of all the stains from blood and other body liquids caused by wounds on the body, as well as the burial style and practices are very constant with the cultural norms and the detailed biblical accounts of the torture and crucifixion of Jesus.

The fact is that the body was laid to rest with the hands over the chest, coins on the eyes, flowers around the head and shoulders, in one long cloth that extended from the feet to head and back to the feet. Add to this the pollens and rock dust studies, combined with the research done on the specific coins placed over the eyes, and flowers imprints found on the Shroud, produce collectively evidence that places the Shroud origins very near Jerusalem in the Spring of the 1st century. The analyses of the dirt and rock fragments found near the feet on the Shroud by an esteemed, world class laboratory identifying the material as a rare form of calcite found near the Damascus Gate in Jerusalem, alone makes the fraud idea far fetched. Add to this the correlations to the Sudarium of Oviedo, an object with a clear direct unbroken historical link to Jesus and Jerusalem of the 1st century and what you are left with is a mounting sum of data supporting the conclusion that the relic is in fact with the highest probability the burial Shroud of Jesus. Only DNA from the actual body of Jesus would positively confirm, but the collected evidence would easily convict in any Western court of law.

The verbal and written tradition tell us that the Shroud of Turin is the Burial Shroud of Jesus, a Jewish master teacher and healer of the first century who was tortured and crucified in a unique and detailed manner. The collected unbiased evidence supports this claim to the

The Silent Gospel

highest probability. This being accurate, one is left pondering the resurrection, a matter of no little importance, being that the crucifixion and resurrection from death three days later are the foundations of a global religion. It is felt by scholars that some very compelling piece of evidence must have existed to propel this small sect of 12 or so individuals into a movement where people submitted willingly to torture and death rather than recant their faith. What evidence was there in that time that assisted this very small group to gain such a following? What did they have that was so astonishing that drew throngs to listen and follow this small splinter group of Judaism? Luke 24:12 gives us a hint. "Then arose Peter, and ran unto the sepulcher; and stooping down, he beheld the linen clothes laid by themselves, and departed, wondering in himself at that which was come to pass."

The Image

The data gathered on the image formation specifically concluded that the physical body that lay within the cloth must have radiated an extremely intense coherent laser like light (energy) for a very, very short period of time, perhaps as short a time as milliseconds. This coherent laser-like brief flash scorched selected fibers producing the unique image. An image encoded with even more unique topographical characteristics that cannot yet be reproduced by any normal picture of a painting or other picture.

This unique flash not only imaged the individual, it imaged the other objects on and around the body, like the flowers and coins on the eyes. So it appears to have come coherently from very near the surface of the body. After all, not much space was left between the body and the cloth. Yet the light/energy was able to image the body and surrounding objects including the markings on the top of the coins. For this to occur the imaging light must have surrounded the body. In short the body could have been the source for the light but the light surrounded the body very near the surface of the skin. This light not only imaged the body but the surrounding objects as well, equally without distortion. This is an important fact because it means that the source was uniform and in no way unidirectional. Sunlight, or any single or multiple light sources produce distortion of the figure like a shadow. This light, however, left a unique dimensional encoding embedded within the fibers. It makes not only the Shroud unique but also photographs of the Shroud unique. Just how unique was best described by the inventor of the NASA VP-8 Image Analyzer, Peter Shumacher in John Iannone's book. He says that, (Dr. John Jackson of the Sandia Scientific Laboratories,) "placed an image (photograph) of the Shroud of Turin onto the light table of the system. He focused the video camera of the system on the image. When the pseudo-three-dimensional image display ("isometric display") was activated, a "true-three-dimensional image" appeared on the monitor. At least, there were main traits of real three-dimensional structuring in the image displayed. The nose ramped in relief. The facial features were contoured properly. Body shapes of the arms, legs, and chest, had the basic human form. The result from the VP-8 had never occurred with any of the images I had studied, nor had I heard of it happening during any image studies done by others. The results were unlike anything I have processed through the VP-8 Analyzer, before or since. Only the Shroud of Turin images has produced these results from a VP-8 Image Analyzer isometric projection study. In short the photographic image of the Shroud was "dimensionally encoded" so that when the ("isometric display") feature was activated the picture projected looked like a 3-dimensional image man lying under a sheet."[16]   I reiterate that this was from a picture taken of the Shroud, not from the Shroud itself. No other photograph, drawing or painting ever processed by this team and their unique device has ever produced these unique anomalous 3-dimensonal characteristics.

After reexamining the data with current even more precise devices then the original 1978 STURP research group had, scholars of the subject of the Shroud image return to the same confounding conclusion. The image was created by highly coherent radiation of some form, for the briefest of moments.

Light and Energy are the same medium with the confounding paradox of being either wave or particle (wavicle). What part of the energy spectrum is not known but is generally assumed to be in the high-energy slice of the spectrum. When one reviews the data the closest model in consideration to have caused the scorching is some form of High Energy Particle Radiation. For it to have produced the even result the medium (High Energy Particle Radiation) occurred in an intense burst for a very short moment in time, in a highly coherent

---

[16] John C. Iannone's 1998 New Scientific Evidence, The Mystery of the Shroud of Turin

manner. This fact is unanimously agreed upon. But the light had to burst forth in a manner that surrounded the body.

The mystery is how this medium of light (energy) was generated and employed to get the astonishing results and unique characteristics embedded within into the image. No single satisfactory theory encompasses this phenomenon, especially from a man near death in antiquity. It is this confounding conundrum that is at the heart of the mystery and continuing global investigation on this article; and it is this specific question to which I'm attempting to give a complete and plausible explanation.

The fact is that when the total sum of material data is viewed in its entirety, it makes it literally impossible for a 13th century forger to have both known about and faked all the materials found on the Shroud. It is especially hard to believe that a forger would, if able, place the evidence with such precision with the intention to fool scientists' seven hundred years later, or for a forger of any historical period to get the extremely unique characteristics that the Shroud image demonstrates under unique investigations specific to the twentieth century.

The facts stated plainly are that even today we cannot recreate the image let alone an image with these uniquely specific complex characteristics. The conclusion we must deduce from this analysis using sound science is self-evident even if initially it goes against logic and common sense; the Shroud of Turin supports the Jesus story as it has been past down to us.

With this entire wealth as foundation I felt comfortable researching the life and teachings of Jesus for collaborating evidence to support my theoretical model that the resurrection and transfiguration stories as told in the Bible reflect parallels to well described outcomes of detailed, long practiced and honed sciences and philosophies of the Indian sub-continent. The value of doing this was to reveal a correlation between their well detailed ancient sciences to that known in modern western science. Take the example of Buddhism. Buddhism relies on self-inquiry and not dogma or supreme deity. It does not ask for faith rather demands debate on experience alone. This experience is codified and passed down from master to student. Out of these came lineages and practices to aid the student in gaining specific levels of experience. Yet again I feel compelled to stress that this is not important to the central question and the solution this book theorizes or to its value to us personally. It just allows a more personalized reading of the material in great measure to the fact that the Jesus story and message is so well disseminated. If the data pointed to a different conclusion, say that it was created in the thirteenth century, the mystery at the heart of the Shroud image would not change, nor would the thesis of this manuscript. Having the evidence point to The Shroud as actually being the burial cloth of the historical Jesus makes it easier to understand. It also puts into context the challenging reality about human potentiality and the process that phase transitions physicality to the domain written in spiritual texts as the *Kingdom of Light*.

Chapter Synopsis

Spiritual Perspective

- Jesus or some other Master realized and mastered at the highest level the ancient science of self-realization, allowing for total, merged, Conscious Union. When conscious union reaches the degree of experience where the Master allows all aspects of individuation and identity to be relinquished, the transition into the Rainbow Body occurs.

- It is a real event that normally occurs at the end of a lifetime of spiritual attunement with the Divine. It happens when all resistance is surrendered and identity is allowed to completely dissolve.

- The Rainbow Body event falls under many differing cultural names. The *Wisdom* or the *Golden Body* are two other popular names from Eastern philosophies while *Heaven*, the *Kingdom of Light,* becoming a *Son of God* are terms used in Middle Eastern cultures. All refer to the highest level of experiential attainment within this reality of existence.

- This *process* of attainment represents levels of physical and virtual attunement that allows expanded degrees of unity experience. A spiritual experience is one of feeling/sensing, *a communion with.* This sense expands to greater and greater degrees of unity, till the point where the line creating separation dissolves.

- "Sacred" is a sense of the Divine, normally experienced

The Silent Gospel

through an aspect of life. The sense of beauty, awe, receptiveness, gratitude, appreciation and allowing are intimately linked with sacred.

- All true spiritual and mystical practices and philosophies are aimed at reducing resistance on all levels, i.e. *to life, what is*, etc. begins with the development of faith in faith itself. They affect those aspects we characterize as; embraced receptive allowing, being genuine and in a state of communion with Self, which from the psychophysical perceptive is self loving-kindness.

- Loving-kindness develops into real compassion as the experience of union stabilizes. Compassion is not empathy, sympathy or pity for another; it is feeling and acting as if you are the other. Separation dissolves and the sense of interconnectedness and communion is enhanced to the level where it is Reality. *Compassion is the only selfless emotion.*

- The highest level of Spiritual attainment allows the Master the Final or Great Completion epitomized by total surrender (dissolving) of all aspects of self (mind). With all aspects of mind dissolved/merged back with the Divine, there is no-thing to act as template for the form in this existence, so it dissolves back to its true nature, which is pure consciousness.

- The Great Completion terminates in the highest form with the Master vanishing from this plane of existence. When describing this event the spiritual text clearly explains that the physical elements (matter) return to their original state of existence. They also tell us that the aware consciousness assumes a higher plane of existence. This plane of existence they tell us is our birthright, to assume the *Kingdom of Light* and become a **Son of God.**

- At the moment the body vanishes from this plane of existence the texts tell us that there is an intense brief burst of light, enhance the term Rainbow.

- This burst of light created the image on the Shroud.

Physics Perspective

- The root foundation to material existence is consciousness.
    1. The agent of consciousness in this plane of existence is mind.
    2. Mind at the core is individualized consciousness/spirit.
    3. Perspective is the lens through which mind filters.
    4. Mind is a byproduct in the creation of Awareness.
    5. Mind is perceived through three main aspects in this reality.
        A. Past or Future (ego),
        B. Present Moment (heart),
        C. No Time (soul).
- Perception can organize from a single aspect or any combination of the three main aspects of mind.
    1. The degree of influence each amount carries determines the organization of the filters through which the lens of perception takes. These filters color the energy interacting with the Quantum Zero Point (QZP) domain and it is from this colored view of Reality that we experience reality.

- The medium of creation at this stage of aware existence is vibration/oscillation with the characteristics of attraction and repulsion. The range of measurable radiation is called the electromagnetic spectrum and it is the palette of material creation. The four known forces generated by the fields of particle/wavicles act as guides in creation but quantum science has clearly demonstrated that these elemental forces do not always come into play.
    1. All objects no matter how small produce resonance.
    2. All objects are electromagnetic phenomena held in self-referencing fields.
    3. These fields are standing waves held in superposition via the bond of self-referencing of resonance, as well as interior and exterior detecting/ observation.

4. The main stimulation for this is the recursive looping (detection/self-referencing), in sentient beings it is the looping of mind called aware consciousness.

- Biofeedback is a looping of what is, with the consciousness creating it.
    1. Biofeedback techniques have been shown to assist in rearranging and balancing neural pathways.
    2. This can lead to emotional and physical stability.
    3. Certain psychophysical states (emotional states) produce more balance and coherency (stability) within the bio-physical systems.
    4. The act of creating and sustaining these specific balancing psychophysical states, broadly termed faith, (loving-kindness/ allowing/openness), and associated states like appreciation, gratitude and awe, with highly advanced training in meditation (concentration and contemplation), literally produces a reduction in resistance (stress) on all levels of physical systems allowing alternative neural pathways to connect.
    5. Internal Resistance *dramatically* shifts when perception is weighted strongly in the non-local witnessing aspect of awareness, i.e., the no-time/soul aspect.
    6. This is not a conceptual shift but an experiential shift of self. Literally, a shift from the time/distance 'my body is me' aspect views, to the quantum non-localized aspect.
    7. Sustaining this perceptual shift in awareness generates radical shift in the biophysical system(s), specifically within the neural, chemical, acoustical, electromagnetic and quantum coupling, processes.
    8. This state allows platforms of oscillation to couple in a highly coherent manner, producing phase synchronization and a shift in the resonance of the standing wave held in superposition.
    9. A shift in resonance shifts the form and what attracts and is repelled by the form.
- The more advanced levels of yogic training allows the

individual to control the branches of the nervous and immune systems, providing greater stability, and allowing an increased ability to stay in concentration/contemplation on a single object. It also has been shown to shift brain functions in research.

- These advanced levels of training produce extremely high degrees of coherency within the physical electromagnetic field due to quantum coupling and coupled platforms of the oscillators operation within the physical system. Oscillators and oscillating systems couple via resonant entrainment.
- At the highest level of training, the vibratory/electromagnetic standing waveform of the physical is modulated totally into a single phased field similar to a type 1 superconductor. The field is in a unique *Phase Synchronization*.
    1. The reason for this from the platform of physics is due to the idealized shape and resonance of the standing wave form held in superposition.
    2. The waveform shape is a phi related torus.
    3. The coupled coherent synchronization is Phi/Golden Mean idealized symmetry.
    4. Phi/Golden Mean synchronization allows scales, in this case scales of oscillation, both wave length and velocities, to nest in fractal resonant attunement, which produces a coherent, unified phase within the field.
    5. The unique synchronization forms a Coherent Scale Invariant Harmonic Fractal Resonance that is in resonance with the Quantum Zero Point Domain. All aspects mirror all aspects regardless of scale. This is a characteristic of the Golden Mean
    6. Other characteristics of Golden Mean are the forms' ability to sustain ideally from within (idealized recursion) (self-generating/self-referencing). This is due to highly coherent symmetry (balance), with symmetrical compression forces, the waves add and multiply harmonically their wavelengths and velocities in a unique scale invariant, highly coupled fashion producing phase synchronization. Because of this the wave-particle distinction melts into light bearing quantal waves.

7. Here the highly ordered organization and synchronization of the various oscillating platforms of the body produces little if any dissonance, and exterior interference of the field of energy is minimized to nil.
8. Coupled oscillators phase to the point that the core phase singularity and space occupied by the standing wave merge to be one.
9. The high degree of internal symmetry creates a phase singularity in phase with the forms core phase singularity at the heart of the waveform. This places it in coherent resonance with the Quantum Zero Point Field.
10. Phase Synchronization continues to the point that a Type-1 superconductor is formed.
11. Quantum coherence/quantum coupling/quantum entanglement on a massive scale occurs.
12. If sustained a phase transition in the elements and structures of the physical occurs.

- What occurs at this moment is that the waveform, now a perfect type 1 superconductor with a single vibrational phase would repel all magnetic invasions. They become diamagnetic which is a form of single frequency photons- no longer particles, but light-bearing quantal waves.
- A Meissner Field would surround the field.
- These antielectron mirrors are ideally in resonance with the quantum Zero Point. The internal resonance perfectly mirrors the energetic resonance of the Still Point, and at that exact moment in time the form under goes a **quantum phase transition** of the constitute elements.
- One perspective of the process is similar to the process of Sonoluminescence.
  1. The symmetry of the internal centering forces produces implosive/compressive forces on the waveform.
  2. The centering/compressive forces implode the waveform with the energies surpassing the speed of light on its way to full compression.
  3. The speed of the compression produced a vacuum.
  4. Quantum field theory predicts that if the detector is

accelerated its ground state can be spontaneously excited even when moving through the vacuum.

5. The Unruh effect predicts radiation by non-inertially moving quantum mirrors, furthermore the accelerated detector will not find a vacuum but a thermal distribution of particles, as if it were in a thermal bath of black-body radiation with a certain temperature coined the Unruh temperature. Simplified, the Unruh Effect is a consequence of a dynamic Casimir Effect. The Casimir Effect has been scientifically shown to be real. Sonoluminescence demonstrates in a dynamic manner the results of these theories.

6. It occurs as the energy pulses past the speed of light forming a plasmic bubble of energy for a millisecond, then it flashes out of human sight creating a photon release at the event horizon of the original energy field. In our case, the Meissner Field surrounding the now single frequency and phase standing wave form of Jesus.

7. The speed of the imploding vacuum produces a temporary black hole and at the event horizon virtual photons are massively released in a coherent flash. This flash photographs if you like, the body template just prior to blinking out of visual sight. This phase transition of a Meissner Field is not a state of invisibility, but of transportation into another dimension of time-space.

8. A secondary result would be that the Meissner Field mirrors the quantum zero point domain and this phase relationship produces a mirror like merging of similarities producing a nil result. An Unruh Effect occurs in the resulting vacuum caused by asymmetry between the fields (two vacuum states).

9. This causes a virtual radiation release of a coherent nature due to the coherent nature of the object in phase transition.

- The imbalance in vacuum to surrounding space, as well as the dynamic Casimir Effect resulting from the non-inertially moving quantum mirrors, produce an intense brief photon release at the Event Horizon of the event which is a phase transition.

- This highly coherent photon releases laser images of the old template of form at the moment of phase transition producing the image found on the Shroud.

The Image Characteristics

When placed in context of the other characteristic known about the Shroud, the questions of how the images photo like depth perception was created and how is the dimensional information, as witnessed in the VP-8 analysis, held and imparted, are the most baffling. Intuition tells us that the answer to both lie in the same process.

If my thesis is correct to this point, we return to the method by which a holograph is formed with *coherent light* (LASERS). Using this understanding as a starting point we again restate that at the core of ALL this material process is a massive *phase transition* of the elements making up the physical structure; a phase transition back to their virtual state.

Since science now sees structure as electromagnetic phenomena, the process can be viewed completely from the electromagnetic thermodynamics. A **phase transition** by definition is the transformation of a thermodynamic system from one phase to another. Phase transitions often (but not always) take place between phases with different symmetry. Generally one phase in a phase transition is more symmetrical (coherent) than the former, this is especially true when discussing Type 1 Superconducting fields.

Golden Mean symmetry produces fractal mirror-like nested phase symmetry. The reason resides in the fundamental characteristic of the Golden Mean. It is the only possible geometric and arithmetic expansion and partitioning (proportional division) of One (unified field) using two terms with the third being one itself. Due to this fundamental characteristic, it represents an archetypal fractal in that it preserves its relationship with itself in the most economical, yet mathematically robust manner. It organically produces a mirroring that when idealized reflects I contend, the ground state of material existence. This level of reflected **wave** (length and velocities)-**particle** (shape of form and resonance) synchronization demands a unique symmetry configuration, one that produced due to its ideal fractal nature, a singularity of phase. In short, the object would be a Type 1 Superconductor in phased resonance with the Quantum Zero Point domain. The chief characteristic of the Quantum Zero Point Domain is also idealized coherency. Quantum Theory contains processes such as Quantum Coherence. Quantum Coherence is the ability of atoms to act as one regardless of distance (Quantum Leap). Related processes are Quantum Coupling and Quantum Entanglement. These characteristics of the Quantum Vacuum married in phase to the coherence of the waveform would produce a *quantum vacuum mirror passing a second*. A dynamic Casimir Effect termed an Unruh Effect would ensue and the accelerated detector would encounter a thermal distribution of particles.

The phase transitioning vacuum bubble like object would be coherently fractal internally and coherently in fractal symmetry to the surrounding zero point vacuum. The two laser-like mirrors would produce radiation with laser like coherent characteristics during the transition. The difference is that the light would not radiate in the normal column (beam) like form of normal lasers. It would instead bathe symmetrically around the whole object more like the sonic massaging during sonoluminescence.

The Sonoluminescence model visually reflects the process, difference being, and a significant difference is that the human field energetically becomes a unique phase singularity with type 1 superconductor characteristic.

It is the Golden Mean ordering that creates the unique characteristics and properties and implies extraordinarily highly coherent waveform symmetry in phase transition. Phase Transition generally transitions to higher forms of symmetry. In this case the mirroring during transition would produce a zero gain result. This highly organized and synchronized fractal process, when quantum coupled would produce a unique holographic lighting environment for the briefest of moments in time, again very similar in process to sonoluminescence. I contend that this laser-like coherent light would, like in the creation of a holograph, embed correct proportional perspective and dimensional encoding to all sides of the witnessing cloth.

A secondary point but one not to be over looked is that this form of perfect Type 1 Superconductor with a single vibrational phase would *repel all magnetic invasion*. The diamagnetic characteristic forms a *single frequency photons*, no longer particles, but *light-bearing quantal waves*. These specific quantal waves (antielectron) are coherently quantum coupled and would mirror ideally the Quantum Zero Point Energy. The internal state would perfectly mirror the energetic state of the Still Point, and at that exact moment in time the form has a **quantum phase transition** of most if not all the elements. The two cancel each other out creating a nil. This form of phase transition produces at the Event Horizon of the event a brief massive release of radiation (Hawking Radiation) with highly coherent characteristics. It is this massive brief intense release of coherent radiation that creates the Shroud Image, as well as the highly unique characteristics.

The *Yellow Brick Road, OZ* and *Parallel Universes*

A tortured man from the first century near or at the moment of death radiated a coherent form of light equally from or very near his entire body for the very briefest of moments. This light embedded the cloth with a brilliant image that has photographic properties mixed with unique *dimensional encoded* characteristics. This occurred at a time when religious cultural values did not support aggrandizement of the person on any level. A brilliant fresh image of a sect's spiritual master would have been slightly more miraculous then actually seeing their spiritual teacher after his torture, death and burial. This might be hard for us in the twenty first century to believe but spiritual miracles were expected… after walking on water and raising the dead it would have been expected that their master would rise above torture and death. But a brilliant photographic witness to His death on a fourteen-foot cloth would have given his disciples faith to move mountains. With the aid of hindsight we can see that they more than moved mountains when this offshoot, small Jewish sect became the state sanctioned religion of Rome and its empire.

This spiritual movement had parallel teachings to the long held beliefs of the Indian Sub-continent. Parallels also exist to the great saints of these spiritual traditions. Parallels between the story of Jesus and Padma Sambhava, the great patron saint of Tibet, allows imagination to connect the resurrection event to the *Great Perfection* of Rainbow Body attainment. The Rainbow Body attainment has different cultural names, The Wisdom Body and The Golden Body are two from the Eastern tradition, but from the early Jewish/Christian perspective one entered the Kingdom of Light and became a *Son of God*. When one takes the time, one can easily see the philosophy, psychology and practices of ancient India in the words and teachings of Jesus. These same well-delineated practices lead to Perfection (Union) in the Eastern Philosophies. As a matter of fact they're similar to other mystical traditions of the Middle East itself, such as those outlined by Sufi and Zoroastrian masters not to mention Hellenistic sects of Jewish mysticism The reason for making these links to the other known spiritual practice is clear when you understand their commonality of idealizing attunement, allowing for a transmutation into the kingdom of *Spiritual Light*, thus becoming a *Son of God*. The reason Jesus was ultimately condemned to death by crucifixion was because he was truthful in agreeing finally that he was a *Son of God*. This was a blasphemous statement in Jewish law that was punishable by death. A side note here that I find interesting is that for most of his life Jesus in the Bible accounts calls himself a *Son of Man*.

Review of the Process of becoming a Son of God

Sri Yukteswar the twentieth century Hindu Swami and Self-realized saint of India, helps us understand the process of *Completion* in his book The Holy Science,

> "In this state, all the necessities having been attained and the ultimate aim effected (end of ignorance), the heart becomes perfectly purified and instead of merely reflecting the spiritual light, actively manifests the same. Man, being thus consecrated or anointed by the Holy Spirit, becomes Christ, the anointed Savior. Entering the kingdom of Spiritual Light, he becomes the Son of God." [1]

Jesus further clarifies the preceding process with his answer to his disciples when he gives them the commandment: *"Love the Lord your God with all your heart and with all your soul and with all your mind. This is the first and greatest commandment. And the second is like it: love your neighbor as*

---

[1] The Holy Science-

yourself. All the laws and prophets hang on these two commandments."

These few lines outline the precise process for the ultimate attunement. But he gives another hint in the Gospel of Thomas, Saying Number 6, on how this love is allowed to fill one heart, soul and mind.

> "His disciples questioned Him and said to Him, 'Do you want us to fast? How shall we pray? Shall we give alms? What diet shall we observe? 'Jesus said, 'Do not tell lies, and do not do what you hate, for all things are plain in the sight of Heaven. For nothing hidden will not become manifest, and nothing covered will remain without being uncovered.' Jesus said to them, 'If you fast, you will give rise to sin for yourselves; and if you pray, you will be condemned; and if you give alms, you will do harm to your spirits. When you go into any land and walk about in the districts, if they receive you, eat what they will set before you, and heal the sick among them. For what goes into your mouth will not defile you, but that which issues from your mouth - it is that which will defile you.'" [2]

Jesus tells his disciples that the most important thing they can do for attainment is to BE TRUTHFUL if you wish to know Truth and inherit the Kingdom of Light. Jesus never demonstrated this more then at the end before Pilate. He was truthful even though he fully realized the implication of doing so.

The final piece to the spiritual illumination puzzle came when I read this profound quote from the revered Indian saint Ramana Maharshi: *"There are no stages in Realization or degrees of Liberation. There are no levels of Reality; there are only levels of experience for the individual."*

For me this quote harmonized with quantum science with a twist. Instead of the individual creating reality out of infinite probabilities, he just created his or her experience of Reality. Ramana is echoing all the illuminated saints throughout time when he exclaims

---
[2] Gospel of Thomas

that there is only One Reality, and that each individual experiences it in accordance to his or her perspective. Ramana is saying that the Kingdom is right here in front of us, it is all Divine. It also helped me understand why there appears no commonality in the expression of spiritual attainment other then "you will know them by their fruits". Manifestation takes many differing appearances with the most exotic being those whose physical structures remain whole after death for varying length of time, to the ultimate, vanishing at the time of death.

So why follow any spiritual practice?

The reason for following these commandments are clearly stated in the first 'Saying' in the Gospel of Thomas; "Jesus said, 'Whoever finds the interpretation of these sayings will not experience death.'"

The Science of Divinity is an attuning of consciousness. The mastery of these things allows for magnanimity to fill the heart, making it ready for the next phase of consciousness growth. Here again Sri Yukteswar clearly states the results, "When magnanimity comes into the heart this makes man fit for the practice of Asana Pranayama, which is control over prana, involuntary nerve electricities, and Pratyahara which is changing the direction of the voluntary nerve currents inward."[3]

The master of great skill and resolve places *all* his attention to the core at the heart of all Stillness and Silence. With all external stimuli closed to attention, the flow of awareness travels inward to the spaciousness of the Absolute. The individual experiences core knowing of Reality gaining direct knowing about the Truth of Being. The Truth, also termed Reality, is the same core for all objective nature. Knowing this Reality experientially gives rise to deep generosity of spirit. This is the moment *magnanimity comes into the heart* and compassion is felt in the heart. When one has gained enough experience in union with this realm and is completely stable in it, they then begin the preparation for the *Final Perfection*.

---

[3] The Holy Science

The Silent Gospel

Final Perfection

Through deep meditation the master dives deep into a death-like state of samadhi to fully merging with the Divine.

The paradox is that even Samadhi has levels of attainment, which are levels of experience. Paramahansa Yogananda in his book <u>Divine Romance</u> outlines his experience, " ...in the initial states of God communion (sabikalpa samadhi) the devotees (students) consciousness merges in the Cosmic Spirit; his life force is withdrawn from the body, which appears as 'dead,' or motionless and ridged (pure stable entropy/homeostasis). The yogi is fully aware of his bodily condition of suspended animation. As he progresses to higher spiritual states (nirbikalpa samahdi), however, he communes with God without bodily fixations; and worldly duties." "Both states are characterized by oneness with the ever new bliss of Spirit, but the nirbikalpa state is experienced by only the most highly advanced masters."

The key word in this narrative is the word "progresses". Again paradoxically, when one delves deeper into the teachings and practices one finds that even this elevated nirbikalpa state has degrees of attainment (experience). These degrees are characterized by the degree and length of time physical stabilization happens after the moment of what looks like death. This is termed Mahasamadhi, maha coming from Sanskrit for "great", samadhi is the last meditation, or conscious communion with the Divine. During which a skilled master merges totally, as all identity dissolves, and physical body surrendered willingly. A master invariability knows beforehand, as did Jesus, the time God has appointed for him to leave his bodily residence. This knowing allows for skilled preparations, which allow this last Great Conscious Communion.

When individuals master samadhi, (continual stabilized God communion) they are endowed with natural powers, called siddhis. Siddhis are the gifts, which appear to be supernatural powers at the disposal of yoga masters because of their ability to create this single pointed concentration. Siddha means literally "one who is successful". The life of Jesus according to the written texts is filled with such extraordinary events, cumulating with the amazing story of the Transfiguration.

As Keiko in chapter 12, <u>Siddhas</u>, explained the process, "I become one with God," (I am) "Beyond body, beyond mind...just soul." (In samadhi I) "…Go deep into self no more sense, no imagination. Just emptiness." (She adds that she), "Become one with the universe."

All the spiritual sciences and disciplines, philosophy, psychology physiology, practices and rituals deal with developing union (purity of heart). The union (attunement) is between the three aspects Jesus mentions as the heart, soul and mind with the Divine. If successful the student is brought to experience the soul or witnessing aspect of the self. This shift creates a radical change in perspective, which allows Purity of Heart and the samadhi experience.

Perfectly Purified - The Immaculate Heart

When the heart becomes perfectly purified, the sacred heart manifests. A unique attunement happens that entrains the entire body allowing for an elevated state of experience. A state where "…instead of merely reflecting the spiritual light, actively manifests the same." (Sri Yukteswar) There are clear physics to explain this statement.

Since Jesus placed the heart first, the soul second and the mind last in His commandments, I chose to do the same. Interestingly medical science has also placed the heart at the apex of the electrical vibrating nature of our bodily systems. The heart is the primary oscillator in coupling all the physical architectures. As we've read objects, including the physical, are basically electromagnetic phenomena with both wave and particle characteristics that organizes and localize into superposition by detection. And most importantly, the communication for this organization originates from impulses arising from the Quantum Zero Point domain. In short, the intelligence pulsing physical responses on a cellular and mind level is ultimately rooted in quantum mechanical processes. Scientifically it has been shown to communicate prior to normal mind awareness. This non-local intelligence one might consider the soul. When the heart and mind are aligned with soul, electrical phase ensues, creating internal electrical balance one could say, and at these moments the emotional feeling is harmony and peace yet the state is love.

Loving-Kindness

Jesus said LOVE your God with all your heart. These three aspects of the self that Jesus speaks about are to be aligned with the qualitative aspect of love and he tells us that living personal truth is a key to gaining this love. This is the same as the Buddhist prompting of Bodhichitta or loving-kindness. Jesus tells us that truth is required first and foremost and then one can love one's neighbor as oneself. This is also similar to the Buddhist teachings. In the end the student learns the skill of being authentic and genuine with the interior reality that he uncovers for himself. Loving oneself comes from being authentic and living it with integrity, moment by moment. The Buddhist teachings assert that the key to this is Mindfulness, which is another way of telling us to be conscious. Caring eventually leads one to one's true nature and the realization that all things are interconnected intimately and with the ultimate realization that all things are of God (wisdom). Knowing experientially this fact prompts one in a genuine way to care for other sentient beings (compassion). Being completely immersed in this state, the physical undergoes subtle changes with enormous ramification. Changes occur in neural pathways as well as the over all resonance of the standing waveform. A shift also occurs in the DNA/RNA cellular exchanges.

The Russian biophysicist and molecular biologist Pjotr Garjajev and his colleagues explored the vibrational behavior of DNA. They found that, "Living chromosomes function just like a holographic computer using endogenous DNA laser radiation," and this "functioning was connected to the vibratory nature of words (language)". I would suggest that it's connected to the resonance of the waveform in the moment similar to research showing that the DNA molecule expands and relaxes during open and peaceful emotional states and contracts during closed, disturbed, contracted emotional states. Garjajev found they could modulate certain frequency patterns (sound) onto a laser-like ray (coherent energy), which influenced DNA frequency and thus the genetic information itself. In short, the DNA and its vast code is not a fixed thing, it is a flexible assemblage of alkaline-pairs that act as a holographic information storage-communication center in the formation of elemental, molecular, and cellular forms. It can only put out information for protein production based on the input received and the environment it's received in. Individuals able to sustain a truly enlightened view of life, individuals skilled at the death-like communion state with the Divine produce a very unique standing wave physically and a resonance that places the physical in an apparent state of suspended animation. These same suspended states can present themselves for varying lengths of time at the end of a saints' life.

The Soul's Perspective

Psyche is the Greek word for soul and is the root for psychology, the study of the reason why we do the things we do. Spoken plainly, the impulse at the core for mental and physical activities as well as intercellular communication and bio-photon sharing, all appear to originate from a non-local intelligence. The Psyche, Soul, Atman, Higher Self, Non-local Self, M-field Consciousness, and the concept of Alternative Perception, are all signposts pointing to the same sense-facet of self.

Grace flows from Faith in Faith itself.

The ego sole aim is survival; it will do, think, and say anything to maintain itself. It acts out of the information imprinted from many sources; parental, social, cultural etcetera. It is easy to know if a thought is originating out of ego because the motion for the movement is always anchored in the past and or the future. And if witnessed for what it is, always has its roots in survival. It is a powerful force in the creation of ones reality for it colors the lens the energy of creation.

Shifting perspective from this forceful facet of mind to the psyche takes Grace. Grace is characterized by a flow of energetic attunement that flows from having *Faith in Life*.

Nirvana means annihilation, not because it destroys the ego but because it *dismantles the grasping* which gives it its prominence. Releasing the grasping allows one to know faith and develop real courage, for it is ultimately through faith in faith itself that one comes to the Truth and what true masters call Enlightenment, Awakening or Illumination. In reality nirvana it is nothing more then stabilizing this *Alternative Perception* and releasing the powerful hold of egoic mind over the creation of ones experiential reality.

Faith and the flow of grace start as a seed in the heart the moment the yearning in the heart to know peace builds sufficient courage to open oneself to *Life*. Faith flows into one's life by the action of *conscious- allowing*. One does not conceptualize faith. One simply allows life to flow and not get paralyzed by egoic fears. One simply is mindful and present to what life (Spirit) brings. This openness of heart generates a receptive space organically. Expanding receptiveness prompts naturally genuine appreciation and deep gratitude.

Receptiveness evolves into inclusive and unshakable courage. No belief or hope can substitute for the grace that comes with sustained faith. Not a faith in something or someone, but faith in faith itself.

The Centering Process

The Aramaic word for Heart, leba, comes from the root that means the *center*, or *best part of one's life*. Depending on the context can mean; the *point of balance and expansion,* the *point of intelligent vitality*, and or *the connecting core of life.*

The meaning of these ancient roots hint at what love truly is. Since, as we learned earlier, that love is the heart's natural tendency. Love might be considered to be a state of *balanced expanding receptiveness,* a *genuine non-judgmental state*. Saint Mother Theresa reportedly said, "If you're judging, you're not loving."

What replaces judgment is genuine appreciation and gratefulness. Yet the process begins with a yearning that comes from the heart, a yearning to know peace and hold its natural tendency. It begins when one finds the courage to listen to the wisdom of the heart. As Jesus himself pointed out, it begins with the heart and interestingly it all literally ends deep within *the connecting core of life.*

Heart Center

Space is the underlying nature of reality. Scientifically our entire objective reality is composed of vibrations swimming in the vastness of space. Everything, even apparently dense objects, when viewing the structure at atomic scales, appear as vibrations vectored in *space*. In physics, chemistry, and engineering an oscillation is a vibrational swing, it refers to a repeated motion back and forth past a central neutral position, or position of equilibrium. An oscillator is something that regulates oscillations; regulates some form of energy. When ever energy is regulated so too is information.

The mechanical regulator for the info-energy dance of the human body is centered in the cardiac matrix. It is the central regulator of rhythm within the human body. When exploring the physiological mechanisms, by which the heart communicates information and energy with the brain and body, scientists found that it communicated with the body in four biological ways.

Neurologically-(through the transmission of nerve impulses)

Chemically-(through hormones and neurotransmitters),

Acoustically-(through acoustic/pressure waves).

Energetically-(through electromagnetic field interactions).

These four information-energy transference communication systems, act in synchronized coupled coherent manner, with the apparent goal of maintaining equilibrium throughout the matrix of human architectures. External environmental components and the / psychological aspects of mind awareness modulating the field, influence all four modes of information-energy transference. But there is a *fifth* more important primal mode of info-energy transference communication system modulating the standing wave matrix, that being one of a quantum mechanical nature. This system is not as easily measured yet is just as real as the others. Ions, photons, electrons and other subatomic oscillating particles share information and energy in and out of a realm beyond the limits of our three-dimensional time-space. The finer communications couples into larger virtual clouds, producing all types of proteins and molecules spontaneously throughout the physical architecture. They communicate and share energy and information in what appears an instantaneous manifestation. The current consensus is that we are all nothing more then complex quantum objects operating through some implicate order termed consciousness. Cleve Backster's Primary Perception, the precognition experiments done by James Spottiswoode at the Cognitive Science Laboratory, Dr. Candace Pert's mind/emotion neurochemistry and Roger Nelson's Princeton Noosphere Consciousness Studies, to name just a few of many, all point to this finer spontaneous communication.

To me the most interesting work is that being done in the field of Biophoton research. Biophotons are photon (light) produced by cell activity, in a phenomenon also known as *ultraweak bioluminescence* and *dark luminescence*. Cells, like all objects animate and inanimate, emit a characteristic *black body* distribution of wavelengths of photons, in a manner directly related to temperature. Scientists studying this phenomenon are detecting a significant variance from the expected distribution of photons, as well as an additional coherence or

The Silent Gospel

coordination of the time when photons are emitted by distinct cells. The exact origin of this emission are unclear, but it is theorized that these emissions are part of a system of cell to cell communication (energy-information transference) that appears to act as a cohering factor, in that it appears that the cell/system stores photons and share via quantum mechanisms. This expanding new field called "Biophoton storage" and research indicates a greater level complexity and inter-relatedness compared to the standard modes of cell communication already known, such as chemical signaling. These new cohering energy-information transferences (communications) are important in the development and sustaining of larger structures such as the organs and it fills an important puzzle piece on the value of coherence in biological wellness. The photons emitted as part of this unknown luminescent process were dubbed "biophotons" by F. A. Popp to indicate simply their origin.

Here's the weird part that the rational mind finds difficult to grasp yet modern science has demonstrated to be real. The info-energy transference happens nowhere and everywhere prior to the point that rational mind consciousness is aware of the impending need. Even the activity of mind itself occurs through quantum coupled/entangled events. So the picture I would like you the reader to imagine is at the core of every organized standing wave form, there exists' a *phase singularity*. Whether an atom or complex organism like a human, the point where the two self-referencing vortexes touch, is the still center point, which electrically is termed a *phase singularity*. This zero point location most likely is in some form of harmonic resonance with the non-local quantum field of information. This field intelligence (M-field), through these four biological modes of info-energy transference, provides input to the heart, which subsequently communicates the info-energy to the brain's function and to all of our bodily systems. It regulates, organizes and influences the ongoing physical symphony of vibratory architectural structures. When a heart beats it does not just pump blood and nutrients to the cells, there is information and energy to produce change that is sent out in a radio-like echo signal to all the cells' DNA and beyond. This information signal radiates out in a 360-degree configuration that can be measured accurately with current devices up to ten feet away from the body. Then magically, the zero point field responds to what will be required in the next beat.

We need to remember that for communication to exist at all it must operate on a two-way street. The flow of information and the energy to carry that information must go both ways, it must be sent and received and the receiving element must respond with information and energy in return for it to be called communication. *Communication* is a prerequisite for *life*, *consciousness* and now apparently, the *foundation of evolution*. The main process and vehicle for all these info-energy transference modes is through the mechanism of resonance.

Resonance at the right frequency can turn on virtual photons or manifest them spontaneously where required for physical processes. The communication for this operation occurs in a precognitive manner as was discovered in studying the phenomenon also known as *ultra weak bioluminescence* and *dark luminescence*. Again they are important in the development and sustaining of larger structures and systems, such as organs and immune. They appear to act as a cohering factor in that it appears that the cell/system stores photons and shares them via quantum mechanisms.

Again, the central neutral position or *position of equilibrium* for the master oscillator (heart) is this zero point place of stillness where all the energies of the waveform vortex into and out of in mirrored symmetry. Yogi's meditating on this still space, called by some the *Cave of Brahman*, begins to entrain the standing waveform field and shift the resonance to one attuned with this omnipresent domain.

Eternal does not mean endless time, it means no-time. It Implies existence prior to time-space.

Regulating Factors

The two key biological modulators of the heart matrix symphony are the breath and emotion. Interestingly these two components are linked, as are loving-kindness and truth. As one slows his/her breath, their emotional state alters in relationship with the breath, and when one's emotions fly off, so does their breath rate shift. One's breath can be seen as a base bio-rhythm. The key modulator of emotion and breath is *consciousness*.

When these psycho-physiological aspects idealize, they do so forming a unique fractal form of coherent resonance, which results in a qualitative psycho-physiological state known as Compassion. The

The Silent Gospel 301

exalted qualitative form of compassion only occurs after self-realization is fully stabilized (anchored in soul/eternal perspective). This degree of compassion mirrors the final state Jesus exhibited just before his death on the cross when he asked Spirit to forgive them, 'for they know not what they do.' It is directly addressed in the commandment to 'love your neighbor as yourself'. Remember, true compassion is to feel *as* the other, which is different than feeling deeply *for* another. **It is the only emotional state of selflessness.**

A Unifying Harmony

Since our objective reality is vibratory in its essence and space is the nature of reality, logic guides us to the conclusion that there is no boundary to reality, there is only our notional perception of it constrained by being based on the experience of our own space-time.

Harmonic and motions not distance change our notion of reality. In effect it is tension affecting the excitation of the waves forming our senses, which forms our perception of space that forms our *sense* of reality. It is the tensions or compression factors of stress that modulates the harmonic and thereby perceived reality. Perception therefore is the simply differences in personal tuning and nothing more.

The science of idealizing the tuning into a unifying harmony, in which the heart, soul and mind can phase harmonically, is the science of attuning the quality of the carrier wave of intention. This is accomplished through a shift in placement of the identity. A shift from the egoic mind (self) to the observing timeless aspect of self called the soul (selfless). It is a major shift in identifying with the survival fear based drives and the timeless observer anchored in the conscious emptiness of no-thingness. This shift allows the carrier wave a resonance that is in alignment with the core field, intelligence, or Presence governing the material show. It tunes to life's creative impulse, which allows for and creates scale invariant phasing of the harmonics. In short it allows heart, soul and mind to phase. This level of phase produces a very unique coherence within the standing wave, as well as a unique over all resonance.

After a time of solidifying (stabilizing) the shift in identity, a union in awareness occurs of all three major aspects of self. At this moment the heart becomes perfectly purified and instead of merely reflecting the spiritual light, it actively manifests the same. Man, being thus consecrated by the Holy Spirit, (life) becomes Illuminated. When fully surrendered to THAT Isness, he enters the Kingdom of Spiritual Light, becoming a Son of God. How the individual experiences this final masterful transmutation is the key to the formation of the image on the Shroud.

Final Meditation

Again the master knows beforehand the time God has appointed for him to leave his bodily residence and prepares accordingly. In the last moments the yogi surrenders totally all aspects of "I" which triggers a cascade of biological events. This normally occurs at the time of death due to the level of entropy/homeostasis and degree of laser like phasing between all the coherent oscillating platforms. The external distractions are minimized to the fewest and the level of internal centering can be the greatest. Another reason why this phenomenon appears to happen at or near the time of death is because life and the gift of life is sacred and relished till the last moments. Deep compassion for those still in darkness impels the master to remain till the intelligence of life calls him or her back for a more evolved role in creation.

Electrical Nature

Spinning down the vortex to the zero point; the great phase singularity of stillness; the local of creativity, potentiality and pure possibility; the womb of life.

All five of the hearts modes of info-energy transference spoken of prior could be used for representing the process that ends in idealized compression symmetry. The truth is that during the Final Meditation they all fall into laser locked step, each one mirroring the other during the final implosive cascade. This is the nature of coupled oscillators entrained by scale invariant resonant coherence. The laser-like quality of mind at that point allows the contemplation and concentration to unify with the silent stillness, producing idealized compression symmetry in the form reflecting that consciousness. The easiest mode of the five to illustrate the process is from the perspective of the electrical nature of all matter.

Physics has demonstrated conclusively that at the core all matter is electric (vibratory/oscillating) phenomena. Imagine the physical body, its structures and systems as independent coherent oscillating platforms operating within a synchronized-coupled environment. The complex vibratory fields of coherent oscillating platforms are coupled together by some mystical force called consciousness.

The symmetric self-referencing energetic field of the body creates a standing wave held in coherent form, hence the term, a standing waveform. The waveform has the overall shape of a torus, which is similar to an apple with the two indented ends that form dual counter rotating vortices that touch at a center point of the field. And it is this shape/waveform that is modulating to varying degrees with each beat of the heart. Even the slightest alteration of the overall shape changes the overall resonance. In truth the shape reflects the fundamental resonance. This was visually demonstrated by Hans Jennys' Cymantics experiments.

Because this field is electromagnetic in nature, even the smallest internal or external generated field can easily modulate these independent-oscillating platforms. These forces have at the core two main principles allowing modulation, those of resonance and entrainment. Neurobiologists have found that the most powerful force forming these two processes is mind. Mind/consciousness forms the point originating internal modulation and as in the case of the master yogi, mind can offset the effects of external modulation. The most powerful aspect of mind is the one with which we are most normally identified.

Shifting the perspective (identity) to the observing aspect of mind allows for changes to take place within the physical structure. The reasons for this are complex from some points of view but simple if it is understood that form follows the musical harmony mind forms. The work of Marcel Vogel, Hans Jenny and others has shown visually this principle in action. Shift the tone or pitch and a corresponding change occurs in the shape being produced. This shift in mind's identity restructures the fluid neural pathways as well as the DNA matrix itself. It produces new emotion bearing proteins to form that allow aspects of the so-called "junk" DNA to be utilized. No longer are massive energies wasted in attempting to maintain balance and harmony. No longer is the input from the five senses controlling the mind, mind rests in reality and as such can withdraw from "physical duties". Through practices, meditation and resolve, the yogi brings the physical under the full control of the Autonomic Nervous System. Sri Yukteswar clearly states the results, "When magnanimity comes in to the heart this makes man fit for the practice of Asana Pranayama, which is control over prana, involuntary nerve electricities, and Pratyahara which is changing the direction of the voluntary nerve currents inward." This as been proven and reproducible over the eons of time, it is a science.

With this science accomplished, the yogi then can direct a more total percentage of attention, focus and concentration on the object of his contemplation, which is normally God/Emptiness. He synchronizes with the creative intelligence/impulse. This level of mediation produces naturally highly coherent organization and synchronization of the various oscillating platforms. The amount of dissonance disturbing this field of electromagnetic coupling is diminished almost to nil. With this degree of mastery the yogi's energetic field, i.e., his standing waveform is sustained in a shape that has unique characteristics. One of these characteristics is the form's ability to sustain ideally from within. It becomes self-generating/self referencing, yet stable. This at the end of the Final Completion is similar to a Type-1 superconductor. This unique torus shaped waveform has as a byproduct highly coherent balanced (symmetric) forces centering in at the center of the phase singularity. When these unique shape/forces are sustained they begin to add and multiply their wavelengths and velocities in a unique scale invariant, highly coupled fashion. If the centering/surrender is allowed to sustain, a critical mass shifts the entire phase relationship of all the oscillating coherent platforms that comprise the body matrix. The diverse oscillating platforms couple in phase and when sustained and complete produces a radical phase transition in the elements and structures of the physical.

What occurs at this precise moment is very rare. The waveform forms a perfect superconductor with a single vibrational phase that repels all magnetic invasions. They become diamagnetic, a form of single frequency photons- no longer particles, but light-bearing quantal waves. A self-referencing Meissner Field surrounds the field. These antielectrons mirror the Quantum Zero Point energy in resonance. The internal resonance perfectly mirrors the energetic resonance of the Still Point, and at that exact moment in time the form has a quantum phase transition of all the elements. The process is similar to the process of Sonoluminescence acoustically. The imploding waveform passes the speed of light on its way to full compression. Quantum field theory predicts that if the detector is accelerated its ground state can be spontaneously excited even when moving through the vacuum. The Unruh effect predicts radiation by non-inertially moving quantum mirrors. In 1996, Steven Lamoreaux, confirmed the existence of this vast field of zero point energy (ZPE) with experiments that demonstrated the Casimir Effect. Yet the Casimir Effect is just one of several phenomena that provided convincing evidence for the reality of this sea of light. This cosmic sea of light known as the electromagnetic zero-point field (ZPF) of the quantum vacuum has enormous energy in every square centimeter.

Another physical phenomenon well established by research is Quantum Leap, technically termed Quantum Coherence. It's the ability of atoms to act as one regardless of distance, even communication between non-physical realms and the physical realms. In certain "special" situations like *coherent light* (lasers) and *superconductivity*, multiple particle aggregations have been proven to become coherent and *behave as if they were single particles*. These coherent systems of particles exhibit quantum properties like quantum non-locality where a force administered to one particle may be **instantly** reflected in a response to another quantum-coupled particle **any distance away**. This coupled response is instantaneous regardless of distance, and is taken to be evidence of communication between the two particles, which is independent of space and time.

Certain researchers like Popp, and Mae-Wan Ho have measured time coherent events in the body, and I predict that other processes using compression on basic elements will be shown to produce light with coherent properties. If atoms or a collection of particles can behave as a single coherent form why can't larger more complex collections? Is it not true that at our core we are simply collections of atoms? And is it not also true that atoms are quantum entangled electromagnetic phenomenon?

The origin of the transition phase occurs when the body's energy synchronizes in Golden Mean, which is another word for scale invariant proportioning. This form of proportioning allows and creates a unique form of relationship and communications. The dance of Spirit, Mind and Body synchronizes under one unique symphonic cosmic rhyth(om). The body then produces and reflects a uniquely coherent resonance, one that allows and forms idealized resonance with the Zero Point Field. When and if this state is mastered (fully stabilized) the individual attains nirbikalpa samadhi. It is this level of attainment that allows for Mahasamadhi, or "great" samadhi. Yet paradoxically, even this highest form of Union has degrees of attainment (experience). This point is important always to remember. These degrees range from stabilization of the physical body for hours, days or eons, after the time of death, to differing degrees of producing full Rainbow Body events. They are characterized by a shrinking yet stable body size, to varying small amounts of the physical body remaining, like finger nails or nasal septum. The rarest form is to completely dissolve leaving nothing at all. It is my belief that when Jesus transitioned to the Kingdom of Light, he left us the image of himself on the Shroud as a testament to His glory and our potential.

Phi phase coherent synchronization is the key. All other forms of phasing i.e. synchronization of the wave characteristics of this medium (EM radiation or light) do not allow for this important level of communication and union. This special form of synchronization allows scales to communicate in a solely constructive way. Remembering the work of Dr. Candace Pert, each emotion is protein specific from which we can deduce that they are energetically/vibratory specific. Love or loving-kindness scientifically sets up within the body these uniquely powerful relationships in the harmonic communications spoken of earlier. When sustained, the main vibratory governor for the physical, which is the heart, produces phi scale invariant synchronization between the various systems. This synchronization is reflected in the electric information instrumentation picks up. Most interestingly is the phasing that happens in the Autonomic Branches of the Nervous system (see HRV). As we've also seen it is this system that controls the other functions of the body. We've also seen that it is this exact system that the yogic master brings under his or her full control in order to go deeper into Silence. So it appears that the ancient teachings are correct, Love is critical to attunement and synchronization. It was seeing this firsthand that moved me into the research that has culminated in this manuscript.

Love is receptive allowing, it is expansive and oddly neutral and having no polarity, it is the isness experienced and as such is our true nature. Hence to be true to ones self is to be with allowing loving-kindness. Remember from Quantum Theory, how we perceive (observe/detect) our reality helps to form/re-enforces our reality. Emotions and their cascade of neuro-chemicals which include hormones, originate from this basic understanding in Quantum Mechanics.

Phase is synchronization of the wave characteristics of the same medium, which is light. Not just the light that we see, but also all of the spectrum and its reciprocal. These all together form a Black-body of thermal radiation at rest, i.e. not oscillating. When it does move, it forms the EM spectrum, which has two main characteristics, wave-particle, Photon and Electron. It appears that this illusion of movement is due to detection and the reflective self-referencing looping of awareness. In other words it is a feature of the way we perceive rather than a characteristic of the core medium. Consciousness allows light to have the characteristics of both a wave and a particle. These two exist as complimentary explanations of light and EM radiation, yet neither is satisfactory in producing a neat symmetry. In other words they are not mutually exclusive, some mixture of both is necessary to represent the phenomena fully. And this pushes us to the conclusion that the irregularities witnessed are a function of our own consciousness interacting with the true nature of the physical world. Loving-kindness originating from the soul produces a unique lens with even more unique outcomes within the physical frame. Truly it is the stuff of miracles.

When the consciousness of the human form is highly experienced thereby able to sustain and stabilize the true nature and tendency of the heart, true blissful joy results. The stabilization allows the master to experience this quantum singularity, the zero-point/Stillness/Silence/ Emptiness. Then and only then can the consciousness truly reflect the True Nature of Reality and is no long inhibited by the mind developed by the outer senses.

With the wave-particle characteristics breaking down, they are no longer held on the holographic screen of awareness. The mirror is gone, but that is all that's gone, the essence we are told remains.

Phi relatedness allows and demands that all relationships unite, allowing both the wave with its photon packets to communicate with its virtual self instantaneously without external dissonance. Quantum Coherence of the field **is possible**. Without space-time distance the individuated subject object relationship is impossible, no-thing can literally exist within this realm. The open phone line to home is formed, idealized communicative laser mirror itself. The resonance produced by this mirroring, produces fused quantum coherence, a coupled union that is in resonance with the domain out of which all matter rises. The two perfectly perfected mirrors pass each other leaving the qualitative aspect from which it originated.

The intelligence of the Field allows creation to take any form. It allows it all to be, this is true love. It does not judge, demand or condemn, it allows the individuated consciousness to play out till all that is left is the yearning to return h(om)e. Truth is Love and it impregnates existence on all levels of experience if one has the eye to see. Love might be thought of as the physical expression of the energetic emotional response to pure allowing, which is pure receptivity, the core feminine principle. This natural response to the experience of this principle is Compassion. Compassion therefore is love in action. We are all examples of that Love.

Human Potential and Human Evolution

In the final analysis, the Silent Gospel of the Shroud is about human potential and human evolution. It is the mirror for the resurrection, the Great Perfection of Jesus. The gospel embedded within the fibers of the Shroud, speaks to our potential and points like a road sign to a future where heaven is experienced here on Earth. When exploring the mystery of the Shroud's image, a reality develops like a photograph in solution, an object created for humanity of this current time.

It shows in a hard and fast object what is possible when all facets of the individual consciousness completely dissolve due to the realization and attunement with Truth. The object reflects the possibilities of love. Loving with all your might 'your God' and 'your neighbors as yourself'. The image is a textural reminder of the gifts that are bestowed when other and self dissolves and death is not experienced ever again.

In the end, exploration of the Silent Gospel produces faith that allows for a total submission to that guiding force we call life and in doing so makes possible total Liberation from ignorance and suffering.

Chapter Twenty One

Purity of Heart

The heart is King, if the country goes into ruin the king too will die.
Love refuses nothing, and takes nothing,
It is the highest and vastest freedom.
All exists through love.

Gospel of Philip

The heart holds faculties for knowing beyond the radar capacities of reason, logical and the five senses. It is a primal intuitive sense that sits beyond the grasp of the three-dimensional mind; it is an immediate and qualitatively knowing termed Heart Intelligence; it is perceived as a sense. The sense of the heart is anchored in the timeless but is perceived in the now. This Wisdom holds our deepest knowing and our truest tendency or nature. If healthy, it is said by the saints, that the heart's knowing will carry you home to receive your birthright, but it must be *allowed* to do so.

Perfecting this knowing with the faculty of discernment is part of the initial process in purifying the heart. Over and over you will see the word 'allowing' coming to the front of the process. The Sufi's use the word submission, the Hindu's use the term surrender, and for Christians the word is faith, though a correct Western translation might simply be understood as *authentic allowing*. *Authentic allowing* is simply an attitude of heart-felt mindfulness to what is present in the moment. I emphasize *authentic* because it must not be merely the outcome of a conceptual action or of moral obligation. It must in the end rise honestly, a genuine outpouring from the heart. Like the mirror it is, the soot of raging emotions and the acids of destructive attitudes may soil heart knowing. We can easily confuse the egoic desires, opinions, social conditioning and fears with the knowing of the heart. Often in the name of following our hearts, we actually follow the desires and fears of the ego mind trapped in the trance of separation.

The heart is a prize for which both spirit and the world compete. These two powerful forces pull with the strength of their collective qualities at the heart for its attention. The heart will assume the qualities of whatever attracts it. Attraction to the limiting qualities, which past and future bring, result at best in a limited reflection of the divine reality. When the goal is total union with the Divine, only total purity will do. For this end only egoic submission or *authentic allowing* of a greater power is required.

In the world of today, how can we know whether we are following the desires of the little self or the guidance of the heart? First the heart does not operate through concepts, propositions or assumptions, it senses and attracts through the *qualitative* aspects of the universe. The pull of the heart when healthy awakens the healing forces of humbleness, gratitude, appreciation and love. These spiritual qualities when authentic rise spontaneously from the heart. One can accomplish this level of being, as Jesus implied, by being *truthful to one's self* and *listening to the call of the Divine echoing within the Cave of one's heart.* It is one's ability to respond to the inner guidance of Love and Wisdom even though this guidance may appear to be irrational and even counter to one's own apparent self-interests. But, you see, that is its beauty and power. The ability to respond to the awakened and healthy heart develops into the quality of compassion, the capacity to submit faithfully, spontaneously and joyfully to the requirements of the moment. For when purity of the heart is reached one knows no fear and always submits to the Absolute with willing gratitude and love for in this moment one knows the ground of Reality. Great teachers will tell you that the complete healing of the soul is possible through the soul's contact with Wholeness through the heart. This is why Jesus in his commandment to the disciples placed it first: "Love Your God, With ALL Your Heart, Soul and Mind."

The principle requisite for attainment of the holy life is attainment of Love, which is the heart's natural tendency. A Purified Heart is one resting in its natural tendency, a state reflecting balance, harmony and great inner peace. As I have mentioned before, this begins with loving-kindness for one self as it is in this moment, not how one wishes it to be in some future moment in time. From this point the creative evolutionary force we call life is embraced and it supports the impulse toward liberation and Perfection.

106   Realization makes a Human Being {Athropos} impalpable and invisible.

        If they were visible, people would enclose them within the bounds of the visible.

        To know the grace of true communion with Him, one must be clothed in clear light.

        In this light we can see His light.

107   Before leaving this world, we must become human beings inhabited by the Breath. (Word/Aum)..."

111:     Spiritual Love is a drunkenness and a balm; those who are anointed by it rejoice.

From the Gospel of Philip Page 78, Plate 124

"Look closely and you will see that all names and forms are but transitory waves on the ocean of consciousness, that only consciousness can be said to be, not its transformations. In the immensity of consciousness a light appears, a tiny point that moves rapidly and traces shapes, thoughts and feelings, concepts and ideas, like the pen writing on paper. And the ink that leaves a trace is memory. You are that tiny point, and by your movement the world is ever re-created. Stop moving and there will be no world. Look within and you will find that the point of light is the reflection of the immensity of light in the body, as the sense "I am". There is only light, all else appears. To the mind, it [that light] appears as darkness. It can be known only through its reflections. All is seen in daylight - except daylight. To be the point of light tracing the world is turiya. To be the light itself is turiyatita. But of what use are names when reality is so near?"

From the book I Am That by Sri Nisargadatta Maharaj[17]

---

[17] Sri Nisargadatta at http://www.angelfire.com/realm/bodhisattva/nisargadatta.html

I AM THAT: Talks With Sri Nisargadatta," (Acorn Press, 1990) ISBN: 0893860220.

Epilogue

Information

I've spoken in this book about Information and Energy as a linked, interrelated thing/event. Where information is present there is energy and where there is energy so too is there information. It is the base for communication and all nature of transference in our objective reality. Yet a new picture is immerging, one where information can exist in a domain prior to energy as we understand it. This new notion is very challenging to get one's mind around, especially after all these years of conditioning that information and energy are linked like two sides of the same coin.

Introducing and explaining these new conceptual understandings would muddy the stream of rational thought, and confuse an already challenging thesis that much more. Yet I feel compelled to introduce it here at the end to further stretch the imagined potentiality of our reality and deepen the link to the ancient mystical wisdoms. Models like those found within String Theory, of multidimensional domains is one thing but a *core realm* of pure Information prior to energy or dimensional existence as we understand it bends the abstract into the absurd, yet this is what new experiential data is pointing to. This is a similar time to those surrounding those leading up to the "Copenhagen Interpretations".

Information in its own realm would be a matrix of pure potentiality and possibility held prior to any and all interference, the god-head if you like, to speak beyond this is only wild speculation and conjecture. What we can speak to currently is that within randomness information is found, within so called empty space stuff is born. The main pursuit in science throughout the electronic age has been to reduce random noise, with the ultimate goal being the full elimination of randomness. This has proven a near impossible task even though our understandings of electronic devices have become very sophisticated. In the final analysis the *echo* of randomness is a constant that appears impossible to totally filter out. Interestingly now some elite scientists are currently adding randomness back into devices resulting in some amazing findings. This *Information* realm is presently being demonstrated via random characteristic to exist in some, as of yet un-

understood, complimentary way with our own. Someday in the near future we will look back on this age like Maxwell looked back on the pre-electronic age. We will develop words and concepts to help move forward our understanding of the characteristics of phenomena.

As of this writing, I can only imagine this infinite potential of pure Information manifesting as a multidimensional holograph compressed into the fabric of Pure Consciousness encoding simultaneously Awareness and Beingness. Beyond this I defer to those experience souls that have explored consciousness in great depth.

> "There is only One God, He is Omnipresent; there is only one religion, the religion of Love; there is only one caste, the caste of Humanity; there is only one language, the language of the Heart."

Sai Baba as quoted in <u>Vision of the Divine</u> by Eruch B. Fanibunda

Final Comment:

This manuscript is a thesis on the value of Heart Intelligence and the inherent depth of human potentiality. The Shroud of Turin is both the direct evidence of this theory, and a silent gospel illuminating a potential path of human evolution. To me it is one of the most amazing artifacts to survive antiquity. Yet this volume is like early animations done by Jules Verne's moon landings. It is crude by the standards yet to soon come. I see this work as a simple seed planted in consciousness for others to fully develop.

> "In order to be truly free, you must desire to know the truth more than you want to feel good. Because, if feeling good is your goal, then as soon as you feel better you will lose interest in what is true. This does not mean that feeling good or experiencing love and bliss is a bad thing. Given the choice, anyone would choose to feel bliss rather than sorrow. It simply means that if this desire to feel good is stronger than the yearning to see, know, and experience Truth, then this desire will always be distorting the perception of what is Real, while corrupting one's deepest integrity. In my experience, everyone will say they want to discover the

The Silent Gospel

Truth, right up until they realize that the Truth will rob them of their deepest held ideas, beliefs, hopes, and dreams. The freedom of enlightenment means much more than the experience of love and peace. It means discovering a Truth that will turn your view of self and life upside-down. For one who is truly ready, this will be unimaginably liberating. But for one who is still clinging in any way, this will be extremely challenging indeed. How does one know if they are ready? One is ready when they are willing to be absolutely consumed, when they are willing to be fuel for a fire without end."

Adyashanti

"Ascension is be coming nonexistent"
   Rumi

Bibliography

What we are looking for is what is looking.

~St. Francis of Assisi

Preface: 1
    Molecules of Emotion - Candace B. Pert, PH.D., Scribner

Chapter One: le Coeur de Mystère: 11
    The Power of Now, Eckhart Tolle, New World Library
    New Scientific Evidence, The Mystery of the Shroud of Turin, John C. Iannone, Alba House, New York
    The Oviedo Cloth, Mark Guscin, The Lutterworth Press, Cambridge
    The Nag Hammadi Library, The Gospel of Thomas, Translated by Stephen Patterson and Marvin Meyer

Chapter Two: Placebo & Faith: 25
    Doctors Orders, Go Fishing, Dean Shrock PhD., First Pub Group Ltd.
    The Psychobiology of Mind-body Healing: New Concepts of Therapeutic Hypnosis, Dr. Ernest Rossi, W.W. Norton & Company Inc.
    Sufi Teachings: The Art of Being, Hazrat Inayat Khan, Element
    Prayers of the Cosmos; Meditations on the Aramaic Words of Jesus, Neil Douglas Klotz, Harper San Francisco
    A New Science of Life: The Hypothesis of Morphic Resonance, Rupert Sheldrake, Park Street Press
    KJV New Testament, Matthew 22:36-40

Chapter Three: The Rainbow, Wisdom or Golden Body 'Ja'-lus in Tibetan: 38
    The Future of the Body, Michael Murphy, Jeremy P. Tarcher – Putnam, member of Penguin Putnam Inc.

Sri Aurobindo, 1950
Autobiography of a Yogi, Paramahansa Yogananda, Self-Realization Fellowship
Meditation the Dzogchen (Dzog Chen) Way, Advice from His Holiness Penor Rinpoche.
Tibetan Book of Living & Dying, Sogyal Rinpoche, Rider Publishing.
The Path of Dzogchen, Master Wang- San Francisco based International Tibetan Qigong Association,
Fr. Francis Tiso a Catholic vicar, *his Internet web Accounts*
http://www.geocities.com/ftiso/rainbb.html
tiso@northcoast.com
www.stmchurch.com
http://www.mercy-center.org/MCM/News/2001Stirrings/Q3-Rainbow_Body.htm

Chapter Four: The Guru Jesus: 52

Nag Hammadi Library, Gospel of Thomas, Translated by Stephen Patterson and Marvin Meyer
Be Thou There: The Holy Family's Journey in Egypt, edited by Gawdat Gabra, The American University in Cairo Press.
The Divine Romance, Paramahansa Yogananda, Self-Realization Fellowship
Words of Light & Dead Sea Scrolls, The Untold Story, Kenneth Hanson, Ph.D. ,Council Oak Books
Bloodline of the Holy Grail, Lawrence Gardner, Element
The Hidden Gospel, Neil Douglas-Klotz, Quest Books
Prayers of the Cosmos, Neil Douglas-Klotz, Harper San Francisco
The Holy Science, Swami Sri Yukteswar, Self Realization Fellowship
The Mystic Heart, Wayne Teasdale, New World Library
The Works of Josephus Flavius Translated by William Whiston, A.M Peabody
M.A., Hendrickson Publishers (Antiquities of the Jews, War of the Jews, The Life of Flavius Josephus- Autobiography)
Rig Veda
Upanishads
Bible Young's Literal Translation (YLT) Mark 1:9-11

Bible The King James Version, Matthew 4:1-11 & Luke 4:1 & Luke 4:16-44
Chapter 1:1-4: of Genesis
The Nag Hammadi Library, The Gospel of Thomas, Translated by Stephen Patterson and Marvin Meyer

Chapter Five: Resurrection: 76
King James Bible
Piste Sophiea Cotice or . "Books of the Savior" "Askew Codex"

Chapter Six: Have Heart: 85
Sufi Teachings, The Art of Being Hazrat Inayat Knan Pg 236
Hazrat Mir Ghotbeddin Mohammad, *Destination: Eternity*, in Principles of Sufism, Nahid Angha, Asian Humanities Press
Babaji and the 18 Siddha Kriya Yoga Tradition, M. Govindan, M.A., Kriya Yoga Publishing
The Holy Science, Swami Sri Yukteswar, Self-Realization Fellowship
The Hidden Gospel, Neil Douglas-Klotz, Quest Books
Prayers of the Cosmos, Neil Douglas-Klotz, Harper San Francisco
Llewellyn Vanghan-Lee; excerpt of his from his web site, www.goldensufi.org

Chapter Seven: Truth: 105
The Power of Now, Eckhart Tolle, New World Library
Nag Hammadi Library, The Gospel of Thomas, Translated by Stephen Patterson and Marvin Meyer
Compassion and the Individual, the Fourteenth Dalai Lama
Gospel of John Bible King James Version

Chapter Eight: Heart Intelligence: 113
Principles of Sufism, Nahid Angha, Asian Humanities Press pg 69
Principles of Sufism, Nahid Angha, Asian Humanities Press pg 21
Scientific Healing Affirmations, Paramahansa Yogananda
Catherine Ingram, www.catherineingram.com
The Power of Now, Eckhart Tolle, New World Library

Chapter Nine: Intent & Compassion: 121

The Knowing Heart, A Sufi Path of Transformation Kabir Helminski
Ammachi. www.ammachi.org
Compassion and the Individual, His Holiness the Fourteenth Dalai Lama
A Heart as Wide as the World, Sharon Salzberg, Shambala
The Coming of the Cosmic Christ, Matthew Fox Harper San Francisco
The Tibetan Book of Living and Dying Sogyal Rinpoche
Loving Kindness: Unsealing the Spring, Sogyal Rinpoche
Ramana Maharshi - The Essential Teaching of Ramana Maharshi , Inner Directions Publishing
Thrangu Rinpoche, as taken from the Oral Instructions on the Karma Pakshi Practice given by Thrangu Rinpoche, @ Samye-Ling, December 1993,
The Hidden Gospel Neil Douglas Klotz,
The Power of Now, Eckhart Tolle,
Awakening the Buddha Within, Lama Surya Da,
Tibet Book on Living and Dying, Sogyal Rinpoche,
Babaji and the 18 Siddha Kriya Yoga Tradition, M. Govindan, M.A., Kriya Yoga Publications

Chapter Ten: Breath: 135

Rig Veda about 3700BC [Hymns to the Mystic Fire: Aurobindo]
The Hidden Gospel, Neil Douglas-Klotz, Quest Books
Hymns to the Mystic Fire: Aurobindo
The Mysticism of Sound and Music, Hazrat Inayat Khan
KJV The Gospel of St. John 1:1
Hazrat Inayat Khan "Mystic Relaxation" in Sufi Message, vol, 4 p.165-166
Babaji and the 18 Siddha Kriya Yoga Tradition, M. Govindan, M.A., Kriya Yoga Publications

Chapter Eleven: Heart Rate Variability (HRV): 142

Yoga Sutras of Patanjali.
The Holy Science Swami Sri Yukteswar, Self-Realization Fellowship

The Divine Romance, Paramahansa Yogananda, Self-Realization Fellowship

Chapter Twelve: Siddhas: 154
Autobiography of a Yogi, Paramahansa Yogananda, Self-Realization Fellowship
Light and Death, One Doctors Fascinating Account of Near Death Experiences, Dr. Michael Sabom, Zondervan Publishing House
The Healing Blade, Edward J. Sylvester, Beck Press Inc

Chapter Thirteen: Awareness; No Subject, Object nor Action An elaborate presentation on No-thing: 160
The Tibetan Book of the Great Liberation
Autobiography of a Yogi, Paramahansa Yogananda, Self-Realization Fellowship
The Holy Science Swami, Sri Yukteswar, Self-Realization Fellowship

Chapter Fourteen: Quantum-Zero Point-& the Holographic Web: 184
Bhagavad-Gita, 12:13-14
Hierarchic Theory of Matter and Field: Water & Biosystems, Vacuum and Duality, Dr. Alex Kaivarainen
Margins Of Reality, The Role of Consciousness in the Physical World, Robert Jahn & Brenda J. Dunne, Harvest Book
The Self-Aware Universe, How Consciousness Creates the Material World. Dr. Amit Goswami, Ph.D., Putnam Books
What is Life, Erwin Schrödinger
Primary Perception: Biocommunication with Plants, Living Foods, and Human Cells, Cleve Backster, White Rose Millennium Press
The Tibetan Book of the Great Liberation

Chapter Fifteen: Resonance: 213
Light After Life, Dr. Konstantin Korotkov, Back Bone Publishing

Chapter Sixteen: Tuning to the Divine; 220

Chapter Seventeen: Quantum Aum: 226
The Holy Science Swami, Sri Yukteswar, Self-Realization Fellowship
Vision of the Divine, Eruch B. Fanibunda
The Essence of Self-Realization Paramhansa Yogananda, Copyright 1990, J. Donald Walters

Chapter Eighteen: Sonoluminescence: 232
Scientific American February 1995 Vol.272,.
Popular Science "A Star in a Jar", December 1998,

Chapter Nineteen: Golden Mean: 244
The Coming of the Cosmic Christ, Matthew Fox (pp 19, referenced from (Hidegard, HB 41, Meditations with Hildegard of Bingen, Gabriel Uhlein, (Santa Fe, N.M. Bear & Co. 1982) & Breakthrough: Meister Eckhart's Creation Spirituality in New Translation, Matthew Fox , Garden City, N.Y.; Doubleday & Co. 1980)
Bernard Haisch, Alfonso Rueda, L.J. Nickisch, Jules Mollere) General Relativity and Quantum Cosmology, abstract 0209016 http://www.arxiv.org/abs/gr- qc/0209016 Update on an Electromagnetic Basis for Inertia, Gravitation, the Principle of Equivalence, Spin and Particle Mass Ratios
http://www.arxiv.org/IgnoreMe
Sacred Geometry, Robert Lawlor, Thames & Hudson pages 46-47 on the Golden Proportion
The Hidden Power of the Heart, Sara Paddison, (c) 1998, Planetary
Professor William Tiller, archive pages of www.tiller.org

Chapter Twenty: Shroud Image Formation - Summary Conclusion: 268
Scientific Evidence, The Mystery of the Shroud of Turin, John C. Iannone's 1998, Alba House New York
The Holy Science, Sri Yukteswar, Self-Realization Fellowship
The Divine Romance, Paramahansa Yogananda. Self-Realization Fellowship\
The Nag Hammadi Library, The Gospel of Thomas, Translated by Stephen Patterson and Marvin Meyer

Chapter Twenty One: Purity of Heart: 309
    The Gospel of Philip, Jean-Yves LeLoup, Inner Traditions
    I Am That: Talks With Sri Nisargadatta," (Acorn Press, 1990) ISBN: 0893860220.

Epilogue, Information exists prior to energy: 313
    Vision of the Divine, Eruch B. Fanibunda, Published by E.B. Fanibunda, for Shri Satya Sai Books & Publications

Glossary found at www.silentgospel.com

ABOUT AUTHOR

James Andrew Barrett is a student of religious and mystical traditions, heart intelligence researcher, author and lecturer, whose company helped to bring about the notion and tools to witness the value of "Internal Heart Coherence", (1996-1997). The original goals of the company were a feedback device that would aid recognition of the *"Hearts Intelligence"* and support personal development of a *Compassionate/Immaculate Heart*. Success came with the help of several individuals, particularly a former U.S. Air Force, control systems analyst in the human-machine interface program at Wright Patterson Air force Base in Dayton, Ohio.

Barrett's company produced and correlated information coming from the use of this novel, first ever, *real-time* heart biofeedback device, data initiating from a diverse spectrum of disciplines scattered around the world.

Resulting conclusions from this innovative approach in combination with the exploding data coming from molecular-neural-consciousness research, spectral analysis of the heart, quantum mechanics and thermodynamics, were producing a new picture of the electromagnetic-self, one brimming with possibility and potentiality.

The new model linked inherent heart-based intelligence with: biological quantum mechanical processes, such as self-organization, emotional intelligence, nerve activity, and wellness, both psychological and physical which implies, to some extent, longevity.

Then, in March of 2000, a life-altering epiphany occurred when his twenty-seven year old son died suddenly. During those weeks of grief Barrett was given a clear vision of a book and a clear personal experience of the witnessing facet of "mind". His priority then changed from developing the cardiac device, its protocols and company, to research, writing and lecturing on the subject of Human Potentiality. *The Silent Gospel: The Science of Divinity - The Creation of the Shroud of Turin,* is a result of this process.

James was born in 1951 in New Rochelle, New York and currently lives in Nevada City, California with his partner Patti.

Printed in the United States
124056LV00007B/33/A